National Politics and Community in Canada

National Politics and Community in Canada

edited by

R. KENNETH CARTY

and

W. PETER WARD

University of British Columbia Press
Vancouver
1986

National Politics and Community in Canada

This book has been published with the help of a grant from the Social Science Federation of Canada, using funds provided by the Social Sciences and Humanities Research Council of Canada.

Canadian Cataloguing in Publication Data

Main entry under title:
National politics and community in Canada

ISBN 0-7748-0248-0
1. Canada - Politics and government - Addresses, essays, lectures. 2. Nationalism - Canada - Addresses, essays, lectures. 3. Federal government - Canada - Addresses, essays, lectures. 4. Political parties - Canada - Addresses, essays, lectures. I. Carty, R. Kenneth, 1944– II. Ward, W. Peter (William Peter), 1943–
JL27.N38 1986 321.02'0971 C86-091116-0

International Standard Book Number 0-7748-0248-0
Printed in Canada

Contents

Contents

1

Canada as Political Community

R. KENNETH CARTY AND W. PETER WARD

In the beginning Canada was a political creation. From the pieces of Britain's North American empire a handful of mid-Victorian colonial legislators fashioned a new state. Lacking a common culture, a common past, or a common interest, they created a common political system to bind themselves together. Since that time the greatest task of national government has been to develop and nourish a Canadian political community. Yet in the past few years this enduring reality has slipped from the view of many thoughtful Canadians. We have come to see this country as the sum of its parts, and in some eyes these parts loom larger than the national whole. As yet there is no consensus on what those parts may be. For some observers region or province is the primary unit in Canada. For others ethnicity, class, income, age, gender, or interest establishes the common basis of the group. But however these categories are defined, the part and not the whole has come to dominate thinking about our society and its most important institutions.

Many members of the academic community have energetically promoted this new vision of our national affairs. Historians have virtually abandoned national history for that of immigrants, workers, women, the poor, or other marginal social groups. Political scientists have maintained a greater interest in the national centre, but many of them have also shifted their primary focus to provinces, social cleavages, and interest groups—from the whole to its components. In some scholarly circles the nation and national institutions have even fallen into considerable disrepute. Consider the title of a recent collection of essays on the history of Canadian regionalism: *Canada and the Burden of Unity*.

It was not always so. There was a time when most students of Canadian political life considered national history and national institutions to be the principal, if not sole, subjects of legitimate enquiry. Not that they held views in common. An enormous gulf stood between the effusions of Georges Dennison, Parkin, and Grant over the glories of Canada's British constitutional inheritance and Goldwin Smith's lamentations over the artificial character of a community with nothing but political substance. Yet, in their very different ways, the imperialists and the continentalists considered the matter of Canada and not its various elements. This overriding concern for the entire nation reached back to the Confederation era, in much of English Canada at least, and it persisted over most of the next hundred years. It left a deep imprint on national intellectual life and moulded the ways in which reflective Canadians thought about their country. Among other things it assigned the primary task of our greatest English-language historians. As Carl Berger noted, "one of the most persistent strands in Canadian historical literature since the First World War has been the concentration on Canadian national history and nationality. Historians have not only attempted to explain how Canada as a nation state came into existence but have isolated the common patterns that affected the country as a whole."[1]

Two primary strains run through the history of ideas about the essence of Canada, one based on the land, the other on the political community. Since the dawn of European settlement, the land has been a challenge to be met intellectually as well as physically. Over the years a complex ideology has evolved concerning the relationship between Canadians and their environment. The crude, deterministic notions some Victorians held about the effect of the northern climate on the Canadian character had little force or influence. But after the turn of the century, the land took firm grip of the Canadian imagination. Witness the Group of Seven, self-proclaimed champions of nationalistic landscape art, whose paintings have become civic icons. (A brief personal digression to illustrate the power of their imagery: one of the editors, a prairie boy born and bred, was schooled in the lessons of nationalist art at the branch of the Bank of Commerce—as it then was—where he deposited the modest weekly profits of his paper route, surrounded by cheap reproductions of Group of Seven canvases. Though these interpretations of the northern Ontario wilderness bore no relationship to any landscape he had ever seen, he grew up accepting them as the essential Canadian environment.) The National Film Board, in its energetic promotion of all things Canadian, has always been obsessed with the national landscape. Its beautiful centennial souvenir, *The Year of the Land,* celebrated a nation almost devoid of people.

The most powerful environmentalist ideas of all came from Harold

Innis. Formulated in the 1920's, his well-known Laurentian thesis emphasized the shaping force of geography over Canada's destiny. To quote Carl Berger once more: "what Innis argued was that behind the pattern of separate regions—an obvious fact that he never denied—there existed a countervailing tendency towards unity, based on the river systems and the Shield, that explained why the various regions were politically united in the first place." These ideas provided solid intellectual underpinnings for the Canadian state and refuted those jeremiahs who considered the nation simply an artificial political entity. "Confederation was, in a sense, a political reflection of the natural coherence of northern America."[2]

But political matters did not interest Innis much. The task of relating these deep geographic forces and their economic manifestations to the creation of Canada fell to Donald Creighton. His mature work analysed the transcontinental linkages inherent in the northern environment, their exploitation by succeeding generations of ambitious entrepreneurs, and their political consolidation in a nation "from sea unto sea." Where Innis implied that Canada was formed by vast, impersonal forces, Creighton saw the hands of many men at work: fur traders, businessmen, navvies, journalists, lawyers, and politicians. But for Creighton one man—Macdonald—towered above all others. It was he who foresaw the possibilities of a new nation. It was he who served as chief architect of Confederation. It was he who shaped the new Dominion's destiny in the first crucial years of its life.

The interplay of nature and man, geography and politics, in the making of modern Canada preoccupied Donald Creighton more than all other national historians. Apart from him, many prominent English-speaking intellectuals adopted the national perspective, but they were much more exclusively concerned with the political community itself. Frank Underhill, like Creighton in his early years, regarded Canadian political parties and behaviour as extensions of economic interest groups. Underhill's views remained partial and impressionistic, however, for he failed to articulate a fully developed theory of Canadian political society. Moreover, his simplistic ideas about the economic roots of political behaviour, derived from Turner, Beard, and other progressive American historians, had limited explanatory power in a society in which the politics of culture had such great significance.

W. L. Morton, in contrast, saw the core of the nation's experience in its political institutions. The central element of the national community, he argued, was its monarchical constitution, which created a political society based on allegiance, not nationality. Canada was thus a non-nationalist state and this allowed—perhaps even encouraged—great diversity within the framework of the state. Shorn of the Anglophile sentimentality and chauvinism so characteristic of earlier conservative thought, Morton's tory convictions sought to reconcile Canada's great ethnic and regional differences with the unifying demands of the state. In his best remembered words he declared that "one of the blessings of Canadian life is that there is no Canadian way of life, much less two, but a unity under the crown admitting of a thousand diversities."[3] For Morton, community in Canada was fundamentally political. But unlike those who held this a weakness, he considered it the nation's greatest strength.

The science of politics did not emerge in Canada until the mid 1940's, and from the outset it was similarly nation-centred. Unlike historians, who sought grand unifying themes in the nation's past, the new political scientists devoted themselves to close formalistic description and cautious analysis. In pioneering textbooks which set the tone of the discipline and influenced a generation of scholars, J. A. Corry and R. M. Dawson wrote extensively about the evolution, nature, and functions of the national government's institutions.The political economy approach—the other major tendency in early Canadian political studies—virtually dictated a national perspective, concerned as it was with the links between environment, resources, social and economic development, and political change. Struck by this overriding concern for Canada as a whole, as late as 1974 Alan Cairns suggested that the "centralist bias . . . characteristic of Anglophone historians and political scientists" constituted "a basic weakness of Canadian political science."[4]

Francophone intellectuals, not surprisingly, never had much interest in an Ottawa-centred view of Canada. From François-Xavier Garneau onward, the greatest French language historians articulated a sense of nation which was rooted in culture. "The traditional historians of French Canada," Ramsay Cook has observed, "concerned themselves chiefly with political, religious, linguistic, and legal questions. Language, laws, and faith were the fundamental bases of French-Canadian culture; politics was the chief means by which these bases were defended against the onslaught of the enemy. The political arena was the scene of that constant 'lutte des races' which was the primary theme of Canadian history."[5] Seen from this point of view the larger national society was at continuous political war with one of its major parts. But what required explanation was the character and experience of the French Catholic minority, not that of its opponents. More recently, the neo-nationalist historians of the "Montreal school," as well as their non-nationalist critics, have approached their own tasks in much the same way. Whatever their particular ideological orientation, each is preoccupied by *la nation française*.

Among students of Canadian politics, the leading French-Canadian commentator on federalism during the past quarter century was prime minister for much of this period. Taking into account his early writing and his conduct in office, it would be hard to deny his commitment to defending the national interest. But perhaps, like some exceptions, that of Pierre Trudeau proves the rule. National governments, national institutions, national policies, and national politics have aroused little curiosity amongst students of politics in francophone Quebec, except a concern for their provincial implications. Even francophone textbooks on the Canadian political system devote a great deal of space to what is essentially Quebec politics.

In the last two decades the nation-centred tradition of enquiry in English Canada has been overturned. Historians, and to a lesser extent political scientists, have abandoned the statist paradigms which once shaped their thinking about Canada. Abandoned is the appropriate term, for these perspectives were not examined, found wanting, and rejected; they were simply discarded like once-fashionable clothes. Why this occurred is not completely clear, but the explanation seems to lie in the changing political world of Canada, and in shifting trends within the two disciplines.

The 1960's buried Mackenzie King's Canada. The Quiet Revolution in Quebec and the emergence of government by federal-provincial diplomacy demanded a reassessment of how Canada worked and of the history leading up to that juncture. A "two nations" view of the country, long a political credo in Quebec, found serious proponents in English Canada. Regional and multicultural conceptions of Canada gained widespread support as the provinces came to play a vastly increased role in the governance of the nation as well as the daily lives of ordinary Canadians. When English-Canadian political scientists and historians turned their attention to these developments, they discovered regional political cultures, institutions, and systems of behaviour, as well as patterns of class action and historical traditions, which seemed to explain these changes.

The growth of a large, new generation of younger scholars reinforced the spread of these fresh perspectives. During the 1960's Canada's burgeoning universities enlarged academic job opportunities enormously. The effect on political science was especially striking—its practitioners grew from about 30 in 1950 to between 700 and 750 by 1980—and the historical profession expanded almost as dramatically. Many young scholars embraced newer conceptions of Canada, and more than a few established their academic reputations with studies which explored some dimension of the larger community or which analysed the country in terms of a system of more basic units or groups.

Canadian political science came of age at the time of that discipline's behavioural revolution, which subordinated the study of political institutions to that of political activity. Together with important changes in the nation's political practices and agenda, and the cry for academic relevance which echoed across the land and through the halls of granting agencies, this development forced the national political community and the nation-building task to the nether edge of disciplinary interest. Those who clung to such traditional concerns found themselves in a shrinking minority. Amongst historians the decline of interest in national—especially political—history resulted in part from the growing appeal of region-focused scholarship, long a subordinate tradition in Canadian historical writing. At the same time, the rise of the new social history asked questions which national history could not answer and required paradigms which it could not provide.

The abandonment of a nation-centred scholarly focus has left us with an incomplete and imperfect knowledge of our national institutions. Innis had emphasized the influence of environment on the making of Canada, Morton and Dawson had discussed its constitutional and institutional arrangements, and Creighton had explored the impact of personality on the national community. But while these approaches offered compelling insights into the fundamentals of the Canadian experience, they had surprisingly little to say about how the national political community actually functioned. What remains largely unexamined to this day is the nation-building process. We still need systematic enquiry into the basis, creation, and management of a national political community in Canada, enquiry which takes at its starting point a centrist perspective. The essays in this book explore some of this neglected terrain. They provide rather less than a comprehensive overview, but together they offer a richer understanding of how the Canadian political community was created and sustained.

The first two essays in this volume address the problem of the basis for a Canadian political community. During the Confederation debates, Christopher Dunkin had responded to Cartier's call for a new political nationality by asking, "how is this plan, in its entirety, going to work?"[6] While Dunkin was convinced that it would not, Macdonald and his associates ignored his constitutional analysis (early political science, reminiscent of much that has been written about Trudeau's constitution) and went about the business of constructing a Canadian politics. Gordon Stewart's paper, part of his important reassessment of the first Canadian party system, explores the foundations of the nation's political culture. As Stewart makes clear both here and elsewhere, Macdonald (good conservative that he was) drew heavily on these traditions as he fashioned the Conservative Party of the later nineteenth century.[7] Though it is generally agreed that the second decade of this century saw the decline of Macdonald's kind of politics in Canada, Stewart's exposition of its underlying attitudes and values points to traditions that remain part of the Canadian political culture today. In answer to Dunkin, the Canadian political community worked in no small part because of the party building activities that Macdonald, and then Laurier, made state building activities. The parties which these leaders created have long vanished; the political culture which they formed has proved rather more resilient.

At first the Canadian political culture was undoubtedly parochial. Margaret Prang challenges us to think about the "nationalizing of sentiment" in interwar Canada. She points to the central role of religious and business elites in creating a public culture with a genuinely national focus and perspective. This provided the basis for Mackenzie King's brokerage politics and his government's increasingly bureaucratic style. In *The Government Party,* Reginald Whitaker argued that the Liberal's ministerialism was "a structural feature of cabinet government in a regionally divided society."[8] Prang puts this argument in perspective by suggesting that it was the emergence of a national elite, selfconsciously defining the character of the Canadian community, which provided the basis for this kind of nationwide politics. Her concluding observations point to new forces at work in the 1920's and 1930's which were shifting the balances that defined the national political culture and thus the basis for political community and nationality in Canada.

The next four essays shift from a concern for the basis of political community to the mechanisms and processes used in its building. Carty and Ward consider the problem of political citizenship. All states must define their own bases of political membership, and most new nations have done so quite deliberately at the time of their inception. In the case of Canada, which had no war of independence based on the proclamation of a common community, one might have expected the nation-building elite to define an exclusive citizenship in law at the outset. They did not. Indeed, no such definition was prescribed until 1976. Membership in the community was identified most clearly by franchise law, an instrument fashioned by tough, competitive politicians, largely for their own partisan ends. In this sense, the national community was explicitly political in early Canada, where party constituted the principal tool of pragmatic nation-builders.

David Smith tackles the issue of the national party system head on. He identifies the dynamics of party-building on a national basis and, in so doing, echoes the major themes of the three previous papers. The process he examines occurred within the malleable boundaries of the political community identified by Carty and Ward and also within the two time periods—with their distinctive forms of party organization and competition—considered by Stewart and Prang. With the end of Macdonald's politics and with the nationalizing of sentiment within English-Canadian elites, a distinct change occurred in the character of the national party system and in the political community which it shaped. Smith observes that the changing face of federal-provincial relations, which now encompasses the regional brokerage processes that once functioned within the two national parties, has weakened the parties' capacity to sustain the community. Smith is uncertain about the outcome of these changes in the party system, but it seems clear that such a fundamental alteration in what historically has been the primary instrument of nation-builders must require new mechanisms for maintaining a national political community.

Stewart makes it clear that political leadership was central to the community-building experience in Canada. John Courtney pursues this theme in his exploration of the changes that the national parties have undergone in their leadership selection activities. His primary concern is the extent to which recent, dramatic changes in the selection of party leaders contribute to the development of a truly national politics and to parties capable of sustaining the political community. His assertion that the national leadership convention is arguably "the most important extra-governmental political institution in Canada" deserves serious consideration. If David Smith's speculations that Canadian parties now are tools for establishing a national "followership" have substance, then Courtney's analysis takes on particular force. As a result, in a clearer understanding of party leadership conventions we may well find the keys to understanding the essence of the emerging forces which will shape the national political community in the future.

The federal-provincial conference has come to replace the politics of regional brokerage as the central mechanism of regional representation in national affairs. Christopher Armstrong explores the origins of this institution. He reminds us of how recent a development the meaningful first ministers' conference is and why it should have appeared when it did. The replacement of political parties by these conferences as the principal institution for resolving interregional disputes represents a shift from political to governmental linkage mechanisms in national policy formation and administration. A change of this magnitude in such an important political function reflects major changes in the character of the country's political institutions, in particular the growth of capable and aggressively selfconscious province-building elites. It also ensures that, henceforth, new forces will be critical in shaping the future of the national community, making the task of its management considerably more difficult than in the past.

The three final papers consider the difficulties of managing the national political community. Because their vantage point is that of the centre, they provide a useful antidote to the large literature of the past two decades which examines the polity from a regional perspective. Peter Waite's essay on the relations between Ottawa and the Maritimes is a grass-roots exposition of how the processes which Stewart refers to actually worked. There was nothing particularly elegant or edifying about the techniques of the first party system. Waite reveals that building a political community in Canada was a slow, piecemeal, gritty business, one that prospered only because the political elite centred on Macdonald had the skill and determination to see the job through.

In his study of British Columbia, Donald Blake demolishes some of the many silly conceptions held about that province as he explores how the issues raised by Smith and Courtney are manifested in the problems faced by national politicians in the disintegrating party system of the 1980's. He too sees the present as characterized by "a decline of party," and he uses the case of British Columbia to explore some of the real consequences of this change for the political community. We are struck by his use of the phrase "the ties that bind" in his conclusions, for this is the image which Margaret Prang uses to describe the interwar creation of national sentiment which marked the emergence of a distinctive and coherent sense of Canadianness in the anglophone nation's political culture. That it should survive behind the confusion of multilevel party politics in contemporary British Columbia is testimony to the existence of an almost primordial sense of political community in Canada.

More than one observer was surprised at the emergence of similar feelings of community in Quebec during the referendum campaign on sovereignty-association, for the "two nations" concept of Canada had taken a strong grip on Canadian intellectuals during the 1960's and 1970's. Rather than attempting to explore the political cultures of French and English Canada, John English analyses the ways in which communal relations were managed through the institution of the French Lieutenant in national government. That much-heralded creature is, in fact, a rather rare bird, for apparently only two mature members of the species have ever been sighted. English does not rehearse the historical record of the successful cases but chooses instead to explore two instances in which attempts to establish a French lieutenancy ended in failure. By considering both Liberal and Conservative episodes, at different times, English removes any partisan sting from the issue. His conclusions are sobering, for he finds that not only is a successful lieutenancy rare, but also that failure to establish such a mechanism has "created much worse problems" than might otherwise have developed. As the management of French-English relations will always be a central task for those leaders who are responsible for sustaining the political community, the conclusions which English draws give pause for reflection. What remains to be seen is whether political parties will, in future, find appropriate mechanisms for communal accommodation or whether other parts of the polity will henceforth manage these relationships.

These papers were originally presented to an interdisciplinary seminar of historians and political scientists at the 1983 Learned Societies conference in Vancouver. Beyond a common interest in subject matter, participants in both disciplines shared an interest in understanding political authority—its origins, nature, functions, and consequences. Despite obvious disciplinary differences in their approaches, the authors address one another's concerns to a remarkable extent; they also identify strikingly similar phenomena at work in shaping the Canadian political community. In addition to their individual contributions, together these essays constitute a powerful argument for further work in a scholarly tradition which still offers us penetrating insights. A fuller understanding demands the tools and approaches of both disciplines, especially as Canada was a deliberate creation whose existence and survival as a political entity has always been somewhat problematic. In recent years respect for traditional disciplinary boundaries has fragmented the study of the Canadian community. The papers in this collection demonstrate the profit to be gained when the disciplines speak to one another. They also suggest that future enquiry will be more fruitful if pursued in an interdisciplinary atmosphere.

NOTES

1. Carl Berger, *The Writing of Canadian History: Aspects of English Canadian Historical Writing: 1900–1970* (Toronto: Oxford University Press, 1976), p. 259.
2. Ibid., p. 98.
3. W. L. Morton, *The Canadian Identity* (Toronto: University of Toronto Press, 1961), p. 111.
4. A. C. Cairns, "Alternative Styles in the Study of Canadian Politics," *Canadian Journal of Political Science* 7, no. 1 (1974): 104.
5. Ramsay Cook, "La Survivance French-Canadian Style," in *The Maple Leaf Forever: Essays on Nationalism and Politics in Canada* (Toronto: Macmillan, 1971), pp. 126–27.
6. P. B. Waite, ed., *The Confederation Debates in the Province of Quebec/1865,* (Toronto: McClelland and Stewart, 1963), p. 107.

7. Gordon Stewart, "Political Patronage under Macdonald and Laurier 1878–1911," *American Review of Canadian Studies* 10, no. 1 (1980): 3–26; "John A. Macdonald's Greatest Triumph," *Canadian Historical Review* 63, no. 1 (1982): 3–33.
8. Reginald Whitaker, *The Government Party: Organizing and Financing the Liberal Party of Canada, 1930–1958* (Toronto: University of Toronto Press, 1977), p. 410.

I

THE BASIS FOR POLITICAL COMMUNITY

2

The Origins of Canadian Politics and John A. Macdonald

GORDON STEWART

John A. Macdonald still stands like a colossus across the landscape of Canadian history. And our image of that colossus is still very much shaped by Donald Creighton's great two-volume biography of the young politician and the old chieftain. Few who have read Creighton's masterpiece can have been unmoved by its achievement. The picture of Macdonald was based on meticulous archival research and was fashioned by Creighton's deeply humane and scholarly mind. Moreover, the two volumes are written in a fluent, literary style (rare in modern historical scholarship) that extended the appeal of Creighton's Macdonald to an audience beyond the narrow academic one. This breadth of appeal was helped by the nationalist theme in Creighton's assessment, a theme which portrayed Macdonald as the far-sighted builder of the Canadian nation. As Creighton depicted his hero, Macdonald was ever gazing steadily into the future in a vigilant effort to create a modern Canada still tied to Great Britain and strong enough to resist absorption into the United States.[1]

That noble vision of Macdonald has been somewhat tarnished as the research and writings of such scholars as Peter Waite and Keith Johnson have filled out some dimensions of Macdonald missing from the Creighton portrait. Keith Johnson has explained Macdonald's deep interest in railway and land speculation in a manner that undermines the image of Macdonald single mindedly pursuing the great political goal that is the focus of Creighton's story.[2] Peter Waite's sensible case that Macdonald's political thinking never ran ahead of public opinion on most issues of the day and his recent work emphasizing Macdonald's preoccupation with patronage deployment remind us that Macdonald was very much a politician of his time rather than an exceptional figure operating in a world of his own.[3]

This essay extends the revisionist assessment of Macdonald. In particular, it shows that Macdonald's view of politics and the constitution, his concept of party leadership, and his understanding of his role as minister of the crown were shaped by the Canadian political world of 1791–1854 and especially by the turbulent years of the 1830's and 1840's. When Confederation was put in place in 1867, Macdonald had been at the centre of the Canadian political stage for about twenty-five years. His ideology, in the sense of his definition of the Anglo-Canadian relationship, was set long before Confederation, but so too was his entire conception of the workings of politics and the constitution. Such a re-evaluation of Macdonald will not radically alter the scholarly understanding of the man and his political outlook, especially if the work of Waite and Johnson is used to qualify Creighton's Macdonald.[4] But if it can be shown that Macdonald's centre of gravity, as it were, was rooted in pre-Confederation Canada, we will be able to view his post-1867 role from a different angle of vision and to weigh afresh his impact on Canadian political culture.

Canadian political culture has its roots in the late eighteenth century. To illustrate how these roots grew into a Canadian system of politics as distinct from a mere repetition of British or American patterns, this analysis opens by placing the late eighteenth-century colonies of Upper and Lower Canada in a comparative context. These colonies possessed many of the same features as the pre-revolutionary American colonies. They had British governors, appointed executive councils, and elected assemblies. In the period between 1800 and 1848, a series of political battles took place between the executive and the assemblies, a political warfare that erupted into actual rebellions in 1837. This kind of conflict between governors and assemblies had also been a basic pattern of politics in the American colonies and, as Bernard Bailyn has shown, embedded in the American political system the concept that executive and legislative branches operated in two separate spheres.[5] The origins of the American separation of the executive and legislative powers were rooted in the politics of the colonial period. It is essential to understand why similar conditions of gubernatorial-assembly political struggles over an extended number of years had a different outcome in the Canadian case.

If the Canadian colonies displayed characteristics that suggested an American pattern might have taken hold, they also exhibited features that might have led to a duplication of British forms or practices in North America. The 1791 constitutions for Upper and Lower Canada left the governor and other heads of departments with strong executive power, a power that was enhanced by the extensive range of crown patronage available to the governor and his fellow high officials. The Catholic

Church in Lower Canada and the Anglican Church in Upper Canada were seen by British colonial policy-makers as potential colonial equivalents to the influential role of the established Church of England. The 1791 constitutional legislation even tried to provide for the emergence of a Canadian House of Lords by arranging for membership of the legislative council to be hereditary through the eldest son. With these types of provisions the Pitt government in England and colonial administrators such as Lieutenant-Governor James Simcoe in Upper Canada expected that the Canadian colonies, rather than repeating the American experience, would follow the British pattern. Yet Canada followed neither the British nor the American pattern. An explanation of why this was so is the key to understanding the origins of Canadian politics. And that explanation can best be set in train by comparing what happened in Britain, America, and Canada down to the 1820's.[6]

In the case of Britain, the best starting point is the outcome of the 1688 revolution. That revolution came about because nearly all important groups within English society came to believe that James II was trying to establish a strong, centralized monarchy similar to the absolutist system that then existed in France. James II's use of prerogative powers to suspend acts of Parliament in pursuit of his Catholicizing policy, his attacks on the Church of England culminating in the trial of the seven bishops, his manipulation of borough charters as part of an attempt to pack Parliament with his supporters, his intervention in the property rights of the fellows of Magdalen College, his appointing of Catholic officers to the army, especially in the Irish garrisons—all these convinced the Whig opposition, and by 1688 most of the Tories, that James II was intent on increasing royal power to the point where it could not be checked. With a weakened church, a subservient Parliament, and a standing army all subject to James II's wishes, English liberty would disappear and English property would be threatened by an overmighty monarchy. With this background to the expulsion of James II, it would have been natural for the revolution to have resulted in a victory for the opposition forces against strong executive power, in seventeenth-century terms a victory of "country" over "court."

Yet, if we look at the revolutionary settlement over the long haul, this was not the case at all. The long series of wars with France between 1689 and 1713 led to an increase in executive weight. Revenue on an unprecedented scale had to be raised, sophisticated credit mechanisms centring on the newly created Bank of England were developed, armies had to be raised, maintained, and deployed. By 1715 the British government was supporting the largest navy in the world. All this required an elaboration of central government power, and most of the leading Whig politicians took to the system like ducks to water. They became "court" Whigs seeking power and office and the emoluments and influence that attached to office.[7] Robert Walpole's rise to fortune and power was typical of this generation of Whigs. The increasing weight of central government was also evident in the energetic and manipulative way in which Queen Anne and her ministers succeeded in getting the Scottish Parliament abolished and bringing that troublesome northern country into a legislative (and subservient) union with England.

Accompanying this growth of the central executive after 1688 was a related phenomenon that helped consolidate a national ruling class in power. The period between 1688 and 1715 was one of intense political excitement as Whigs and Tories argued over all the religious, constitutional, and foreign policy issues left open after the revolution. There were frequent general elections, more frequent in fact than in any other period in British history. All these elections and the size of the stakes involved made politics an expensive business. As J. H. Plumb has shown, this meant that by the 1720's English national politics was controlled by an oligarchy composed largely of the landed magnates who had enough money and influence to manage elections and administration.[8] Thus, the great paradox of this period of British history is that the revolution to topple a tyrannical executive ended up with a stronger executive controlled by a narrow national ruling class. Principled "old" Whigs and disgruntled Tories might tilt at this "court" Whig hypocrisy, middle-class audiences might laugh at its depiction in John Gay's *Beggar's Opera,* but the Whig oligarchy was securely entrenched by the 1720's. They had even extended the period between general elections to seven years, which gave ministers ample time to manage and influence Parliament. All these developments were made tolerable because of the image of papist tyranny that James II still represented and even more importantly because this central government kept its hands off local government in the counties.[9] For the remainder of the eighteenth century, the growth of strong national government capable of defeating France and extending the empire coexisted with an absence of intervention in the localities. James II had so intervened. His successors, the Hanoverian kings and their ministers, learned that if they kept their hands off local government, they could in the name of national security and prosperity build up an executive power unimagined by James II. The re-emergence of Toryism as a political force from the 1790's on, the reaction of the English propertied classes to the French Revolution and social unrest, increased the role of English national government as ministers made responses to dislocations caused by the twin impact of industrialization and war. By the 1830's the national government was prepared to make a whole series of interventions into society, even now into local government, and the pattern was securely established of strong national government.[10] In the British case "court" had triumphed over "country."

In the American case the result was just the opposite. By the 1820's the federal administration was, to use John Murrin's phrase, "a miniscule government in a giant land."[11] Such a divergence from the post-1688 British path was not the foregone conclusion it seems from today's perspective, although it must be acknowledged that the geographical extent and economic diversity of the colonies, the absence of an hereditary landed class, the presence in society of a much larger percentage of property-owners and franchise-wielders, and the failure of the established church to extend its binding influence to the colonies all conspired to make it difficult for a "court"-style political system to take root in eighteenth-century America. A fundamental difficulty in this respect was the weakness of the royal governors. Powerful enough on paper, in practice they had few means of influence to manage the colonial assemblies in the ways Hanoverian ministers managed Parliament. Governors did not have enough funds free of assembly control, they did not have executive spokesmen in the assemblies, they did not have enough patronage, and they did not have sufficient backing from locally influential social groups to build up weighty executives that could reach into society. Most governors found themselves on the defensive from the 1690's to the 1760's as colonial assemblies manoeuvred to circumscribe the power they had on paper.[12]

This pattern of weak executive, strong assemblies was particularly well-defined in the southern colonies where local constitutions worked in a typical "country" fashion. The economic, social, and cultural conditions led to this emasculation of central power. There were no towns in the southern colonies equivalent to New York or Boston or Philadelphia functioning as economic and social magnets for increasingly integrated hinterlands. Economic centres were more local and scattered. Perhaps most important of all was the nature of the planter class in the south. Dispersed over the countryside, dealing individually with British merchant houses, enjoying local status and prestige, they were not a suitable base upon which governors might hope to build a client class dedicated to the strengthening of central authority. Like the parliamentary gentry of pre-1640 England, these local notables in the southern colonies wanted small and frugal government, low taxes, and as much liberty as possible to organize the labour and production on their estates. It was no socio-political accident that during the revolutionary period it was this southern planter class which produced the most eloquent spokesmen of the "country" ideology. Set on their country estates, having no need of complex fiscal mechanisms of a central government, with their poor effectively controlled as slaves, the Virginia planters like Thomas Jefferson were one class in the Anglo-American world of the mid-eighteenth century that could embrace unreservedly the "country" ideology (protecting property from the Crown and from the poor) as the best guide to organizing government and society. Conditions in Virginia made this a self-evident truth.

It was not quite so self-evident in Boston, however. In spite of the formidable obstacles, several characteristics of the "court" political system did show signs of taking root in Massachusetts and other northern colonies. In Massachusetts, under the administrations of William Shirley, Thomas Pownall, and Thomas Hutchinson, the royal governors attempted with some success to use patronage and influence to build up a class of officeholders and Anglicans who would be equivalent in function to the ruling oligarchy in England and who would act as a counterweight to the levelling tendencies in colonial society. As Bernard Bailyn has summed up Hutchinson's view of the matter, "For Hutchinson, as for Ramsay and the ruling whig governments in England the ultimate fact of political life . . . was the logical necessity for an absolute and unitary authority to exist somewhere in every government; in its essential definition that is what government was: a unit of absolute and undivisible authority."[13] In the same way as the executive controlled and influenced the English state in the eighteenth century, so Hutchinson looked to the local equivalents emerging in the colonies. This being so, he sought to use his gubernatorial power to encourage the acceptance of those social and religious distinctions which marked out the ruling groups of eighteenth-century England. It was this drift towards an Anglican ruling class knit together by patronage, a drift that would become a strong current if governors could get their hands on the revenue to be raised by new acts in the 1760's, that so disenchanted propertied, educated, and influential men like John Adams who were not included in Hutchinson's circle of influence. The opposition began to articulate more assertively a "country" critique of the Hutchinson regime as a local system of executive influence and patronage that would grow to the bloated size of the corrupt administrations in England.

Under the pressure of the 1763–74 attempts by Britain to make parliamentary imperial policies more effective in the colonies, the colonial patriot ideology came to rely heavily on this classical "country" critique of corrupt and overpowerful central authority threatening long-cherished local liberties, local wealth, and property. The increase of officials, especially in the customs service, the use of admiralty courts, the quartering of troops, the attempts to raise revenues beyond assembly control, all these measures were taken by the colonial patriots as evidence that George III's ministers were seeking to duplicate in the colonies circumstances that already enabled them to suborn Parliament in England.

The revolutionary experience transformed this "country" critique into a republican ideology complete with a formal separation of powers that had been the practice in the colonial period and with great emphasis on elected rather than appointed officials.[14] This new republican ideology seemed to be generally accepted by the 1780's, but as the new nation experienced fiscal, economic, social, and diplomatic problems of the first order, the concept of strong central government akin to the post-1688 version in England took on a new lease of life. To Alexander Hamilton and like-minded Federalists, the new republic could very usefully adopt those features of English government which had made that country the dominant economic power in the world. The Federalists wished to build a government strong enough to maintain domestic law and order, to defend the frontier in the northwest, to protect American shipping on the high seas, and to stabilize the economy by establishing a central bank similar in function to the Bank of England.

The Federalists' greatest strength throughout the 1780–1815 years lay in the New England states where, during the colonial period, some approximation to a "court" political and social culture had flickered fitfully into life. But the anglophilia of the Federalists, their hankering after hierarchy and deference, convinced too many democratic Americans that revolutionary achievements and republican ideology were being threatened by the reintroduction of a British-style, quasi-monarchical definition of national government. The Democratic-Republican opposition, solidly strong in the southern states where economic growth was not seen to require elaborate initiatives by central government, redoubled their efforts under Jefferson and his Virginian successors to preserve the virtuous republic which had been created by freeing American from corrupt British practices of government. These Democratic-Republicans won in 1800 and so thwarted Federalists' hopes of building up a more directive central government. Over the next decade and a half, the Federalists declined as a political force, unable to imprint their more traditional view of government and society on the geographically expanding, ethnically varied landscape of democratic and republican America. Without a national ruling class, without (as yet) an integrated national economy, with deep sectional differences, with its characteristic localism, and with its revolutionary myths to cherish, America was fertile ground for the apotheosis of the "country" view of government. In America the long-term consequence of revolution was small and weak central government, "frugal" government as Jefferson would put it. If by the 1830's the "court" had triumphed in England, in America the "country" had vanquished all.[15]

Placing the Canadian colonies in this Anglo-American context produces an odd result. Conventional wisdom has it that Canada's politics and constitution fall somewhere in between the British and American patterns, but taking stock of conditions in the 1820's shows that Canada's local constitutions were even more "court" in their workings than that of Britain. The governor of Lower Canada and the lieutenant-governor of Upper Canada were able to run their colonies with a minimum of reference to the assemblies. Most of the executive's income came from crown revenues not susceptible to assembly control. The entire patronage of each colony was in the hands of the governor and his appointed council, and in both colonies powerful networks of local notables were built up by patronage distribution. The governor appointed not only his executive councillors but also the legislative council, which, in a manner similar to the House of Lords in Britain, could amend, delay, or stop legislation coming up from the assembly. Both Canadas then by the 1820's had thoroughgoing "court" systems of politics.[16]

There were four reasons for this extreme development. The first is that Canada differed from the colonies that rebelled in 1776 in that it had been conquered by the army and navy of the British Crown in 1759–60. This fact of military conquest made Canada fundamentally different from the thirteen seaboard colonies, as Benjamin Franklin and other patriots clearly understood. The whole patriot case elaborated against Britain in the 1760's rested on the argument that the colonies had not been acquired by presettlement military conquest. They had originated as settler communities in the seventeenth century with charter privileges granted by the Crown. This was the essential starting point for making the case that an array of colonial settler rights stemming from seventeenth-century foundations could not be invaded or dismantled by later parliamentary authority.

One of the most interesting and telling confirmations of this frame of reference comes from Nova Scotia during the 1760's. That colony had been ceded to Britain by the Treaty of Utrecht, most of the French-speaking settlers were expelled by the British army in the course of the Seven Years' War, and during the 1760's new settlers arrived from eastern Connecticut, Rhode Island, and southeastern Massachusetts on the invitation of the British governor. These settlers were accustomed to local self-government in New England, where township officers were elected. Immediately they moved into a colony acquired by British arms, doubts surfaced as to the applicability of these traditional New England ways. They tried to duplicate the New England form of township government, but the governor and council in Halifax intruded appointed officials into the localities, and in their petitions of protest, the New England settlers were clearly ill-at-ease about what legal grounds they stood on. Instead of tradition-sanctioned assertions about colonial rights that came so easily to their relatives back in New England, the settlers in Nova Scotia wrote hesitatingly about rights they conceived they might have. They understood that moving onto crown land acquired through conquest put into doubt the entire basis of colonial rights.[17] For French Canadians in the newly acquired colony of Quebec, the stark fact of conquest was even more evident. They knew the French population of Nova Scotia had been physically removed, they knew that Catholicism was illegal in England, they knew that to protect property and church they would have to co-operate with the British military executive and after 1764 the British civilian executive. The Catholic church co-operated so well that the British accepted Briand as the new bishop of Quebec in 1766, and from that time on the church was a solid underpinning for the Crown.[18] In short, the fact of conquest created favourable conditions for the growth of executive influence.

The second reason for Canada's "court" orientation was the result of the values of the French-speaking community. Throughout the period of French rule, they had accepted royal authority and government by royal officials appointed by the intendant. They had also accepted military authority, all males between sixteen and forty being called out regularly for militia duty. They expected government to come from above by way of royal officials and military officers without any mediating force of representative institutions. They were used to hierarchy in society. All these traditional values of French Canadians predisposed them to accept a "court"-style constitution. Their acceptance was all the more willing since the British took pains to adjust government as far as possible to meet the needs of his majesty's new subjects. The Catholic church was legitimized, and the Quebec Act of 1774 maintained the Canadian border at the Ohio and formally recognized existing French law and custom. The absence of an assembly that produced such protests in the thirteen colonies (and among some English merchants in Montreal) was simply not an issue for French Canadians. The increasing prosperity of Quebec from the 1770's on as the West Indian markets opened up to them and as the British increasingly turned to her North American colonies for naval supplies during the wars with France deepened French-Canadian attachment to a British regime which Americans could only see as tyrannical.[19]

If the fact of conquest and the values and predicament of the French

Canadians gave initial shape to constitutional forms in Canada, the third conditioning factor was the influx of thousands of loyalists who settled in pockets along the north shore of the St. Lawrence and Lake Ontario. The loyalist migration and later additions created both an English settler society west of Montreal and a problem for the government of William Pitt in London. As long as the population remained almost entirely French, the London government could justify its assemblyless constitution, but with an English population now in place, it became necessary to concede that mixed or balanced constitution with its representative component that the eighteenth-century English believed to be a birthright both in the mother country and the colonies.

The loyalists believed this too, but their concepts of government and society were, by this time, different from the patriot defenders of assembly rights against encroaching executive power. Loyalist values were a peculiar mixture based on British and colonial practices but affected by their experiences at the hands of American rebels during the war years. As a guiding credo, loyalists believed that the American patriots were extremists who pushed their criticism of royal and gubernatorial authority to the point where familiar features of the Anglo-colonial landscape were destroyed. As we have seen in the case of Thomas Hutchinson, loyalists thought that an effective, unitary executive power with legitimate means of managing and influencing the assemblies was as essential for political and social stability in the colonies as it was in Britain. Loyalists further believed that deference was an essential characteristic of the good society. In this sense they were practical believers in the benefits of that classical concept of deference which J. G. A. Pocock has described as the basis of conventional eighteenth-century political thought.[20] They reasoned that in the English and colonial settings where administrations did not possess the policing power of absolute monarchies, deferential social interaction was the key to preserving constitutional liberty. Without deference, government would degenerate into chaotic democracy. Intimately tied to their penchant for deference, the loyalists were deeply attached to the concept of monarchy with all its associated techniques of appointive rather than elective administration. In the increasingly open and competitive colonial societies of the 1760's and 1770's, the loyalists (although many were critical of British policies) came to regard monarchy as the constitutional and psychological means of assuring hierarchy, deference, and stability. Once that anchor was abandoned, the whole social fabric would unravel.[21] These early English Canadians, in contrast to Jefferson, had no faith in "the people." Their outlook was much closer to conservative Federalists, if one can imagine Federalists still operating in a monarchical setting.[22]

Still, the loyalists, as creatures of the eighteenth-century Anglo-American world, did believe in representative institutions. So too did Pitt's government in London (at least where propertied Englishmen were concerned), and the loyalist influence forced the British government to draw up a new constitution for Canada. And this leads to the fourth factor moulding the early Canadian polity—the outlook of the Pitt administration in the early 1790's. As they approached the Canadian matter, Pitt and his ministers bore in mind two contemporary worrisome developments. There were signs that the French Revolution was not going to be as limited and respectable as England's bloodless revolution in 1688, and, secondly, Pitt's administration was concerned about the beginnings of political unrest arising from the dislocating impact of industrialization. From 1790 on, Pitt's government became increasingly Tory in its cast of mind.[23] Beyond that, most British ministers who bothered to think about colonial matters in the late eighteenth century were convinced they had learned a lesson from history. As they recalled the successful revolution of the thirteen colonies, they believed they could focus in on the fundamental weakness of those old colonial constitutions. The problem had been that governors were weak and assemblies were strong. The Canadian constitution was to be so constructed as to avoid a repetition of the destructive pattern of American colonial politics.[24]

The 1791 Canada Act (31 George III, c.31) did several things to ensure this outcome. To strengthen the governor's hand, the 1774 Quebec Revenue Act (14 George III, c.88) remained in effect, an act which gave the executive revenue free of assembly control.[25] The entire patronage of each colony lay with the governor and his appointed executive councillors. Appointed legislative councils were also established in the hope that they would become local equivalents of the House of Lords. The 1791 act provided explicitly for this possibility, stipulating in section VI that the crown-appointed legislative councillors would have "a hereditary right of being summoned to the Legislative Council."[26] This was in effect an attempt to coax into existence a Canadian peerage. Besides the hereditary upper house, the 1791 act also provided for public support of a church establishment, principally by setting aside public land in each township for parsonages or rectories "according to the Establishment of the Church of England."[27] In savouring this provision for a state church, the first lieutenant-governor of Upper Canada, John Graves Simcoe exulted that he was " to have a Bishop" and explained that "the state propriety of some form of public worship practically considered arises from the necessity there is of preventing the enthusiastic and fanatic teachers from acquiring that superstitious hold of the multitude.[28]

With provision for a strong executive, a hereditary upper house, and support for a church establishment, the 1791 act gave a decidedly "court" orientation to the Canadian constitution—an orientation, it must be understood, that was even more weighted to the executive than the current British one. Ever since the events of 1688–89, the British parliament had met in annual sessions to make appropriations for his majesty's government. The executive still retained a wide discretion on use of appropriations, but even that was changing by the 1780's and 1790's as public opinion and Pitt's administrative reforms led to parliamentary scrutiny of public accounts. In short, the ministers of the crown in Britain knew they had to bring Parliament along with them if they hoped to win approval of expenditures.[29] In contrast, the situation in Canada meant that the governor and executive councillors had little need to consult or work with the assembly in the systematic way Pitt and his ministers worked with Parliament. On top of all this, all British governors of Upper and Lower Canada between 1791 and the 1820's were military men, most of them former officers of the Duke of Wellington. The fact of the long French wars between 1793 and 1815 was one factor and so was the need to have men of military experience for matters on the American frontier. Whatever the reason for such appointments, this meant that the men at the head of the Canadian executives had no parliamentary experience and no interest in building up a working relationship with the colonial legislatures in the way that Pitt and all eighteenth-century British first Lords of the Treasury had to build up a relationship with Parliament. The end result was that local executive power was more unchecked in the Canadas than it was in Britain. Putting Canada, the United States, and Great Britain along the "country"–"court" spectrum, by the 1820s, Canada was emphatically furthest to the "court" end.

The 1791 constitution was intended to be the "image and transcript" of the British constitution transplanted to North America. As Lord Grenville summed up British policy, the "general object . . . is to assimilate the constitution of that Province to that of Great Britain as nearly as the differences arising from the manners of the People and from the present situation of that Province will admit." Simcoe believed that the political and social stability guaranteed by such a British constitution would attract immigrants from the fragmented American democracy. In Canada they were "establishing a free, honourable British Government and a pure administration of its laws which shall hold out to the solitary immigrants, and to the several states, advantages that under the present form of government they do not and cannot enjoy."[30] Grenville, Simcoe, and the Pitt government hoped that the 1791 constitution would lead to stability and good government and thus present an exemplary counterpoint to the

United States with its ineffective central government and its formless democracy. But these hopes were dashed. Far from producing stability, the 1791 constitution led to forty years of bitter political divisions culminating in armed rebellions in both Canadas in 1837. The 1791 constitution simply did not work.

It did not work because there was a fundamental disjunction between the hopes of the British policy-makers and social and cultural conditions in North America. In this sense the British had learned no lesson from the American Revolution, for they were well-nigh ignorant of colonial circumstances that precluded the emergence of British social groups and institutions. Take the legislative councils, for example. It was intended that they would develop into colonial equivalents of the House of Lords, influential chambers filled with men of property possessing some reach in society that could become a pool for ministers and a legitimate conservative counterweight to the more representative assemblies. Simcoe had been optimistic on this score in the 1790's, but by the 1830's even colonial Tories understood that the councils were falling far short of any such significant role. John Beverly Robinson, attorney-general of Upper Canada and a member of the ruling Tory group, was reduced to lamenting, as he watched the rise of a democratic opposition, that there was "no counteracting influence of an ancient aristocracy, of a great landed interest or even of a wealthy agricultural class."[31] That venerable old Tory loyalist Richard Cartwright complained in the same vein about conditions "where almost universal suffrage prevails, where the great mass of the people are uneducated and where there is little of that salutary influence which hereditary rank and great wealth exercise in Great Britain."[32]

Some belated efforts were made in the 1830's to increase the influence of the legislative council by enlarging its size and thus pulling in more members with some status in the localities, but it was a fruitless endeavour. As John Macaulay, another Tory jeremiah, conceded, there "is no country in the world [where] materials can be found for a legislative body corresponding in influence with the British House of Peers."[33] Throughout the entire period since 1791, the legislative councils were composed of officials and lay members usually inclined to support the prerogative powers of the governor. They were extensions of officialdom rather than institutions with influence in the country. In his characteristically forthright manner, Lord Elgin, the Whig governor general of Canada from 1847 to 1856, summed it up when he wrote to his masters in London that the legislative councillors "were worse than useless . . . they have no weight whatsoever in the community."[34]

If the hopes of making the legislative councils into a House of Lords were futile, so were the expectations that a state church could emerge in

Canada. The 1791 constitution envisioned the established church playing a central role similar to the function of the Church of England since the 1688 revolution. It was to encourage religious uniformity, enable a link to be maintained between Anglicanism and office-holding, inculcate reverence for the 1791 constitution, and uphold the benefits of social deference and hierarchy. John Strachan, a tireless toiler on this quest and a tireless smiter of non-Anglican denominations, obtained a royal charter for Kings College in 1827 which required the teaching staff to take the test by subscribing to the thirty-nine articles and insisted that only Anglicans benefit from the land reserved for clergy. For his pains, he was made first bishop of Toronto in 1839. But it was all in a losing cause. Far from contributing towards stability, the privileged position of the Anglican church led to increasingly bitter religious turmoil. The privileges of the Church of England, particularly the granting of clergy reserves in each township, were challenged first by the Presbyterians (cleverly insisting that they too were an established church) and then by Methodists, Baptists, and other dissenters. These dissenting interests constituted a majority of the population, and they turned to politics to press their case. The religious issue inflamed politics until in 1854 the most galling of the Anglican privileges were abolished.[35] The church establishment that Simcoe had been so hopeful about in 1791 turned out to be a house of cards.

Perhaps in an even more fundamental way the 1791 constitution was at odds with British norms because it provided no encouragement for a working relationship to develop between governor and executive councillors on the one hand and the elected assembly on the other. The starting point for understanding the issue here is to understand how the British constitution actually worked in this period. Earl Grey, the British Whig leader, prided himself on his knowledge of constitutional matters and set out in his *Parliamentary Government* the importance of appreciating the difference between theoretical formulations of the British balanced constitution and how it actually worked.

> Since the establishment of Parliamentary Government, the common description of the British constitution as one in which the executive power belongs to the Crown while the power of legislation is vested jointly in the Sovereign and the two Houses of Parliament, has ceased to be correct, unless it is understood as applying only to the legal and technical distribution of power. It is the distinguishing characteristic of Parliamentary Government that it requires the powers belonging to the Crown to be exercised through Ministers who are held responsible for the manner in which they are used, who are expected to be

> members of the two Houses of Parliament, the proceedings of which they must be able generally to guide and who are considered entitled to hold their offices only while they possess the confidence of Parliament and more especially of the House of Commons.[36]

The structure set up in the Canadas could hardly have been less conducive to preventing such British practices from working. The governor was appointed, the executive councillors were appointed as officials rather than as members with political weight in the assembly, and the entire executive got much of its revenue up to 1834 from the 1774 British Act of Parliament. Far from having to possess the confidence of the assembly as British administrators had to possess the confidence of the House of Commons, the Canadian executives had little need to establish a systematic relationship with the elected chamber. As Lord Durham succinctly summarized the situation in his 1839 report, "the natural state of government in all these Colonies is that of collision between the executive and the representative body."[37]

Whereas in Britain successful government depended on a working harmony between ministers of the Crown and Parliament, there was no similar intermingling of executive council and assembly in the Canadas. Governors and their executive councillors could function almost independently of the assemblies. The executive councillors were chosen by the governors in consultation with the imperial government. Down to the 1830's most members of the executive councils in both Upper and Lower Canada, whether British- or Canadian-born, regarded their appointments as individual patent offices to be held for life. These men were not the equivalent of British cabinet members but permanent crown officials, "gens de place" as the opposition in Lower Canada called them.[38] So entrenched were members of the executive council that even the governors sometimes had difficulty in making the council work as an administration since each member kept exclusive control of his department. The governor and his councillors had extensive control of crown revenues and complete control of patronage, and they used these powers to build up a series of local patronage networks loyal to the regime.[39] The designation by frustrated Reformers of the ruling groups as the Family Compact (in Upper Canada) and the Chateau Clique (in Lower Canada) were terms of abuse intended to emphasize the criticism of executive exclusivity. By the 1830's there was widespread lack of confidence in these executives because as William Hamilton Merritt so cogently phrased it, they were "beyond the control of the people."[40] Instead of bringing the much vaunted stability so complacently anticipated in 1791, the constitution had in fact proved to be a recipe for systematic instability.

One of the most comprehensive and insightful critiques of the working of the 1791 constitution, all the more informative because it did not come from a Reformer, was that penned in 1839 by Poulett Thomson (subsequently Lord Sydenham), the governor sent out to calm the post-rebellion atmosphere and prepare the ground for whatever constitutional changes his London masters decided upon as a solution to the troubles in Canada. Thomson was a conservative, much in the mould of Robert Peel in England, who considered himself moderate and who distrusted alike the old, exclusive Toryism and the more forward Reformers whom he judged to be too democratic. As he assessed the sorry state of affairs in the Canadas, Thomson drew attention to the isolation of the adminstration. "A deeply rooted animosity appears to prevail against a majority of the officers of the Executive government," he observed. He emphasized that this animosity was not simply an opposition cry but was shared by many who were utterly loyal to the governor. The antagonistic view of the executive was "not confined to the popular party alone but [was] shared extensively by those who claim to be supporters of the prerogative of the Crown."

In his analysis of the constitutional defects in the Canadas, Thomson focused on what to him was very odd—that the local executives, while accused of being tyrannical, were weak by British standards. They were weak because there was no concerted policy-making by the executive councillors. Government in the two colonies consisted of a collection of individual place-holders rather than a cabinet administration in the British sense. Individual executive councillors secure in life appointments were not always amenable even to the wishes of the governor. When issues of public import did arise, government business was conducted by these "five or six individuals in town" who could agree as to public measures. The government in Upper Canada, concluded Thomson, was "a mere clique in the capital." Under the British system, Thomson noted that the Crown's ministers had "the duty . . . to initiate and perfect the measures necessary for the good of the country, and, above all, to endeavour to give to the action of those Bodies [the legislative councils and assemblies in Canada] the direction which will make their labours more efficient. This duty, one of the most important that can devolve on a Government, has hitherto been entirely neglected in Canada." According to British norms, the governors and their executive councillors should have tried to build up a working relationship with the assemblies, but in the Canadas the executive had "pursued the opposite course." Instead of trying to manage and work with the assembly, they had preferred to function in a separate executive sphere. "The local government," pointed out Thomson, "has not only abstained from taking the initiative in measures of

Legislation but it appears to have studiously repudiated these legitimate means of influence without which it could scarce be carried on.'' There was never a leader of the administration in the assembly ''authorised or instructed to explain to the House the views of the Government.''[41] The local governments in the Canadas had no British-style relationship with the assemblies. They believed they had no need to manage and influence the assemblies because the 1791 constitution had up to 1834 given them the means to administer largely by use of prerogative powers backed by Parliament-sanctioned revenue. In Upper Canada by the 1830's, this meant, as Thomson critically observed, that the assembly was ''in a most disorganized state'' because it had become nothing more than a forum for excluded or discontented elements. The result was that ''the government has little power in it [the assembly] owing to the want of a system.''[42]

In 1850, Lord Elgin, three years into his governorship, attempted a detached and historical assessment of the 1791 constitution to understand why it had been so trouble-prone and why it had created such unstable political conditions by the 1820's. Under the 1791 constitution, Elgin reasoned, the Canadas had continued to exhibit characteristics that had created political difficulties in the American colonies. The system in the thirteen colonies had disintegrated because the assemblies had ''excluded every member of the Cabinet from their legislature.'' This led to a lack of co-operation between assemblies and executive, a co-operation that Elgin, like Earl Grey and all other British constitutional experts, believed essential. This lack of co-operation was typical of countries like France and the United States which, according to Elgin, had weak governments and unstable politics when compared to Britain. In both these countries, there was ''so little to secure the co-operation of the Legislative and Executive powers.'' Indeed, Elgin was convinced that the fatal flaw of the American system, after independence, was the perpetuation of the divide between executive and legislative spheres that had developed in the old colonial system. ''The fact is,'' he concluded, ''that the Yankee system is our Old Colonial system, with, in certain cases, the principal of popular election substituted for that of nomination to the Crown.'' Drawing on his recent gubernatorial experience in Jamaica, a colony still moulded on the old pattern, Elgin illustrated his case by suggesting that ''Mr. Fillmore [the U.S. President] stands to his Congress very much in the same relation in which I stood to my Assemblies in Jamaica.'' The constitutional weakness in Jamaica, in the old thirteen colonies, in the independent United States, and in the Canadas after 1791 was ''the same absence of effective responsibility in the conduct of legislation—the same want of concurrent action between the parts of the political machine.''[43]

Thus, the 1791 constitution, which had been designed to ensure

British-style government in the Canadas, turned out to be fundamentally at odds with British constitutional and political custom. Power was exercised by appointed officials and nominated councillors who were not required to respond to concerns among the people or within the assembly.

The critique by Elgin of the workings of the 1791 constitution appears to bring the analysis full circle. If it was true, as Elgin and Thomson and other informed contemporaries argued, that the Canadian system, like the one in the thirteen colonies, had reverted to the executive and legislature operating in two distinct, antagonistic spheres, then it seemed very much on the cards that an American definition of politics would emerge in these remaining British North American colonies. After all, the analysis provided by Elgin and Thomson fits exactly the model of executive-legislative colonial warfare that Bailyn saw as lying at the origins of the American concept of separation of the executive and legislative powers. Yet this classic American pattern did not take hold in Canada. It did not because the mainstream opposition in the Canadian assemblies remained thoroughly "court" in orientation.

There were several reasons why this was so. The first conditioning factor was the very existence and geographical proximity of the United States. The United States invaded Upper Canada during the War of 1812, in the aftermath of that war an elaborate system of canals and fortifications was constructed to defend against another attempt, and in the late 1830's and 1840's there were a series of scares about American invasions on behalf of the 1837 rebels. In addition to this apprehension of the United States as aggressively expansionist, most Canadians viewed American society and government as a failure, so thoroughly democratic that order, deference, and stability had well-nigh disappeared.[44] Any Canadian politician who could be branded as an American-style democrat and republican suffered at the polls. In the 1836 election in Upper Canada, this anti-American cry was a potent weapon that unseated from the assembly William Lyon Mackenzie, the most radical Reform leader.[45] In Lower Canada the church hierarchy never failed to remind the habitants that British and monarchical institutions protected their language, culture, and religion where American democracy would destroy them. It was because of this worldview that French Canadians would be the ones to fire the last cannon shot in defence of British institutions in North America.[46] Any Canadian political party that appeared to draw too near to American political values did so at its peril, for it could so easily lead to self-inflicted wounds. This was one fact that prevented the adoption of American-style solutions to the 1791 constitutional problems.

To understand the other factors, we must examine the opposition Reform parties in Upper and Lower Canada. For the French Canadians in Lower Canada, representative institutions like the assembly were novel. Their response to the new British regime after 1791 became more complex than during the 1760–91 period, when they had accepted the customary government from above. Because of their overwhelming demographic superiority, the French Canadians were able from the outset to control the Lower Canadian assembly. This numerical preponderance could not be brought to bear on government because the 1791 constitution gave the assembly only a marginal role. The political situation became tense as early as 1800, by which time economic and social conditions produced sharp resentments against the regime, resentments that were voiced through the francophone majority in the assembly. The period between 1760 and 1847 witnessed a rapid increase of the French-Canadian population, from about 70,000 to 610,000. The prosperity associated with the French wars and the growth of urban markets in Montreal and Quebec led to the emergence of a new social class of middle-class professionals.[47] Educated at the *collèges classiques,* these men were entering society in such numbers that they came directly up against the barriers protecting the exclusive governing and official class which controlled the whole range of public service appointments through patronage. Untrained, and for the most part uninterested, in the world of business (in what was still largely an agrarian economy for French Canadians), these new men (as the British governors described them) formed *le parti canadien,* and from their position of strength in the assembly, they mounted a campaign against the Chateau Clique which monopolized public offices throughout the colony from its base in the executive.

Since the conflict took place within the anglicized institutional context created in 1791, it might have been expected that a classical "country" ideology would develop in the assembly directed against a bloated executive. But such a "country"-style opposition never took root in Lower Canada. The mainstream opposition in Lower Canada remained "court" and statist in orientation. They did not wish to destroy the world of executive patronage; they wanted access to it. They did not wish to sink the government ship; they wished to be taken aboard. They did not even wish to change the captain, for as the events of the 1840's and 1850's were to confirm, the French Canadians were perfectly willing to accept British monarchical and gubernatorial rule providing they could fully participate in it. This statist mentality had deep roots in the French colonial past and has remained a pervasive influence in the political development of modern Quebec, as has been amply demonstrated by the phenomenon of the "state middle classes" in Quebec of the 1970's and 1980's.[48] The goal of the opposition in Lower Canada was to break open the exclusive system of patronage and share in it to the fullest extent justified by overwhelming demographic strength (about 610,000 to 80,000 in 1848).[49] Insofar as the opposition achieved popularity, it was not on the basis of "country" shibboleths but because the struggle could be cast in nationalist terms of fighting against the largely anglophone imperial "*gens de place*" and their local allies, the remnants of the seigneurial class from the French colonial period. When economic distress and the surprising intransigence of the British Whig governments after 1830 finally drove some opposition leaders into armed rebellion in 1837–38, this nationalist dimension made the outbreak a more serious affair than its counterpart in Upper Canada.[50] But most French Canadians turned their backs on such radical solutions, the Church worked hard to deepen loyalty to existing institutions, and in the aftermath of the disturbances, opposition leadership fell into the hand of Louis-Hippolyte LaFontaine, a moderate dedicated to working the system to the benefit of French Canadians. The core of LaFontaine's position was simple. He wished the governors to choose their advisors from leaders in the assembly. In that way French Canadians would be in charge of government and patronage. The British Whig ministers understood that LaFontaine was no radical on these matters. Grey observed to Elgin in 1851 that LaFontaine "seems to me to have had more of the gentleman about him than any other public man in Canada."[51]

It took longer for opposition to become effective in Upper Canada. For the first two decades the population of Upper Canada was so small, scattered, and preoccupied with survival that the executive was as unchallenged as the 1791 constitution intended it to be (although there were individual critics). The military and diplomatic tensions with the United States which culminated in the outbreak of war in 1812 and the large proportion of American-born settlers led the governing elite to stick hard to its constitutional privileges. After 1815, as immigrants began to flow in from the troubled post-Waterloo British society and as the economy of Upper Canada expanded, the number and social importance of those excluded from the system increased to the point where systematic and organized opposition began to appear in the assembly. As in Lower Canada, the contemptuous intransigence of the ruling alliance and the deaf ears of post-1832 Whig governments in London led some Reform leaders into radical positions by the 1830's. In his final furious stage, following his election defeat in 1836 (largely because the governor Sir Francis Bond Head portrayed him as a radical pro-American), William Lyon Mackenzie came out for independence, republicanism, and democracy (besides biblical egalitarianism). But Mackenzie was a demented, isolated figure by 1837. The mainstream Reformer view was better presented by Robert Baldwin, who emerged as the leader of the opposition and along with LaFontaine in Lower Canada took leadership of the struggle after 1837.

The basic conservatism of the opposition view of executive power was demonstrated time and time again in the critical decade from the rebellions to the governorship of Lord Elgin in 1847. While the rebellions were abject failures in military terms, they did force the British government to take stock of their post-1791 policy in Canada. They sent over Lord Durham to help them make this reassessment. Durham's analysis focused on the lack of co-operation between executive and legislature, the governor and the assemblies. He argued that the governors would have to change their ways and develop a working relationship with the assemblies. "The Crown in Canada," he urged," would have to submit to the necessary consequence of representative institutions." This meant that the governor would have to select as his advisers political leaders with standing in the community. Administration must be carried on "by means of those in whom the representative body has confidence." This line of argument of Durham's is the one students are most familiar with, but it is of great importance for appreciating the nature of Canadian politics at this formative moment to understand that Durham's main emphasis was on the need to *increase* the weight and reach of executive power. "The defective want of administration," he explained, "commences at the very source of power; and the efficiency of the public service is impaired throughout by the entire want in the colony of any vigorous administration of the prerogative of the crown." Lest any could mistake his point, Durham emphasized that he "would not impair a single prerogative of the crown; on the contrary I believe that the interests of the people of these colonies require the protection of prerogatives which have not hitherto been exercised."[52] Under the old ways, the Family Compact and Chateau Clique had operated the executive in exclusive and personal ways that had fragmented gubernatorial authority and led to perennial battles with the assemblies. If governors now chose their executive councillors from the assemblies, they would be more effective and powerful heads of administration.

Baldwin and LaFontaine, the Reform leaders between 1837 and 1851, accepted this point about the need for strong executive power. Neither man was a democratic politician in the American sense. Lord Elgin once described Baldwin as "the most Conservative public man in Upper Canada."[53] LaFontaine was somewhat aloof as a political leader and in public took on aristocratic airs.[54] The changes Baldwin wished to implement, he took pains to make clear, "would be accomplished without in the least entrenching upon the just and necessary prerogatives of the Crown which I consider, when administered by the Lieutenant-Governor through the medium of a Provincial ministry responsible to the Provincial

Parliament, to be an essential part of the constitution of the province." In 1842, Baldwin reiterated his view that his goal was "a strong Government . . . not one like those in the neighboring states blown about by every wind and bowing before every storm."[55]

While there was an apparent agreement between Durham's views and those of the Reform leaders in the aftermath of the rebellions, there was one critical disagreement that led to the first-class political and constitutional crisis in 1844. The British view, shared by Whig and Tory ministers, and even by British Colonial reformers,[56] was that the governor should remain the centre of gravity in the colonial government. He would now choose his councillors from the assembly, but he would choose them as individuals, listen to their advice as individual heads of departments, and then determine what government policy should be. Under this scheme of things, the governor would also retain control of the actual running of administration and would remain the sole dispenser of patronage. This was unacceptable to the Reform leaders. They distrusted governors as political heads of administrations. The governors since 1791 had been Tory partisans distributing patronage for about fifty years to individuals who met Tory social and religious requirements. If things were to change in a genuine way, this power had to be broken and the public service of the colony opened to a much wider section of society represented by the Reformers. Thus the Reform leaders would only agree to become members of the executive council if they could act as a ministry with a majority in the legislature, giving them a consequent constitutional right to set policy and make appointments. Unless the centre of gravity shifted to this party leadership, there would be a perpetuation of "the old system of government—viz: the will of the Governor."[57]

That this question of control of patronage, whether it should be done by the governor or by the party leaders who sat on the council and controlled a majority in the assembly, was at the centre of things was amply demonstrated by the last great crisis in 1844 during the governorship of William Metcalfe. In a characteristically Canadian fashion, the crisis occurred when Metcalfe refused to allow Baldwin and LaFontaine, who were members of his council, to take away any of his prerogative rights to make appointments. Metcalfe complained that from the beginning of his governorship there had been "an antagonism between his views and those of his ministers on the subject of the prerogative." If he submitted to his council members on the patronage issue, that would leave the governor as "solely and completely a tool in the hands of the Council. The Council are now spoken of by themselves and others generally as 'the Ministers,' 'the Administration,' 'the Cabinet,' 'the Government' and so forth. Their pretensions are according to this new nomenclature. They expect that the policy and conduct of the governor shall be subservient to their views and party purposes.''[58]

The outcome of the 1844 crisis was a close run thing. If Metcalfe had not had to contend with his face being eaten away by cancer, he might have pulled off a political triumph, for there was a good deal of sympathy for his view even from such liberal men as Edward G. Wakefield and Egerton Ryerson. But even in the struggle to win, Metcalfe and the governors were being thrust aside by more powerful social and political forces. Once he had dismissed Baldwin and LaFontaine, Metcalfe turned to the moderate Tory William Draper to lead his council. In order to shore up Draper's strength in the assembly, Metcalfe had to concede to Draper what he had felt it so important to deny to the Reformers—extensive use of patronage for partisan purposes.[59] The Reformers' great strength was in the electorate, especially the French-Canadian electorate that remained solidly behind LaFontaine. This was the ace up the Reformers' sleeve. LaFontaine understood that the French Canadians were in a commanding position because of ''the confidence which they place in their public men.''[60] It was this bloc vote that was the rock upon which gubernatorial hopes were dashed. As M. Errol Bouchette observed, ''in reading the history of our first fifty years of constitutional struggles one is struck by the great power of the French-Canadian electorate.''[61]

Metcalfe left Canada in 1845. In 1846 a Whig government, returned to power in Britain, appointed Lord Elgin as the new governor general of Canada. Elgin had been instructed by Earl Grey to end the political turmoil in Canada by accepting the Reformers' version of responsible government. He appointed a Baldwin-LaFontaine ministry and allowed them to set policy and control patronage and thus make the governor more of a figurehead than the active government leader conceived by Metcalfe. Once in power the Reformers employed their executive powers to the full. As disenchanted colonial reformers in England perceived, the Reformers were determined ''by engrossing all the patronage to make themselves as powerful a family compact as that which they have trodden down.''[62] Jacques Monet has well summed up the phenomenon as it worked in Quebec:

> For two generations since 1800 the Canadian professional class had been struggling to secure an outlet for its ambitious; so now with a kind of bacterial thoroughness it began to invade every vital organ of government and divide up among its members hundreds of posts as Judges, Queen's Counsels, Justices of the Peace, Medical Examiners, school inspectors, militia captains, postal clerks, mail conductors, census commissioners. And as the flatteries and salaries of

> office percolated down to other classes of society—from merchants who wanted seats on the legislative council down to impoverished habitants on the crowded seigneuries—the Canadians came to realize that parliamentary democracy could be more than a lovely ideal; it was also a profitable fact.[63]

The triumph of the Reform party in 1848 was not then a victory for frugal government but a thoroughgoing confirmation of how deeply the "court" orientation to politics had moulded Canadian political culture.

The policy of Elgin towards the Baldwin-LaFontaine ministry ushered in responsible government in Canada, a form of responsible government which, instead of being governor-centred as Durham and then Metcalfe had envisaged, gave power and glory to the party leaders who controlled a majority in the legislature. During the course of the nineteenth century, all the other white settlement colonies of the empire went through this transition from gubernatorial to party rule, from oligarchic control of government to more democratic control of government. But it is essential to understand that in no other colony was the transformation so prolonged, so embittered, and so violent as it was in Canada. The political heat was so intense that permanent features were moulded onto the Canadian political landscape, a phenomenon that can be instructively assessed in the career of the greatest politician to have emerged in the 1840's, John A. Macdonald.

This period between 1828, when the Canadian opposition began to feel its strength, and 1848, when the Elgin version of responsible government was achieved, was the equivalent in Canada to the tumultuous 1689–1714 years in England (which saw more general elections than at any other period in English history) and the transforming revolutionary years between 1774 and 1789 in the United States. In both England and the United States these periods of high political activism led to basic definitions about the constitution and the working of politics. While there was no revolution in Canada, elections became frequent and bitterly contested as they had been in England when fundamental questions about the constitution were yet to be decided. In Upper Canada elections took place in 1828, 1830, 1834 and 1836, and in the Union of the Canadas in 1841, 1844, and 1848—seven elections within twenty years. At every one of these elections contemporaries believed fundamental questions about the constitution and the working of politics were at stake. In Lower Canada there was no series of elections in the 1830's, but the situation was even more tense because the French-Canadian Reformers could so easily control the assembly. There was a direct constitutional clash between the governor and the assembly as the assembly used the new Canadian Revenue Control Act (1 and 2 William IV, c. 23) to attempt a stop of supplies. In 1838 the constitution was suspended altogether, and Lower Canada was run by a specially appointed council until representative institutions were restored by the Union. Throughout this period governors and lieutenant-governors were convinced they were fighting a decisive battle for the British constitution against American-style democratic alternatives. Victory by the Reformers would lead to the end of monarchical authority in Canada and even to the loss of the colonies. To contemporaries it seemed "the fate of the Canadas" was at stake.[64]

The political turbulence erupted into open rebellion in 1837, as frustrated Reform leaders despaired of wringing any changes coming through a system so easily manipulated by the governors and their Tory allies, backed, so it seemed, even by Whig governments in London. These rebellions further deepened the already bitter partisanship as Tories came to believe all Reformers were traitors to the British connection and resented behaviour of imperial authorities like Durham giving countenance to such disloyal creatures. By the late 1830's the Tories, or "the Constitutional Party" as they tried to call themselves, were "incensed beyond all expression"[65] at developments in Upper Canada. If anything, politics after the Union was established became even more heated as French Canadians fought against anglicization, as moderate and compact Tories argued over the best definition of a conservative course that would protect the British constitution in Canada, and as Tories and Reformers fought the climactic battle that would decide whether governors or party leaders would exercise power. Having four governors within the space of five years only increased the sense of political flux. In 1845 that old Anglican Tory John Strachan lamented that ever since the Union had been established "all is political agitation."[66] Canadian parties fought as they had never fought before to gain control of the legislature and so impose their version of constitutional government. The Tory outrage of the Rebellion Losses Bill in 1849, leading to extended mob violence in Montreal during which the parliament buildings were burned, was the culminating example of how deep political feelings ran during these troubled years. "Never had party ferocity reached such a pitch in Canada" wrote J. C. Dent in one of the earliest histories of these years.[67] Etienne Parent, who was active in French-Canadian Reform politics throughout the period, summed it up as "une époque mémorable de notre histoire."[68]

A lasting consequence of all this for Canadian political culture was that the language of politics was exceptionally bitter and vituperative. All observers of Canadian politics from Durham and Elgin in the 1830's and 1840's to the French political scientist André Siegfried in 1900 were struck by this phenomenon. This characteristic of Canadian politics crystallized in this period of turmoil. Opposition leaders in the assembly with no hope of gaining office and with few hopes of checking executive power "by that habit which is second nature are demagogues rather than politicians."[69] As Lieutenant-Governor Arthur noted in November 1839, "there was a very bitter feeling . . . between the Reform and Constitutional parties," and Poulett Thomson reported in a similar vein to Russell that "the people are split into factions violently excited against each other." In spite of the fact that the great mass of the people were loyal, Thomson was surprised to note that charges of treason were "unsparingly levelled against a large proportion of people" on the Reform side.[70] When Lord Elgin arrived in Canada in 1847, he found the language of politics to be "incredible" in its vindictiveness. He thought the years of struggle between a prerogative-based executive and a frustrated assembly was the root cause: "to revile the one was the surest test of Patriotism, to denounce the other, of Loyalty."[71] In 1874 Lord Dufferin was discouraged that "party spirit runs so high and is so unscrupulous."[72] And Siegfried, writing at the turn of the century and basing his judgment on his knowledge of politics in France, Britain, and the United States, thought elections in Canada roused more fury than anywhere else.[73]

Macdonald, entering politics at the climactic moment of the struggle, was forever branded by these heated characteristics of Canadian politics. To the end of his life, he viewed opposition as factious and, even more seriously, as disloyal. He thought that once the church question had been decided in the 1850's, there was no excuse for continued Reform opposition;[74] after the 1864 coalition was formed and Confederation achieved, he viewed the persistence of Grit opposition as disloyal; the Conservative party of the 1870's accused the opposition of "veiled treason," and in his last great campaign during the 1891 election, Macdonald pursued the traditional theme that the Liberal opposition was thoroughly disloyal.[75] He and his supporters habitually referred to the opposition as "the enemy." Macdonald had few qualms about employing all means available to the executive to circumvent or weaken the opposition. To him the opposition always carried a taint of treason; it was illegitimate. That kind of thinking was a product of the 1840's.

So too was Macdonald's concept of executive power. The question at the centre of the crisis years 1837–46 concerned the power of the governor. Beginning with William Draper (Macdonald's mentor in politics), the party leaders took over the prerogative powers of the governors in the vast realm of patronage. In the case of Draper, this had limited consequences, for he was not strong in the legislature and, indeed, in an old-fashioned way, he kept himself distant from popular politics in the constituencies.[76] Macdonald understood much better than his mentor that the old ways were gone forever and that the Conservatives must abandon the remnants of compact Tory exclusivity. The Tories' great weakness, Macdonald understood, was that they "had no strength in numbers" and that they could not "abide promotion or employment of any one beyond their pale."[77] Macdonald had a much harder task than Baldwin and LaFontaine in building and maintaining party strength.[78] To do so, he used the old prerogative powers of the governors to the full, which, in combination with his strength derived from party leadership, enabled him to accomplish what Metcalfe and Draper had tried to accomplish in 1844. Like all of his contemporaries in the 1840's, Macdonald believed in the need for a strong executive, and he understood better than others how the party leaders could use their new powers to achieve that end. As J. C. Dent tellingly phrased it, Macdonald aspired to "far more than vice-regal power,"[79] and on his return from Britain in 1883 a supporter welcomed him back as "the Prince of Canada who has friends by the thousand who are most demonstrative in their joy at his being home because of the offices in his gift to bestow."[80]

Macdonald took over the powers exercised by the governors since 1791 and appointed only his party's supporters to posts throughout the public service from judges to tidewaiters in the customs service. He even evolved a constitutional justification for such a thoroughgoing deployment of patronage for party purposes. "By constitutional practice," he insisted, "appointments are vested in the Crown and the whole responsibility of appointments rests with the ministry of the day." There was no doubt in Macdonald's mind that "whenever an office is vacant it belongs to the party supporting the government."[81] Macdonald's comprehensive understanding of the possibilities now open to party leaders comes out clearly when he is compared to Draper. As the *Montreal Courier* wrote insightfully, politicians like Draper "ne sont introduits dans la politique que pour obtenir des sièges sur le banc judiciaire; ce ne fût pas le parti qui les poussa à travailler dans la chambre mais le banc."[82] Even the two great Reform leaders, LaFontaine and Baldwin, left politics for the bench in 1851. It was this use of crown patronage, now available to party leaders who controlled the executive, that was Macdonald's "long game" strategy for the rest of his career. "Depend on it," Macdonald told M. C. Cameron in 1872, "the long game is the true one."[83]

No British prime minister in the 1870's could have made the statements Macdonald made about the legitimacy of partisan patronage.[84] It was a distinctively Canadian growth, rooted in the 1791–1847 political world. In this context Macdonald remained much closer to eighteenth-century British political culture than to contemporary Victorian England.

Goldwin Smith caught this characteristic when he described the Canadian Conservative party as held together "by an artificer who, in the course of a long career has acquired a thorough knowledge of all the men, the interests and passions with which he has to deal, uses that knowledge with considerable skill and shrinks from the employment of no means of influence, while, like Walpole, in the midst of corruption, he remains personally pure."[85] On the purity scale, Macdonald comes out well ahead of Walpole, but the parallel between the two men's use of executive patronage and influence is illuminating. Dufferin shared the same insight when he remarked of Macdonald that he was "certainly the best statesman in Canada though too prone to maintain his power by expedients condemned by the higher moral standard of modern politics."[86]

Besides taking over and adapting crown patronage in such a calculating, comprehensive, and thoroughly partisan manner, Macdonald inherited another characteristic approach to politics from these formative years. During the political turmoil of the 1830's and 1840's, lieutenant-governors and governors had not hesitated to use their powers to manipulate the electoral system or to influence elections by use of the prerogative. In 1836, for example, Sir Francis Bond Head worked hard to disqualify voters he thought would support Mackenzie. In the tense first years of the Union, Lord Sydenham used his gubernatorial powers to sway elections in favour of the administration. By proclamation, for example, he altered electoral boundaries in Canada East as part of a plan to favour English and urban districts which would elect administrative supporters. In LaFontaine's own constituency at Terrebonne, the polling place was moved to the Scots and Irish settlement of New Glasgow in preparation for organized intimidation of Reform voters. Sydenham relished this kind of detailed electoral battling. "The governor plans and talks of nothing else," noted T. W. C. Murdock, his civil secretary. Such tactics, Sydenham believed, were a legitimate exercise of his powers. In a phrase that Macdonald himself might have used in later years, Sydenham wrote exultantly in June 1841, "I fought the whole battle myself."[87]

Macdonald, like Sydenham, relished these details of applying to the fullest extent all the executive techniques available. He "tried to do everything" by himself.[88] Again, this was a distinctive development for Canadian political leadership. Macdonald conceded ruefully in the midst of the Pacific Scandal that had he been a British party leader, he would not have spent so much time himself on the fine points of electoral manipulation. As Macdonald explained to Carnarvon, he "should have left it to our Carlton and Reform Clubs."[89] But it was a hallmark of Macdonald that to the end he did keep paying attention to such details. There is an undated document written in his own hand sometime in 1889 which shows Macdonald painstakingly figuring out the political complexion of Q.C.'s and lawyers eligible to be Q.C.'s in Ontario.[90] The gerrymander of 1882 can be comprehended as part of this same tradition of electoral manipulation. So can the Franchise Act of 1885, which Macdonald hoped would enable the Conservative party to hold onto its position in Ontario (by allowing him to appoint federal revising officers). Macdonald described the Franchise Act as "the greatest triumph of my life." That has been a difficult self-assessment for modern scholars to explain, but Lord Sydenham would have understood what Macdonald meant.[91]

The full scope of Macdonald's deepest hopes about how far he could build up executive power and influence are revealed by his view that the provinces created in 1867 would decline to become mere municipalities. Macdonald was badly wrong on that, but understanding the political world from which he emerged explains why he had such hopes. One of the apparent consequences of the last crisis years 1844–47 was that the party that controlled the legislature would have no challenges to its exercise of executive power. In contrast to Britain, where the Commons had to contend with the House of Lords and the residual influence of the Crown, or the United States, where the House of Representatives was checked by the Senate and the presidency, the Canadian legislature seemed all-powerful after 1848. R. B. Sullivan lamented as he saw Canada sliding towards responsible government that the Canadian legislature "would possess a power superior to that of the House of Commons, the House of Representatives and any other body we know of short of despotic authority."[92] But R. B. Sullivan and the other Tory doomsayers were as wrong about the future as Macdonald was. They were unable to see into the future and imagine the possibility that the new provinces could act as counterweights to the seemingly limitless power of the party that controlled the Commons. Canada was too extensive geographically, too diverse ethnically, too fragmented economically, and it had no national ruling class to sustain Macdonald's vision of central power. Above all, it had powerful provinces like Ontario and Quebec that were able to build up their own "court" counterparts to Macdonald's federal executive. Macdonald could not pull off his final triumph because he was confronted with rival "court" governments in Ontario and Quebec. This phenomenon led to another distinctive characteristic of Canadian political culture. The "country" challenge to "court"-style administration was a failure, but rival "court" governments in the two huge provinces did the job of circumscribing central power.

This assessment of Macdonald against an extended analysis of the origins of Canadian politics in the 1791–1854 period shows the extent to which Macdonald's views on party, political leadership, executive power, and patronage were shaped by his understanding of the past. Donald Creighton's emphasis on Macdonald as a statesman gazing steadily into the future puts out of focus the image of Macdonald as a party leader. Like most politicians, indeed like most mortals, he marched into the future with his gaze fixed firmly on the past. Macdonald's longevity carried into thc 1870's, 1880's, and 1890's political and constitutional values and attitudes that had been moulded in the turbulent formative period of Canadian politics. Macdonald, as Waite and Johnson have pointed out, had no great or original ideas on what Siegfried called "the race question in Canada" because, as J. C. Dent observed long ago, it was Macdonald's "misfortune to enter political life under auspices unfavourable to the speedy enlargement of his mind."[93]

NOTES

1. Donald G. Creighton, *John A. Macdonald: The Young Politician* (Toronto, 1952), and *John A. Macdonald: The Old Chieftain* (Toronto, 1955).
2. J. K. Johnson, "John A. Macdonald: the Young non-Politician," Canadian Historical Association, *Historical Papers* (1971): 138–53. Johnson has made a more extended re-evaluation of Macdonald in the editorial comments he has made in the volumes of Macdonald's early correspondence and his family correspondence. See J. K. Johnson, ed., *The Letters of John A. Macdonald 1837–1861,* 2 vols. (Ottawa, 1968–69); and *Affectionately Yours: The Letters of John A. Macdonald and His Family* (Toronto, 1969).
3. Peter B. Waite, *Macdonald: His Life and World* (Toronto, 1975); and *Arduous Destiny: Canada 1874–1896* (Toronto, 1971). On the usc of patronage to pacify the Maritimes, see Waite's article in this collection.
4. Such an understanding of Macdonald is also supported by the work of Rod Preece, who has argued that Macdonald worked within a political context derived from the views of that great late-eighteenth-century English conservative political philosopher Edmund Burke. See Preece, "The Political Wisdom of John A. Macdonald," *Canadian Journal of Political Science* 17 (1984): 459–86.
5. Bernard Bailyn, *The Origins of American Politics* (New York, 1968).
6. The following comparison between English and American political development after 1688 is based on the illuminating comparative study of John M. Murrin, "The Great Inversion, or Court versus Country: a Comparison of the Revolutionary Settlements in England (1688–1721) and America (1776–1816)," in J. G. A. Pocock, ed., *Three British Revolutions 1641, 1688, 1776* (Princeton, 1980), pp. 368–453.
7. Ibid, pp. 379–81; J. R. Jones, *Country and Court: England 1658–1714* (Cambridge, MA, 1979) provides a fine synthesis of scholarship on this period.
8. J. H. Plumb, *The Growth of Political Stability in England 1675–1725* (London, 1967).
9. W. A. Speck, *Stability and Strife: England 1714–1760* (Cambridge, MA, 1979), pp. 11–30; Caroline Robbins, *The Eighteenth-Century Commonwealthmen* (London, 1959); Bernard Bailyn, *The Ideological Origins of the American Revolution* (Cambridge, MA, 1967), pp. 35–37.

10. E. Neville Williams, *The Eighteenth Century Constitution 1688–1815* (Cambridge, 1960), pp. 75–76; Norman Gash, *Aristocracy and the People. England 1815–1865* (Cambridge, MA, 1979), pp. 1–128; A. D. Harvey, *Britain in the Early Nineteenth Century* (New York, 1978); G. B. Finlayson, *England in the 1830's: Decade of Reform* (London, 1969); Oliver MacDonagh, *Early Victorian Government 1830–1870* (London, 1977); W. L. Lubenow, *The Politics of Government Growth* (Newton Abbot, 1971).
11. Murrin, "The Great Inversion," p. 425. The following assessment of colonial, revolutionary, and early national political development comes from this Murrin piece.
12. Bailyn, *The Origins of American Politics, passim;* Jack P. Greene, *The Quest for Power: The Lower Houses of Assembly in the Southern Royal Colonies 1689–1776,* Chapel Hill, 1963, *passim.*
13. Bernard Bailyn, *The Ordeal of Thomas Hutchinson* (Cambridge, MA, 1974), pp. 78–79.
14. Gordon S. Wood, *The Creation of the American Republic* (Chapel Hill, 1969), pp. 143–50.
15. Murrin, "The Great Inversion," pp. 425–26.
16. The Constitutional Act (31 George III, c. 31) 1791 is printed in W. P. M. Kennedy, ed., *Documents of the Canadian Constitution 1759–1915* (Toronto, 1926), pp. 207–20. For the reasoning behind the act and assessments of how it operated, see Gerald M. Craig, *Upper Canada: The Formative Years 1784–1841* (Toronto, 1963), pp. 9–41, and Gilles Pacquet and Jean-Pierre Wallot, *Patronage et Pouvoir dans le Bas-Canada 1794–1812* (Quebec, 1973), pp. 17–34, 75, 136.
17. Gordon Stewart and George Rawlyk, *A People Highly Favoured of God: The Nova Scotia Yankees and the American Revolution* (Toronto, 1972), pp. 13–23.
18. Hilda Neatby, *Quebec: The Revolutionary Age 1760–1791* (Toronto, 1966), pp. 1–124.
19. Ibid., pp. 125–248; Fernand Ouellet, *Histoire Economique et Sociale du Québec 1760–1850* (Montreal, 1966), pp. 1–212.
20. J. G. A. Pocock, "The Classical Theory of Deference," *American Historical Review* 81 (1976): 516–23.
21. Janice Potter, *The Liberty We Seek: Loyalist Ideology in Colonial New York and Massachusetts* (Cambridge, MA, 1983), pp. 15–61.
22. Jane Errington and George Rawlyk, "The Loyalist-Federalist Alliance of Upper Canada," *American Review of Canadian Studies* 14 (1984): 157–76.
23. Ian R. Christie, *Wars and Revolutions: Britain 1760–1815* (Cambridge, MA, 1982), pp. 20–44, 181–222.
24. Neatby, *Quebec, 1760–1791,* pp. 257–63; Craig, *Upper Canada, 1784–1841,* pp. 14–15.
25. Kennedy, *Documents on the Canadian Constitution,* pp. 136–39, 149–50.
26. Ibid., pp. 208–9.
27. Ibid., pp. 215–17.
28. Simcoe to Henry Dundas, 6 November 1792; Simcoe to bishop of Quebec, Kingston, 30 April 1795; Simcoe Memorandum, 28 February 1794, in E. A. Cruickshank, ed., *The Correspondence of Lieutenant-Governor John Graves Simcoe* (Toronto, 1923), 1:251–52; 2:167; 3:348–49; Grenville to Dorchester, Whitehall, 20 October 1789, in *Public Archives of Canada Report* (1890), pp. 11–12.
29. Christie, *Britain 1760–1815,* pp. 20–44.
30. Simcoe to Sir Joseph Banks, 8 January 1791, in Cruickshank, *Simcoe Correspondence,* 1:18.
31. J. B. Robinson to Sir George Arthur, London, 23 February 1839, in Charles R. Sanderson, ed., *The Arthur Papers,* 3 vols. (Toronto, 1957–1959), 2:62.
32. J. C. Dent, *The Last Forty Years: The Union of 1841 to Confederation* (Toronto, 1881 [1972]), p. 82.
33. John Macaulay to Sir George Arthur, 15 September 1839, in Sanderson, *The Arthur Papers,* 2:263.
34. Elgin to Grey, Montreal, 27 August 1849, in A. G. Doughty, ed., *The Elgin-Grey Papers 1846–1852,* 4 vols. (Ottawa, 1937), 2:452.

35. Craig, *Upper Canada 1784–1841,* pp. 145–64; J. M. S. Careless, *The Union of the Canadas* (Toronto, 1967), pp. 150–84.
36. H. J. Hanham, ed., *The Nineteenth Century Constitution* (Cambridge, 1969), p. 13.
37. Charles Lucas, ed., *The Durham Report* (Oxford, 1912), 2:73. As Colin Read has succinctly phrased it, the 1791 act had set up "a contentious framework of government." See Read, *The Rising in Western Upper Canada 1837–1838* (Toronto, 1982), p. 5.
38. Helen Taft Manning, "The Colonial Policy of the Whig Ministers 1830–1837," *Canadian Historical Review,* 33 (1952): 352.
39. S. F. Wise, "The Upper Canadian Conservative Tradition," in Morris Zaslow, ed., *Profiles of a Province* (Toronto, 1967), pp. 26–29; Pacquet and Wallot, *Patronage et Pouvoir, passim.*
40. Dent, *The Last Forty Years,* pp. 53, 56.
41. Thomson to Russell, Toronto, 15 December 1839, in Sanderson, *The Arthur Papers,* 2:346–49.
42. Thomson to Arthur, Toronto, 11 December 1839; Arthur to Colborne, Toronto, 9 May 1839, in ibid., 2:144, 338.
43. Elgin to Grey, Toronto, 6 June and 1 November 1850; Grey to Elgin, London, 25 November 1850, in Doughty, *The Elgin-Grey Papers,* 2:683–86, 733–35.
44. S. F. Wise and R. C. Brown, *Canada Views the United States: Nineteenth-Century Political Attitudes* (Toronto, 1967), pp. 16–97.
45. Craig, *Upper Canada 1784–1841,* pp. 226–40.
46. Jacques Monet, *The Last Cannon Shot: A Study of French-Canadian Nationalism 1837–1850* (Toronto, 1969).
47. Ouellet, *Histoire Economique et Sociale,* pp. 599–602, 196–212.
48. Henry Milner, *Politics in the New Quebec* (Toronto, 1978), pp. 19, 85–105.
49. Pacquet and Wallot, *Patronage et Pouvoir,* pp. 137–141.
50. Social and economic factors also deepened the crisis. See Ouellet, *Histoire Economique et Sociale,* pp. 325–440.
51. Grey to Elgin, London, 21 October 1851, in Doughty, *The Elgin-Grey Papers,* 3:900.
52. Lucas, *The Durham Report,* 2:101–3, 277–80; Peter Burroughs, ed., *The Colonial Reformers and Canada 1830–1849* (Toronto, 1969), pp. 95–96, 145–46. Ged Martin, *The Durham Report* (Cambridge, 1972) points out the backward-looking nature of Durham's emphasis on a strong Crown-controlled executive.
53. Elgin to Grey, Toronto, 23 March 1850 and 28 June 1851, in Doughty, *The Elgin-Grey Papers,* 2:51, 609; Dent, *The Last Forty Years,* pp. 224–31.
54. Monet, *The Last Cannon Shot,* p. 59; Grey to Elgin, London, 21 October 1851, in Doughty, *The Elgin-Grey Papers,* 3:900.
55. Baldwin to Peter Perry, 16 March 1836, in Sanderson, *The Arthur Papers,* 1:7; Dent, *The Last Forty Years,* p. 90.
56. *Colonial Gazette,* 21 September 1844, in Burroughs, *Colonial Reformers 1830–1849,* p. 168.
57. Egerton Ryerson, *The Story of My Life* (Toronto, 1884), p. 333. This summing up of LaFontaine's case was made during a conversation with Governor Metcalfe—so Higginson, Metcalfe's civil secretary, told Ryerson. See also Dent, *The Last Forty Years,* p. 177.
58. Careless, *Union of the Canadas,* pp. 79, 80, 83; Ryerson, *The Story of My Life,* pp. 312, 320, 320–25; Louis P. Turcotte, *Le Canada sous l'Union 1841–1867* (Quebec, 1871–72), pp. 164, 174–75, 199; Dent, *The Last Forty Years,* pp. 115, 125.
59. Elgin to Grey, Montreal, 14 March 1849, in Doughty, *The Elgin-Grey Papers,* 1:308.
60. Montreal Gazette, 6 October 1851, in Doughty, *The Elgin-Grey Papers,* 3:904.
61. *Mémoires de Robert S. M. Bouchette* (Montreal, [1903]), pp. 119–20.
62. *The Colonial Gazette,* 21 September 1844, quoted in Burroughs, *The Colonial Reformers 1830–1849,* p. 169.
63. Jacques Monet, "Les idées politiques de Baldwin et LaFontaine," in Marcel Hamelin, *The Political Ideas of the Prime Ministers of Canada* (Ottawa, 1969), pp. 16–17.

64. Arthur to Glenelg, Toronto, 24 June 1839, in Sanderson, *The Arthur Papers,* 1:178.
65. Arthur to Sir John Macdonald, Toronto, 27 February 1839, ibid., pp. 66–67.
66. John Strachan to Henry Phillpots, bishop of Exeter, 11 May 1845, in J. L. H. Henderson, *John Strachan: Documents and Opinions* (Toronto, 1969), p. 176.
67. Dent, *The Last Forty Years,* pp. 141, 171–73.
68. Turcotte, *Le Canada sous l'Union,* part 2, p. 5.
69. *The Spectator,* 19 February 1848, quoted in Burroughs, *The Colonial Reformers 1830–1849,* p. 171.
70. Arthur to Thomson, Toronto, 9 November 1839, in Sanderson, *The Arthur Papers,* 2:306; Thomson to Russell, Toronto, 15 December 1839, ibid., pp. 345–46; Dent, *The Last Forty Years,* p. 139.
71. Elgin to Grey, Montreal, 30 April 1849, in Doughty, *The Elgin-Grey Correspondence, 4:1460.*
72. Dufferin to Carnarvon, Ottawa, 10 October 1874, in C. W. Dekiewiet and F. H. Underhill, eds., *The Dufferin-Carnarvon Correspondence 1874–1878* (Toronto, 1955), p. 108.
73. André Siegfried, *The Race Question in Canada* (Paris, 1906). Quotes are from the edition edited by F. H. Underhill (Toronto, 1966), p. 117.
74. Dent, *The Last Forty Years,* p. 291.
75. Joseph Pope, *The Day of Sir John Macdonald* (Toronto, 1920), p. 176; Waite, *Canada 1874–1896,* pp. 221–25.
76. George Metcalfe, "William Henry Draper," in J. M. S. Careless, ed., *Pre-Confederation Premiers: Ontario Government Leaders 1841–1867* (Toronto, 1980), pp. 70, 78.
77. Macdonald to Ogle Gowan, 30 April 1847, in Frederick Armstrong, "The Macdonald-Gowan Letters 1847," *Ontario History* 63 (1971).
78. J. K. Johnson, *Letters of Sir John A. Macdonald,* p. 26; Stewart, "Macdonald's Greatest Triumph," *Canadian Historical Review,* 63 (1982): 13–15.
79. Dent, *The Last Forty Years,* p. 106.
80. J. Farnelly to Macdonald, Belleville, 6 October 1881, *Macdonald Papers,* P.A.C., Vol 25 II.
81. Macdonald to A. Watts, 26 February 1880, in Joseph Pope, ed., *Correspondence of Sir John A. Macdonald 1840–1891* (Toronto, 1921), pp. 271–72; Norman Ward, "Responsible Government: an Introduction," *Journal of Canadian Studies* 14 (1979): 3.
82. Turcotte, *Le Canada sous l'Union,* part 2, p. 32.
83. Stewart, "Macdonald's Greatest Triumph," pp. 23–24, makes the case that it was the game of patronage and influence that Macdonald had in mind.
84. Peter G. Richards, *Patronage in British Government* (London, 1963), pp. 30, 37, 41, 50, 60–61.
85. *The Bystander,* April 1883, p. 90.
86. Dufferin to Carnarvon, Ottawa, 18 March 1874, in DeKiewiet and Underhill, *The Dufferin-Carnarvon Correspondence,* pp. 13–14.
87. Careless, *Union of the Canadas,* pp. 41–44; Paul G. Cornell, "The Genesis of Ontario Politics in the Province of Canada 1838–1871," in Zaslow, *Profiles of a Province,* p. 60; Turcotte, *Le Canada sous l'Union,* p. 104n1.
88. J. K. Johnson, "Macdonald," in Careless, *Pre-Confederation Premiers,* p. 214.
89. Macdonald to Dufferin, 9 October 1873, in Joseph Pope, *Memoirs of the Rt. Hon. Sir John A. Macdonald* (Toronto, 1894), p. 553.
90. Stewart, "Macdonald's Greatest Triumph," pp. 26–27.
91. Ibid; Creighton, *The Old Chieftain,* p. 427.
92. Sullivan Report on the State of the Province, June 1838, in Sanderson, *The Arthur Papers,* 1:164.
93. Dent, *The Last Forty Years,* p. 158.

3

Networks and Associations and the Nationalizing of Sentiment in English Canada

MARGARET PRANG

Writing about Canadian federalism in the 1950's, J. A. Corry discerned "the nationalizing of sentiment" among elites and opinion makers as a factor in understanding the willingness of citizens to assign to the federal government an increasingly definitive role in their affairs: "Sentiment is rapidly being nationalized among the élites . . . the leaders of minority groups, the persons whose occupations or interests lead them into close relationships with government or into sustained reflection about it." Corry perceived a series of cross-country networks composed of people who, in their encounters and work in various national associations, had come to "breathe the large air of broader understanding and sympathies" than those characteristic of earlier generations. Thus he identified welfare, trade union, business, agricultural, and educational elites, whose influence he believed was proving to be decisive in tipping Canadian opinion in favour of strong leadership from Ottawa.[1]

It was not always so, although clearly those loose associations of family, friendship, and interest which lie well below the surface of politics have always been of some relevance to the political process in democratic societies, and perhaps nowhere more influential than in the thinly populated and vast expanses of Canada. Despite their importance in helping to create the universe of discourse in which Canadians have fashioned a society, these relationships and the cumulative loyalties they foster are too amorphous and elusive to be easy subjects of investigation by scholars, with or without benefit of statistics and computers, and they have been little studied.

To suggest that networks of individuals or groups, whether informal or more structured, have some bearing on how Canadian federalism has functioned in the past or might do so in the future is not to deny the force of economic, constitutional, and political factors or the role of government itself in shaping political culture. However, this paper runs the risk of being received as an example of sociological reductionism.[2] Those who are reluctant to find explanations of political developments in other social phenomena or are unable to accept a degree of impressionistic speculation in historical discourse should read no further.

Until well after the beginning of the twentieth century, English Canada was overwhelmingly a collection of rural societies in which local values and allegiances were dominant, as they had been in the decades before Confederation. In these circumstances, the political parties and the patronage system provided a minimal organizing and unifying force in a country where most of the citizens rarely felt the impact of the national government on their lives.[3] Paradoxically, the parties served this unifying function by emphasizing local issues. At election time, party leaders might discuss national issues such as the tariff or the imperial connection, but there is much evidence to suggest that few political contests were determined by such major issues. As the contemporary journalist W. D. Lesueur observed in 1872 in a comment valid for several decades to come: "Localism is rampant . . . the special interests of [an M.P.'s] constituency not the general interests of the country are those over which he has to watch with the greatest vigilance and for his dealings with which he will be held to the strictest account."[4] The means by which the local members were held to account was the patronage system. Thus, "in the absence of ideology, tradition, communications, and even formal governmental structure, the locally centered party, based upon corruption in its many forms"[5] was the focus of interest for local politicians who had little incentive to think about matters beyond the operation of the local pork barrel.

At the federal level, Macdonald was the primary architect of this form of politics based on vigilant cultivation of a complex patronage system, as Mowat at the provincial level was the master of a similar system in Ontario. Despite economic and social changes which were making Canada an industrialized and urbanized society with a business elite whose members saw their interests less parochially than their fathers had done, Laurier managed to perpetuate this system to the great advantage of the Liberal party. How great these changes were only became apparent when the old system fell apart in the election campaign of 1917, bringing to power a new coalition of economic and social interests intent on defining and serving a national interest.[6] Henceforth, national politics would matter more to more voters, and the elite now needed new means of forming their own opinions and influencing government, especially on issues relating to the settlement of the West and the development of a transcontinental economy.

In the last two decades of the nineteenth century, a host of networks and associations whose existence reflected these changes were born. Focused essentially in Ontario at first, they included the Canadian Manufacturers' Association, the Dominion Wholesale Grocers' Guild, the Canadian Bankers' Association, the Retail Merchants' Association, and numerous other specialized groups such as those formed by the retail jewellers and the cotton manufacturers. After the turn of the century, these associations expanded their membership and activities, especially in the new cities of the West, and they were joined by new groups designed to promote the interests of specific segments of business and industry. At meetings of such organizations and in railway club cars travelling east and west, a growing number of Canadian businessmen came to know one another. Often their most immediate concerns were ways and means of limiting competition or preventing the growth of trade unions, but they also exchanged views on the social, religious, and political issues of the day.[7] T. W. Acheson's study of leading Canadian manufacturers in the late nineteenth and early twentieth centuries tells us a good deal about the origins and mobility, both social and geographical, of one segment of the Canadian business elite.[8] Robert McDonald has shown how the growth of a transcontinental economy created a Vancouver business elite, many of whose members were central Canadians or Maritimers who had begun their business careers in prairie cities, often in the service of national business concerns, and thus had connections across the country.[9]

Members of the business elites were not the only Canadians to develop transcontinental associations and personal networks. The farmers' perception of the threat posed by rural depopulation in Ontario and the Maritimes, and by the growing power of eastern financial interests in the economy of the prairies, was indicated by the formation in 1910 of the Canadian Federation of Agriculture. At the same time, labour aspired to a larger share of the prosperity of "Canada's century." Although the Trades and Labour Congress of Canada had been bringing representatives of workingmen together since 1886, trade union membership and activity increased enormously in the first decade of the century. While rapid industrialization gave labour leaders much to discuss, ideological and regional differences inhibited the growth of unity and the development of any strong political influence. Nevertheless, before the First World War there was a small labour elite whose members were endeavouring to shape policies reflecting their position in a national economy and political system.

Although the study of economic elites provides some clues to understanding the creation of national sentiment, so too would an investigation of internal migration among the general population. There have been many bands of "hopeful travellers" in Canadian history, usually moving westward, but we know all too little about the consequences of the transfer of their social and cultural baggage. Thus, in a general way the influence of the migrating Pictou county Scots on education, religion, and commerce has often been noticed but seldom studied. The reasons for the migration of Huron-Grey-Bruce County farmers in the 1880's have been explored,[10] but our understanding of the process by which those migrants ensured "the triumph of Ontario democracy"[11] in the new physical environment of southwestern Manitoba would be enhanced by a knowledge of how kinship ties with those who stayed behind may have contributed to this result. David Breen has portrayed the distinctive web of family, business, and cultural associations which tied the ranching community of the foothills to Montreal, London, and the Pacific coast and created a British Canadian society which saw itself as a distinctive part of the larger prairie West. The influence of this group was ater challenged by the development in the first decade of the twentieth century of another economic and cultural network oriented toward Chicago and representing the traditions of the American ranchers who created a flourishing range cattle industry in the southeastern section of the new province of Alberta.[12] Another network even more regional in character is described in a recent study of private boys' schools in British Columbia which shows how an institution imported by British immigrants contributed to the province's continuing British orientation and educated several generations of boys quite unconnected with the graduates of private schools in central Canada whom other scholars have seen as constituting a national elite.[13]

Until 1921, the prairie provinces and British Columbia were peopled mainly by first generation immigrants. Thereafter, population growth in the Pacific province continued to rest heavily on immigration from Britain and the rest of Canada, but by 1941 the native-born or foreign immigrants constituted over 90 per cent of the prairie population. As Peter Ward has argued, the fact that so many prairie people had family and cultural ties with the outside world but not with the rest of Canada must have contributed a good deal to the growth of a regional consciousness.[14] In the short run, the newcomers, especially the non-Anglo-Saxons, rarely joined the ruling elites of prairie society, but now their grandchildren do so in increasing numbers. That process, and the possible role of informal associations and networks in it, may be worth examination. So is the influence of the thousands of prairie residents who migrated to British Columbia after the Second World War with values and attitudes shaped by their experience of the Great Depression. There is considerable impressionistic evidence to suggest that these prairie refugees played a role disproportionate to their number in the public life of their adopted province.

A major focus of localism in individual communities throughout the years were the churches. Yet, from at least the late nineteenth century onward, the churches were also often the challengers of that localism. At a time when a majority of members of the Canadian elites acknowledged a formal religious affiliation, the churches constituted national networks that had considerable influence in shaping their members' vision of Canadian society and informing their opinions on such matters as prohibition, the recurring schools issues, the Ne Temere decree, or the imperial connection. To the extent that they exercised their minds on questions like these, both Protestants and Roman Catholics were engaged in consideration of concerns larger than those of local congregations and national in their import. In the last two decades of the nineteenth century, there developed a national ecumenical Protestant network composed of the often interlocking leadership of various temperance and missionary societies, the YMCA and YWCA, and the Lord's Day Alliance, culminating in the formation in 1907 of the Moral and Social Reform Council of Canada. These organizations gave expression to the ''Christianizing and Canadianizing'' programme which embodied the response of most Anglo-Saxon Canadian Protestants to the influx of foreign-born immigrants.

Nowhere was a network based on religious affiliation more evident than among the peripatetic ministers of that most Canadian of denominations, the Methodist church. Required by church polity to move to a new pulpit every four years, Methodist ministers frequently served congregations from one end of the country to the other during their careers. They thus came to know Canada well and to know and be known by a large crosssection of the Methodist community. And in the pages of the *Christian Guardian,* the ministers and their congregations were informed about those religious, national, and international issues deemed by the editors to be the concern of a Christian conscience. In the later decades of the nineteenth century, no Canadian journalist needed to yield place to the *Guardian*'s editor, Dr. E. H. Dewart, in enthusiasm for the growth of a distinctively Canadian culture, nor after the turn of the century to Dr. W. B. Creighton in his use of ''Canada's National Religious Weekly,'' as the *Guardian*'s masthead proclaimed it, as a vehicle for discussion of the character of the Canadian community. Under Creighton's editorship, the *Guardian* had a circulation of about thirty thousand, distributed across English-speaking Canada roughly in proportion to population—a circulation equal to that of the widely read secular weekly, *Saturday Night*.

Within the Methodist community, there was a more worldly and possibly more powerful subnetwork than any composed of parsons. Among the financiers who organized the capital that fuelled the business expansion and the great consolidations of the prewar years were E. R. Wood, J. H. Gundy, G. A. Cox, W. E. Rundle, G. H. Wood, and J. W. Flavelle, Methodists all. Although there is no evidence that these Toronto financiers had any exclusive preference for doing business with other Methodists, they were closely associated both financially and socially with local Methodist manufacturers and merchants such as the Masseys, the Eatons, and H. H. Fudger of Simpson's, and after 1900 this group dominated Toronto business to a remarkable degree.[15] They developed business ties with Methodists across the country, including J. A. M. Aikins, Sanford Evans, and J. H. Ashdown in Winnipeg and David Spencer and W. H. Malkin on the west coast, and they vigorously supported Methodist missionary activities in the west. Indeed, Joseph Flavelle's life-long interest in the Canadian west is said to have begun at his mother's knee as he listened to her account of a Methodist missionary's glowing predictions about the future productivity of what was then still Rupert's Land.[16] It was an interest that served well the boy who was to become Canada's wealthiest meat packer. Among the many things these men and their families had in common was that they did not drink, go to the races, or engage in other pursuits equally wasteful of time and money, which for some also included playing cards and attendance at the theatre. This disposition separated faithful Methodists from Anglicans, and from many Presbyterians. Common social mores formed the basis for an apparently high rate of marriage within the Methodist community, an impression which can be derived from a reading of *The Christian Guardian* over any substantial period of time. John Webster Grant has observed that "in the 19th century, Methodists were all related. The leaders in the Methodist church in Canada were all married to each other," and this contributed to a "family network of religion" and to "commercial and regional networks which were very powerful."[17]

Of course, there were Presbyterian and Anglican networks as well, although the clergy of these denominations moved about less frequently than their Methodist brethren. Despite the Scottish origins of many of its members and the close personal and intellectual ties they maintained with Scotland, the Presbyterian Church in Canada clearly displayed its "Canadianism" as early as the union of 1874, and in the later nineteenth century, few Canadian leaders were listened to on national issues with more respect than Principal G. M. Grant of Queen's. In that tradition, after the turn of the century other Presbyterian ministers, including R. A. Falconer who became president of the University of Toronto in 1907,

J. G. Shearer, first secretary of the Moral and Social Reform Council of Canada, and Charles W. Gordon (Ralph Connor), articulated a Presbyterian "national gospel," an amalgam of social Christianity and Canadian nationalism which they hoped would meet the threats to the social fabric of the nation from industrialization, urbanization, and immigration.[18] Presbyterians who attended church with any regularity and read their denomination's publications could scarcely escape the conclusion that they had some responsibility for the quality of Canadian national life and that politics, whatever the corruption of some politicians, was an honourable calling.

One of the most perceptive of the many Britons who published accounts of their travels in Canada in the early years of the century observed: "The Presbyterians struck me as much the most Canadian . . . of the churches. . . . Presbyterianism seems to have a marked unity all over the Dominion, Western ministers having been educated down East and being personally acquainted with Church leaders in Montreal and Toronto. In 1913 three or four wealthy laymen arranged to pay the fares of every minister in the Dominion and his wife to and from the General Dominion Assembly of that year. . . . The Presbyterian Church is clearly one of the forces acting to bring scattered Canada together."[19]

Although the Church of England was not lacking in concern for the common good, Anglicans' interest in Canadian public life, like that of English-speaking Roman Catholics, was often diluted by trans-Atlantic ties which fostered and perpetuated continuing attention to social and political issues "back home." The observer cited above viewed the Anglican church in western Canada from the vantage point afforded by several months' stay in the home of a cousin, an Anglican deaconess in North Battleford, Saskatchewan, and came to conclusions in accord with those of contemporaries and of later students. Despite her deep admiration for the devoted service of individual Anglicans on the prairies, it seemed that their work was adversely affected because their church was "not Canadian but English," owing to the perpetuation in Canada of ecclesiastical and theological divisions originating in England, as well as to the paucity of Canadian-born or trained clergy. "How surprised I was . . . at a lunch following a deanery meeting, when conversation ran persistently on Mr. Lloyd George and the Insurance Act, not a Canadian question! Listening and looking around I realized that almost all the men were English."[20]

Reflecting as well the decentralization of a diocesan form of organization, inhibitions arising from its position as the state church in England, and the relatively more limited role assigned to laymen, the Anglican church was less likely to make pronouncements on public issues than were Methodist and Presbyterian Church courts, and its members, both clerical and lay, were usually underrepresented in interdenominational movements for social reform. Few Anglicans were enthusiastic about the temperance movement, and many were sceptical about efforts to legislate "the good life."

Baptists were numerically fewer than members of the three other major Protestant denominations and were more loosely organized, yet they developed an identifiable national business elite, including William and Ross McMaster of the Steel Company of Canada, the agricultural implement manufacturer Alanson Harris, meat packers William Davies and Carey Fox, the jeweller James Ryrie, S. J. Moore, distributor of business forms, John Northway, tailor and retailer, and the financier Albert Matthews. All of these men were deeply involved in the financial support and governance of McMaster University. That institution was the principal spawning ground of what A. R. M. Lower, amazed that the denomination could produce such a phenomenon, identified as a Baptist intellectual elite that was of some importance in Canadian religious and academic life in the first half of this century.[21] Like their Methodist counterparts in the great debate over "higher criticism" of the Bible at Victoria College ("the Jackson controversy"), the Baptist business and intellectual elites came down on the liberal and victorious side when in the 1920's McMaster was torn by a similar struggle centring on the influence of the fundamentalist T. T. Shields in the university and the church.

Since women were without the vote until the First World War, they clearly possessed less direct political influence than their fathers and husbands, but they were a significant part of the religious networks, despite their exclusion from official church courts and from the ordained ministry until well into the twentieth century. Before the turn of the century, the women's missionary societies of the several denominations were among the largest national organizations of any kind in the country, and they may have been the largest. One major concern of these societies—the nature of the new society that was emerging in western Canada—was expressed through their home mission enterprises, which brought women face to face with a variety of social and political questions. A broader network of friendship and interest was created by women in interdenominational endeavours such as the Women's Christian Temperance Union and the Young Women's Christian Association. Many of the thousands of upper- and middle-class women who were active in these associations also belonged to others of more secular origin such as the Imperial Order of the Daughters of the Empire (1900) and the Women's Institutes (1897). The leaders of these and other groups came to know one another in the National Council of Women, where attention was frequently directed to national issues, especially those bearing on the lives of women and children. Typically, the activists in the women's networks were the wives of the business and professional men, and clergymen who constituted the male networks. One can only speculate about the influence of dinner table conversations dominated by such parents on the rising generation.

In the decades between the two world wars, the influence of informal networks and voluntary organizations on the political culture of English Canada was more visible than ever before. In the 1920's the national feeling aroused among English Canadians by the war brought fresh vigour to many existing associations and led to the formation of scores of new ones representing a wide spectrum of economic, religious, educational, sporting, and cultural concerns. Thirty years later, Brooke Claxton, then a member of the federal cabinet and at one time a central figure in a network which included many young intellectuals and business and professional men, observed that in the decade following the war, "every kind of organization, national and local, cultural and religious, political and commercial, was at a peak of activity hardly equalled since. . . . All these were manifestations of national feeling—it was nationwide, spontaneous, inevitable. It cut across political, racial, and social lines; indeed it was curiously a-political."[22]

Thus when the Association of Canadian Clubs, founded before the war, despatched its newly appointed national secretary, Graham Spry, on a drive to establish new clubs, he found a ready response. In 1926–27 alone the number of clubs increased from 53 to 120, with a membership of over forty thousand, and there were few cities or towns of any size without a Canadian Club, or often two, since women had their own clubs. In 1928 the Native Sons of Canada boasted a hundred assemblies across the nation with thirty thousand members devoted to promoting Canadian sentiment. Although its roots lay in the prewar years, the movement which created the United Church of Canada in 1925 owed something to the national feeling of the decade, insufficient though that was to carry all the Presbyterians into an institution "as Canadian as the maple leaf and the beaver."[23] The Royal Canadian Legion, which brought together several organizations of war veterans in 1925, kept alive the memories and loyalties of the war years. In 1936 the Legion organized a pilgrimage of six thousand veterans and many wives and children to the unveiling of the Canadian war memorial on Vimy Ridge on the twentieth anniversary of the battle which symbolized Canadian suffering and achievement in the Great War. It was a time for the renewing of old friendships and the forming of new ones, and for the expression of a heightened national pride that was shared by the thousands more at home who listened to the official ceremonies on the radio.

The 1920's saw the formation of many new national organizations with more specific purposes than the promotion of a generalized Canadian patriotism. What they had in common was a belief that some of their interests could best be articulated and pursued within a national context. Such groups included the Canadian Chambers of Commerce, the Canadian Teachers' Federation, the Catholic Women's League, the Canadian Authors' Association, the National Conference of Education, the Canadian Federation of University Women, and the Student Christian Movement, the first national organization of students and the creator at the end of the decade of the larger National Federation of Canadian University Students.

Ever since the 1880's, the Royal Society had provided a meeting place for intellectuals in the sciences and the humanities and had consistently clamoured for more scientific research in Canada, a plea that was now yielding some results since the programme of the National Research Council, established by the federal government in 1917, was underway. And in the new National Conference of Canadian Universities, university presidents had created a forum for considering the role of their institutions in promoting the national interest. At about the same time, historians in Canada formed the Canadian Historical Association, and in the following decade the Canadian Political Science Association was born. These and other academic societies intended to serve particular academic disciplines formed a web of interest and friendship, all the stronger because it was relatively small, which was a conspicuous feature of English Canadian academic life until the great expansion of the universities in the 1960's.

Among the new groups of the postwar decade one of the smallest and short-lived, but perhaps the most influential, was the Canadian League. It began in 1924 when a group of Ottawa men, led by the lawyer W.D. Herridge, became aware of similar groups in Montreal, Toronto, and Winnipeg whose members shared their alarm that all was not going well in Canada and that some elements in the community found Confederation a burden. Soon, J. M. Macdonnell, a prominent Toronto lawyer, was visiting the cities of the west to establish groups there and lay plans for the founding convention of the Canadian League in Winnipeg in the autumn of 1925. Among the thirty-four men in attendance were many who had known one another in the Association of Canadian Clubs or in the League of Nations Society. In Winnipeg they declared their intention to "foster the national spirit as opposed to sectionalism," to stimulate interest in public affairs, and to promote "such special objects for the benefit of the country as may be decided upon." Self-consciously elitist and believing that the group was composed of those most able to influence government, the members of the League were mainly lawyers and other professionals, businessmen, and university professors. Membership never exceeded five hundred and by 1932 the League had ceased to exist, apparently because of its failure to agree on any specific objective or program.[24] That did not mean that the group had failed. A leading member in Winnipeg, the life insurance executive E. J. Tarr, reported that his group "had never agreed upon a single thing," but it was "very successful because its members . . .as the result of the discussion . . .exercised a substantial influence through the press, platform, and various other contacts.[25]

Although its life as an organization was brief, the influence of the Canadian League carried on well into the future. In 1932 men who had come to know one another in the League were organizing the Canadian Institute of International Affairs to promote the development of a more informed opinion on Canada's external relations and achieved considerable success in realizing that objective.[26] Some, notably Graham Spry, Alan Plaunt, and Brooke Claxton, had organized one of the most successful pressure groups in Canadian history, the Canadian Radio League, a body which played a major role in the establishment of public broadcasting in Canada.[27] Later, the same constituency was organized to support the formation of the National Film Board. The more radically minded formed the League for Social Reconstruction, composed largely of academics in Montreal and Toronto, and began to plan for a democratic socialist society in Canada. Still others, many of them officers of the extension departments of the universities, joined with the leaders of rural social movements such as the New Canada Movement and the Antigonish Movement to form the Canadian Association for Adult Education with E. A. Corbett as president. Through such programmes as the "National Farm Radio Forum" and "Citizens' Forum," that association demonstrated how effective the CBC and the Film Board could be in furthering adult education. During the Second World War, the adult educators formed the core of the group which framed and administered the policies of the Wartime Information Board.[28]

Graham Spry, who was probably associated with more of these organizations than anyone else, has referred to the "quite extraordinary pattern or web of personal relationships and friendships extending from coast to coast" in the 1930's, "a web informal, intimate, trusting, confident, strong, but really unorganized . . . .Through this web it was not merely possible but often simple to set an idea upon its course, to have it thrashed out across Canada and ultimately expressed either in terms of voluntary action or governmental action."[29]

The existence of such a web and the conviction that it had influence no doubt had some bearing on the eagerness of voluntary organizations to submit briefs to the grand enquiry into the working of Canadian federalism, the Rowell-Sirois Commission. Further, many members of its large research staff and the commissioners themselves, including the chief architect of their report, John Dafoe, were members of the elite network. As many observers noted at the time, the commission's enthusiasm for the federal government's central role in the development of the nation was scarcely surprising. A decade later a similar influence was clearly visible in the membership of the Royal Commission on National Development in the Arts, Letters, and Sciences. Its chairman, Vincent Massey, had been an active member of several of the earlier voluntary organizations, as had another commissioner, N. A. M. MacKenzie. The major recommendation of the Massey Commission, the establishment of a "Canada Council for the Encouragement of the Arts, Letters, Humanities, and Social Sciences," accorded well with views the educational and cultural elite of English Canada had been developing for more than two decades.

In the 1950's Corry thought that the voluntary associations had been highly effective in breaking through "the two solitudes," and he was optimistic about the effect this would have on the Canadian future. Closer examination shows that although a few distinguished French Canadians were associated with some groups, including the Canadian Radio League and the Canadian Institute of International Affairs, they formed a very small part of "the web" and were unable to interest many of their fellow Quebecers in organizations which were so clearly dominated by English Canadians. Even scarcer was labour participation, an exception being Tom Moore, one of the most conservative leaders of the Trades and Labour Congress of Canada.

In the larger, more complex Canadian society of the second half of this century have informal associations been more or less influential than they were earlier? Has the advent of the electronic age and the global village dissolved the old networks and created very different ones? Certainly the old, often overlapping networks composed of a relatively small number of upper- and middle-class English Canadians are less dominant. Rarely now does one hear newcomers to Canada, especially Americans, exclaim, as so many of them did twenty-five years ago: "In this country everybody knows everybody else!" Now Canadians who come from outside the British 'charter group" are among the activists in many national associations, and a variety of nationally organized ethnic organizations have added their perspectives to the discussion of Canadian issues. Despite rapid secularization, churches continue to form networks of some importance, and their social concerns create interchurch agencies more ecumenical than the earlier bodies for they now often include Roman Catholics. At the same time the mainline churches are challenged by the growth of more conservative or fundamentalist churches with their own networks and often opposing attitudes on what constitutes the public good.

Throughout our history, many Canadians, possibly a majority, have had relatives in the United States and have thus been part of a personal north-south network. At the same time, large numbers of Canadians have belonged to associations which were branches of larger American organizations. Have kinship and organizational ties with the United States declined or grown in recent years, and what effect do they have on how Canadians perceive themselves and their government? And how has national sentiment been affected by the growth of sport and of the associations which support it and bring together thousands of athletes and spectators within Canada and from outside? (During any Canadian-Soviet hockey game there could be no doubt about the answer!)

One important change in the context in which voluntary associations operate comes from increased government involvement in almost every aspect of life. This has encouraged informal and loosely organized societies to become formal pressure groups to secure a hearing for their concerns and often to focus on very specific objectives. As part of that, the increasing power of provincial governments has fostered the growth of provincial branches of national organizations and has heightened the influence of regional and provincial networks.

"The ties that bind" English Canadians may be easier to identify in the history of the first half of this century than they are through the complexities of the second half. If modern technology creates an increasingly impersonal society, it also facilitates a new degree of mobility and communication. Today it seems probable that a larger proportion of Canadians than ever before know fellow citizens in other regions of the country. Although difficult, attempts to understand the nature of their associations and its effects on English Canadians' image of their country are worthwhile studies.

NOTES

1. J. A. Corry, "Constitutional Trends and Federalism," in A. R. M. Lower, et al., *Evolving Canadian Federalism* (Durham: Duke University Press, 1958), pp. 109–10.

2. For a discussion of this hazard, see Alan C. Cairns, ''The Governments and Societies of Canadian Federalism,'' *Canadian Journal of Political Science* 10 (December 1977): 695–725.
3. Gordon T. Stewart, ''Political Patronage under Macdonald and Laurier 1879–1911,'' *American Review of Canadian Studies* 10 (Spring 1980): 3–26.
4. Cited in Gordon Stewart, ''John A. Macdonald's Greatest Triumph,'' *Canadian Historical Review* 63 (March 1982): 30.
5. John English, *The Decline of Politics: The Conservatives and the Party System 1901–20* (Toronto: University of Toronto Press, 1977), p. 29.
6. Ibid., 222–29.
7. Michael Bliss, *A Living Profit: Studies in the Social History of Canadian Business, 1883–1911* (Toronto: McClelland and Stewart, 1974), explores the minds of businessmen.
8. T. W. Acheson, ''The Social Origins of the Canadian Industrial Elite, 1880–85,'' in David S. Macmillan, ed., *Canadian Business History: Selected Studies, 1497–1971* (Toronto: McClelland and Stewart, 1972), pp. 144–74; Acheson, ''Changing Social Origins of the Canadian Industrial Elite, 1880–1910,'' *Business History Review* 47 (Summer 1973): 189–91.
9. Robert A. J. McDonald, ''Business Leaders in Early Vancouver, 1886–1914,'' (Ph. D. diss., University of British Columbia, 1977).
10. David Gagan, *Hopeful Travellers: Families, Land, and Social Change in Mid-Victorian Peel County, Canada West* (Toronto: University of Toronto Press, 1981).
11. W. L. Morton, *Manitoba: A History* (Toronto: University of Toronto Press, 1957), ch. 9.
12. D. H. Breen, *The Canadian Prairie West and the Ranching Frontier 1874–1924* (Toronto: University of Toronto Press, 1982).
13. Jean Barman, *Growing Up British in British Columbia* (Vancouver: University of British Columbia Press, 1984); John Porter, *The Vertical Mosaic* (Toronto: University of Toronto Press, 1965); Wallace Clement, *The Canadian Corporate Elite: An Analysis of Economic Power* (Toronto: McClelland and Stewart, 1975).
14. W. Peter Ward, ''Population Growth in Western Canada, 1901–1971,'' in John E. Foster, ed., *The Developing West: Essays on Canadian History in Honor of Lewis H. Thomas* (Edmonton: University of Alberta Press, 1983), pp. 174–75.
15. Michael Bliss, ''Better and Purer: The Peterborough Methodist Mafia and the Renaissance of Toronto,'' in William Kilbourn, ed., *Toronto Remembered* (Toronto: Stoddart Publishing, 1984), pp. 194–205; Margaret Prang, *N. W. Rowell, Ontario Nationalist* (Toronto: University of Toronto Press, 1975), *passim*.
16. Michael Bliss, *A Canadian Millionaire: The Life and Times of Sir Joseph Flavelle, Bart. 1858–1939* (Toronto: Macmillan, 1978), pp. 7–8.
17. Unpublished Summary of Proceedings of Conference on ''Canadian Missionaries and East Asia,'' University of Toronto, 22–23 April 1983, pp. 23–24.
18. For a discussion of the origins and content of this ''national gospel,'' see Brian J. Fraser, ''The Christianization of Our Civilization: Presbyterian Reformers and Their Defence of a Protestant Canada, 1875–1914'' (Ph. D. diss., York University, 1982).
19. Elizabeth B. Mitchell, *In Western Canada before the War* (London: John Murray, 1915; reprint, Saskatoon: Western Producer Prairie Books, 1981), pp. 83–84. The author, a Scot, distinguished Oxford graduate, and town planner, spent nearly a year in Canada in 1913–14.
20. Ibid., pp. 85–86. An unsuccessful attempt to refute the frequently argued view that the Anglican church was slow to ''Canadianize'' is David A. Nock, ''Patriotism and Patriarchs: Anglican Archbishops and Canadianization,'' *Canadian Ethnic Studies* 14, no. 3 (1982): 79–94.
21. A. R. M. Lower, *My First Seventy-Five Years* (Toronto: Macmillan, 1967), p. 301.
22. Cited in E. A. Corbett, *We Have with Us To-night* (Toronto: Ryerson Press, 1957), p. 104.

23. Porter, *The Vertical Mosaic*, p. 519.
24. Ron Faris, *The Passionate Educators: Voluntary Associations and the Struggle for Control of Adult Educational Broadcasting in Canada 1919–52* (Toronto: Peter Martin Associates, 1975), pp. 9–12. This volume contains names of many of the participants in various voluntary associations of the period.
25. Cited in ibid., p. 11.
26. Edward D. Greathed, ''Antecedents and Origins of the Canadian Institute of International Affairs,'' in H. L. Dyck and H. P. Krosby, eds., *Empire and Nations* (Toronto: University of Toronto Press, 1969).
27. Margaret Prang, ''The Origins of Public Broadcasting in Canada,'' *Canadian Historical Review* 46 (1965): 1–31; Graham Spry, ''The Origins of Public Broadcasting in Canada: A Comment,'' Ibid., 46 (1965): 134–41.
28. William R. Young, ''Making the Truth Graphic: The Canadian Government's Home Front Information Structure and Programmes during World War II'' (Ph. D. diss., University of British Columbia, 1978), ch. 2.
29. Spry, *The Origins of Public Broadcasting*, pp. 136–37; on their participation in the Winnipeg and Toronto groups of the web, see Lower, *My First Seventy-Five Years*, chs. 14–15; Escott Reid, *On Duty: A Canadian at the Making of the United Nations 1945–1946* (Toronto: McClelland and Stewart, 1983), pp. 8–9.

II

BUILDING THE POLITICAL COMMUNITY

4

The Making of a Canadian Political Citizenship

R. KENNETH CARTY AND W. PETER WARD

George Etienne Cartier's call for a new political nationality is perhaps the most cited phrase of the Confederation Debates. Cartier sought a limited, political nationality for the new dominion because one based on culture could not be achieved. In his words, "the idea of unity of races was utopian—it was impossible."[1] Whether or not one agrees with Cartier's assumptions (and there has been plenty of hot debate in the intervening years), his remark inadvertently raised a question fundamental to all modern political societies, Canada included. Who should have membership in the national political community?

The term citizen bears several definitions, and therefore it is important at the outset to explain what we mean by the concept.[2] Modern notions of citizenship derive from eighteenth-century political theory. The American and French revolutions fashioned republican forms of government which rested on beliefs about citizenship derived from Lockean notions of allegiance. These theories emphasized that the relationship between governors and the governed was consensual and contractual. As the revolutionary assembly of France declared in August 1789, "no body and no individual may exercise authority which does not emanate from the nation expressly." Government was rooted in the free association of individual citizens, united by consent in allegiance to the state. In revolutionary America and France, political citizenship was defined by proclamation, each declaration based on the doctrines of the victors.

These theories denied older, monarchical doctrines which spoke not of citizens but of subjects. Whereas republican allegiance was voluntary, conditional, and institutional, monarchical allegiance was natural, perpetual, and personal. Citizens bound themselves to the state only as long as their rulers governed with their assent. Subjects owed allegiance to their sovereign in his or her person; their obligation derived from natural law and therefore could not be set aside. Lord Coke, the British jurist whose early seventeenth-century judgements framed the subsequent evolution of citizenship law in England, declared that "God and nature, not men and laws, made natural born subjects." He argued that "the legitimacy of every kingdom and state rested upon the hierarchical principles of the natural order."[3] In Coke's age, few British subjects had any active political role. Over time, however, membership in British political society greatly expanded. But unlike the French and American experiences, this growth was basically evolutionary. Successive British Parliaments extended the rights of representation and participation in the national legislature, propelled more by pressures from those who were denied these rights than any ideological commitment.

The evolving concept of citizenship in Canada rested on British precedent. Before 1947 there were no Canadian citizens as such, only British subjects resident in Canada. Those who acquired the rights of membership in Canada, either through birth or naturalization, in reality acquired the rights of British subjects. Political rights were among the most important of them, of course, and much of the nascent sense of Canadian citizenship (in the republican sense of the term) which took form in the half century after confederation centred on the achievement of these rights. Gradually a hybrid form of nationality emerged, which combined elements of both republican and monarchical principles. For thirty years after 1946, a Canadian citizen was simultaneously a British subject. In practice this meant that one owed allegiance to the British crown while exercising political rights in Canada. The ambiguities of these circumstances have only recently been clarified.

This paper treats Canadian citizenship in an important, but restricted, sense, exploring the evolution of a distinctive sense of "political citizenship" in Canada since Confederation. In addition, it examines some of the more important implications of this process for the national political community. The citizens spoken of here were not citizens in the republican sense of the term; nor were they subjects in the broad sense of the term. The political citizens discussed here were those who had the legal capacity to play a direct role in the political process in Canada. In this sense possession of the franchise defined active membership in the political community; the vote constituted participation at its most fundamental level.

In Canada even more than Great Britain, pragmatism has ruled the making of a national political citizenry.[4] When he called for a new political nationality in 1865, Cartier had no high ideals—perhaps not even any clear thoughts—in mind but rather a practical recognition of the apparently insoluble problem of merging the British North American colonies. The general question of citizenship was so awkward a problem that those who drafted the confederation agreement largely avoided it. Thereafter, Canadian politicians generally dealt with the matter of political citizenship as expedience dictated. Consequently, the achievement of popular democracy in Canada was not a simple process of gradually broadening liberties as it has sometimes been thought to be. There have been significant retreats as well as notable advances. And changes, when they occured, were not measured against any great principles but were implemented "with a sharp sensitivity to shifting pressures and to political advantages."[5]

In Canada as elsewhere the franchise has always been the instrument which defines the political citizenry, for it establishes the minimum criteria for participation in national political life. But other factors have had an equally powerful impact on this process of definition. Since long before Confederation, the country has been the destination of millions of immigrants. For this reason immigration and naturalization policies have left a deep imprint on the face of the political community. The need to deal with a dispossessed and supplanted indigenous population has also influenced decisions about the boundaries of political society. The bicultural fact in national political life has brought conflicting pressures to bear on policy areas touching all these issues. What follows is an attempt to explore the interplay of these factors as national governments have exploited them in shaping and reshaping the Canadian political community.

The issue of who might become political citizens has obviously been deeply influenced by the nation's immigration policies. Until the Great Depression, the federal government placed few barriers before prospective white immigrants. The law always excluded people on the basis of physical, mental, and moral incapacity, and for brief periods of time, enemy aliens, pacifists, and unpopular visible minorities were also barred from the country.[6] Immigration was also retarded during serious recessions, ostensibly to prevent large labour surpluses from accumulating. But before 1930 Canada generally pursued an open door policy.

Over the past half century, however, immigration requirements have been tuned much more finely to national manpower requirements, although lingering ethnic and racial prejudices and humanitarian sympathies have modified this principle. But even though more selective, Canada's immigration policies remain among the most open of all western societies. An important consequence of this has been that since the Second World War, Canada's electorate has grown more quickly than that of any other liberal democracy except Israel. This flow of new Canadians has been a critical factor in dissolving the imperial link and in stimulating what attempts have been made to create a distinctive Canadian citizenship. If in the 1946 debates on the first Canadian Citizenship Act "the continuity of the British connection was the single theme that filled most pages of Hansard,"[7] the steady stream of migrants in subsequent years made the connection increasingly anachronistic. The Liberal party, which lived off these new citizens in metropolitan Canada, recognized this anachronism and moved to sever the connection in the 1976 Citizenship Act.

Until recently, however, the open door policy was not extended to non-white immigrants. From the 1880's to the 1960's, successive national governments employed widely varied strategies to limit Asian and black immigration. The King government's policy of deporting Canadians born of Japanese ancestry in 1945 and 1946 was an even clearer statement of prevailing assumptions about Canadian citizenship. By and large these policies worked. Before the advent of colour-blind admission (1967), the proportion of non-whites in the Canadian population was extremely small.[8]

The racial, ethnic, and class preferences of successive governments have been as evident in their recruitment programmes as in their exclusion policies. The great immigration promotion schemes of the Laurier years, unprecedented before and unequalled since, sought potential Canadians far more energetically in Britain and the American midwest than elsewhere. Until the 1960's most policies encouraging migration reflected the assumption that northwestern Europeans and Americans of like descent made the best prospective citizens. Recruitment has also had a marked class bias. The express desire for migrants with specific levels of education, skill, and wealth—the early twentieth-century preference for unskilled agricultural and industrial workers as much as the recent bias toward the well-educated and highly-trained—has also moulded the social structure of the Canadian community.

The law of naturalization has had an equally profound impact on the shape of the Canadian citizenry. In general, since 1867, the concept of citizen implicit in Canadian naturalization requirements has shifted from imperial to national foundations, from cultural preferment to universalism, and from familial to individual bases. This marked the slow transformation from monarchical to republican assumptions about the basis of citizenship. Confederation made no change in the status of resident British subjects, though uniform requirements for naturalization soon replaced the various measures formerly in place in the several colonies. Henceforth, naturalization was based upon a few simple requirements: three years' residence, good character, and an oath of loyalty to the Crown. In accordance with established British practice and patriarchal assumptions about the nature of the family, women were deemed to acquire their husband's citizenship at marriage and minor children to possess that of their fathers. The naturalized, like the native born, became subjects of the British Crown, not citizens of the new Dominion. Canadian naturalization was among the most open in all western societies. Birth or naturalization throughout the Empire conferred political rights in Canada, the requirements for naturalization were few and easily met, and the naturalized suffered no special disadvantage vis-a-vis the imperially born.

Of the many amendments to the law of naturalization since 1867, three groups of substantive changes bear directly on the fundamental concept of citizen. The first was the very late evolution of a distinctive sense of Canadian citizenship. For three decades after 1946 Canadian citizenship still conferred British subject status. Only since 1976 has a sharp line been drawn between these once coterminous concepts. The status of British subject has been replaced by one of Commonwealth citizen, a rather murky condition which seemingly bears no significant obligations or privileges.

The second series of changes was made in the early twentieth century, when massive foreign immigration provoked a marked upsurge in Canadian nativism. Urged on by assimilationist aspirations and an Anglo-Canadian vision of the preferred society, the Borden government impeded the naturalization of all but British immigrants. It amended the law of naturalization to require a minimum of five years' residence and an adequate knowledge of English or French.[9] Electoral expediency played no little part in the calculations which led to these changes: this was the government which deprived naturalized citizens of enemy alien ancestry of the vote during the First World War. Further alterations also gave the secretary of state widespread discretion in the administration of naturalization regulations. The resulting legal bias, favouring British over all other immigrants, persisted until the mid-1970's, when new revisions placed all aliens seeking citizenship on the same footing.

The third change, embodied in a series of amendments dating from 1931, gave women increasing independence—and ultimately autonomy—from their husbands in the determination of their national status. These developments were in keeping with the contemporary removal of other legal restrictions upon women and also with the ongoing twentieth-century challenge to corporate and patriarchal assumptions about the family.

This brief overview of the national government's policies regarding naturalization suggests that there have not been any clearly defined guiding principles underlying the system. Policy has evolved slowly and unevenly. Changes in law have almost always been governmental responses to the changing nature of the populace rather than tools to mould the character of the country. The end to British preferment was simply a belated admission that Britain no longer served as the principle source of new Canadians. Finally, it should be noted that in all these developments pragmatic electoral considerations were rarely far from the minds of the politicians who enacted them. Canadian citizenship, at least in so far as the immigration and naturalization processes reveal, has been a concept rooted more in electoral need than in any highly developed principles.

At Confederation the political foci of the new community were the assemblies in which Canadians were to be represented. The process of deciding upon rights to membership in them provides one clear indication of the pragmatism which characterized the first Canadian definitions of political citizenship. As early as 1867 the two maritime provinces moved to prohibit members of the national House of Commons from sitting in their legislatures. Within a decade, dual representation had been abolished, by politicians in Ottawa, for the other provinces.[10] For the most part, the decision to separate the assemblies in this way reflected no reasoned debate on constitutional principles or on the political rights of the citizenry. It stemmed from the political calculations of groups of politicians seeking to maximize their strength in the new system. In this battle the Nova Scotians went so far as to disenfranchise federal employees.[11]

All this activity was a signal to Canadians that two distinct, if intertwined, political citizenships were being created—one provincial, the other national. Since then, as Alan Cairns and others have reminded us, governments have constantly promoted the growth of selfconscious provincial communities through state-building activity and continuing jurisdictional disputes.[12] Any comparison with the post Civil War United States reveals the federal government's continuing difficulty in asserting the primacy of national citizenship except in time of war. In the absence of any hard evidence, one might also speculate that this segmentation inevitably worked its way into the major political parties by distinguishing their national and provincial wings in each province. At a time when parties were little more than cliques of parliamentary notables, and yet remained the only available instruments for nation-building and national integration, this fragmentation worked against the interests of a national community and of a common political citizenship.

If native birth, migration, immigration policy, and naturalization law have provided the raw materials of the Canadian political citizenry, the franchise was the tool used in its making. Therefore, the history of franchise law lies at the heart of our enquiry. While the contents of franchise regulations have varied widely over time, all such laws have had two fundamental consequences. First, they have defined the basic units of political society (and thus the boundaries of the source of governing authority, at least since the dawn of responsible government). Second, in so doing they have identified that segment of the population which was to be propitiated, solicited, organized, and manipulated by practicing politicians in their competition for office. In this sense these laws established the fundamental task of electoral politics.

At Confederation the new Dominion inherited a melange of franchises, for each former colonial legislature had previously determined its own electoral requirements.[13] All of them reserved the vote to male British subjects, including Jews and Roman Catholics who were emancipated in British North America before their co-religionists in Britain. All but one invoked property or income qualifications, though the precise requirements varied from one colony to the next. (The only exception was British Columbia, where manhood suffrage prevailed at the time of union.) In 1867 expedience dictated that these various laws be used to define the new national electorate, and they remained in force until 1885, when Parliament established the first Canadian franchise.

This new electoral law neither departed from past principles nor imposed a uniform franchise on the country. Without really intending to, it extended the privilege of voting somewhat, but this extension was limited and uneven, for the act produced a franchise "more diversified than the varied provincial qualifications it supplanted." The result was "an astonishing hodge-podge that discriminated between provinces, social classes, and racial groups . . . a situation which Sir John drily explained away by a desire not to insist on 'pedantic uniformity.' "[14] Given the primitive character of electoral administration, there was undoubtedly even more diversity in practice than provided for in law. Here was no concern to define a common political nationality, no attempt to make the choice of government a collective act of the citizenry. It was a narrowly partisan scheme, for the fundamental significance of the act lay not in its principles or its practices but in its purposes. As Gordon Stewart has recently argued, the new franchise law—which Macdonald deemed "the greatest triumph of my life"—was intended to strengthen the Conservative government's control of the electoral system and thus defend the party, the patronage apparatus, and the legislative programme which Sir John A. had laboured throughout his political lifetime to create.[15]

By the end of the next decade, however, five of the seven provinces had embraced manhood suffrage. At the same time, the flaws and inconsistencies in the federal law had become all too apparent. As a result Macdonald's greatest triumph seemed inadequate and inequitable. But after 1896 the new Laurier government saw no easy path to a reformed federal franchise. The prime minister himself opposed the principle of manhood suffrage, and two provinces—Quebec and Nova Scotia—still required property qualifications for the vote. With all but one of the provinces then in the hands of Liberal administrations, political expedience once more dictated the adoption of the various provincial franchises as the basis of the federal. Ironically, while this permitted some inconsistencies in voter requirements to persist, it reduced their number significantly. Thus, by 1898, manhood suffrage in the federal sphere had been achieved in all but two provinces. The first victory of liberal democracy had been a partial and undramatic triumph. Perhaps more important, from the perspective of a developing Canadian political citizenship, 1898 marked a retreat. The national Parliament handed back to the seven provincial assemblies the decision regarding who could vote and on what terms they were to do so; Ottawa had abrogated its right to define membership in the national political community. True to the one consistent principle operating throughout the period, this was done solely for reasons of political expedience.

By 1900 the greatest potential for further expansion of the national electorate lay in female enfranchisement. Within two decades, this had been achieved, but in a manner rather different from earlier franchise reforms. In this case alone change came in response to broad, popular demand which could not be denied indefinitely. With no national franchise, provincial governments held all the keys to reform, and therefore each one became the target of a separate campaign. Reformers largely overlooked the federal government. But when the five westernmost provinces enfranchised women in 1915 and 1916, in an atmosphere of heightened wartime idealism, the Borden government could not long ignore the implications of such changes for federal voting requirements. In the notorious War-time Elections Act of 1917, it gave the vote to women with close relations in the armed services and then, one year later, extended the federal franchise to all women on the same basis as men.

The popular nature of the campaign for suffrage reform apart, other pragmatic political concerns played an important part in the way Canadian women obtained this political right. The absence of any national standards constituting a minimum political citizenship meant that these rights were not fully extended until 1940, when women in Quebec obtained the provincial vote. In his last ditch opposition to female enfranchisement, Cardinal Villeneuve gave pride of place to the argument that "it [was] contrary to familial unity and hierarchy."[16] Obviously, the assumptions which underlay the Victorian family, as well as the Victorian constitution, persisted longest in Quebec.[17] But this was only one striking example of how varied political rights in the Dominion could be.

The move toward a renewed national franchise began during the First World War when the War-time Elections Act provided a uniform electoral law for the entire country. It broadened the male franchise slightly, extended the vote to selected groups of women, and took it away from pacifists and many naturalized citizens. As a partisan manoeuvre, it was audacious even by previous Canadian practice. The purpose of the measure was freely admitted by its advocates. In the words of Arthur Meighen, who shepherded the bill through the Commons, "I do believe that the majority of those in the trenches . . . [and] of those whose near relatives are overseas fighting the foe would rather support this Administration than support one formed by the leader of the Opposition."[18] For the Union government this had the happy consequence of assuring electoral victory in 1917. For the Conservatives, the measure allowed the reassertion of the British character of Canada. But the act also made it clear that, half a century after Confederation, the national government had yet to grapple in any realistic fashion with the basic concept of a Canadian political citizenship.

In 1920, Parliament finally enacted the first uniform national franchise law since Confederation. Prisoners were disenfranchised on grounds of their offences against society, lunatics because they were deemed incompetent, poor house inmates owing to their status as public charges, judges by reason of their apolitical office, and electoral officials owing to their intimate links with the polling process. In law, however, universal suffrage had virtually been achieved. But law and practice did not necessarily coincide, and for the next twenty years, electoral arrangements restricted the opportunity some citizens might have to exercise their basic political right. Throughout the 1920's, the new national franchise continued to depend on provincial voters' lists, appropriately altered, and no satisfactory scheme for preparing such lists emerged until the Dominion Elections Act of 1938.[19]

Still, during the slow evolution of a single national franchise, the egalitarian political ideals commonly associated with suffrage reform in a liberal democracy were always qualified in Canada. Women apart, the most obvious qualification was the longstanding denial of franchise rights to several racial and ethnic minorities. All treaty Indians and Eskimos, save veterans, were disenfranchised before 1960, ostensibly because they were wards of the Crown. Until the later 1940's, the law also prohibited most Canadians of Chinese, Japanese, and East Indian descent from voting—provisions designed to appease popular opinion in British Columbia.[20] Doukhobors, too, were excluded from the franchise throughout much of the twentieth century, allegedly because of their unwillingness to bear arms. Whatever the immediate rationale, fundamentally these groups were precluded from voting on racial and ethnic grounds. Of all the minorities in post-Confederation Canada, they were the most unpopular. And so long as no clear concept of a Canadian's political rights existed, members of these groups found that their claims to the franchise varied as they moved from province to province.[21] The denial of franchise rights embodied common prejudices in law while affirming the popular conviction that these minorities were less than full citizens. As long as such restrictions persisted, racial and ethnic origins were criteria which determined admissability to the national political community.

In postwar Canada, newly ascendent liberal views on race and ethnic relations challenged traditional biases in electoral law, and, in response, governments dismantled these barriers one by one. But not until 1960 was universal suffrage, the proclaimed goal of popular democracy, truly achieved.[22] Finally, with the Constitution Act, 1982, every Canadian citizen has seen his or her democratic rights entrenched in a Charter of Rights and Freedoms, 115 years after Confederation.[23] In one sense this represents the triumph of an individualistic and egalitarian citizenship. Yet, references in the new constitution to the rights of the two charter language groups and the rights of aboriginal peoples suggest that the triumph is not complete. Quite the contrary, they remind us of the enduring reality of those collective rights traditionally exercised in national political life by some social groups. They are present in the Charter for pragmatic political reasons, and they are indications of the difficulties confronting any national government which attempts to define the essence of Canadian political rights.

Historically, the unique role of francophone Quebec in the federal system, and the character of Canadian federalism more generally, has always constituted a challenge to the equalitarianism implicit in the building of a Canadian liberal democracy. Professor Arthur Silver has observed the post-Confederation emergence of "a peculiar Quebec view of the Parliament of Canada, a body seen less as representing all the Canadian people, as Canadians, than as representing the provinces, which were the constituent members of confederation."[24] In the aftermath of Riel's execution, Quebec francophones—who until then had considered the province the only French homeland in North America—claimed a new pan-Canadian role for themselves and insisted that their language and religious rights be defended across the nation.[25] The implication of these aspirations was that Canada was a federation of races rather than provinces, a community of two equal cultures rather than of individuals. Henri Bourassa was the most persistent advocate of the two nations concept in early twentieth century Canada, just as the Pearson and Trudeau Liberals have been its leading practitioners during the last two decades. But Mr. Trudeau's success in institutionalizing his version of French-English equality in the charter of individual rights has not settled the matter. It guarantees that group and individual definitions of citizenship will continue to lie at the heart of the nation's political conflicts.

Nor has Quebec been the only source of challenges to liberal democratic ideals. At one time or another most provinces have represented the nation as the sum of its provincial components or, at least, of its regions. Alberta, the most recent champion of this view, can draw on a rich inheritance of similar declarations when pressing this assertion, many of them first uttered by the oldest and most persistent advocate of the compact theory—Ontario. But all such claims, whether based on the assumption that the nation is composed of cultures, regions, or provinces, deny a fundamental principle of liberal democracy: that citizens are *individually* and *equally* incorporated into the political community.

From time to time this same denial has been linked with political dissent in Canada. This was perhaps inevitable given the lack of any clear vision of Canadian citizenship and the manipulation of political rights by governments seeking partisan advantage. To the extent that the small groups of socialist radicals in the early twentieth century West eschewed direct action for electoral and parliamentary politics, they upheld class-based models of political society at variance with the individualistic assumptions of liberalism. During the 1920's the group government theorists in the Alberta wing of the Progressive party made this challenge explicit. But despite the legacy it inherited from both traditions, the CCF repudiated such notions of class or group politics. Indeed, among the national political parties in Canada, the CCF and its successor have been the staunchest defenders of the liberal democratic ideal. What little political support was offered to Japanese Canadians in their quest for the franchise came from the CCF.[26] This was hardly the electoral pragmatism that characterized its more successful opponents.

In ideological terms, however, the choices confronting all politicians—left, right, and centre—are not always so easy. There may well be confusion about the specific demands advanced by the contemporary native rights movement, but one general point is abundantly clear: native leaders have rejected the view that the political rights of citizens are essentially individual. The whole thrust of their current campaign is to attain special collective political and constitutional rights for aboriginal peoples. Because their numbers are relatively small and they are thinly distributed across the nation, they cannot exercise power as natives unless they can embed themselves in the polity as a collectivity.[27] How our political leaders might accommodate these aspirations, in the face of a general commitment to the liberal democratic vision of political citizenship, seems unclear. Nor, given the long tradition of dealing with these fundamental issues on a partisan level, is there much reason to expect that national politicians will find the incentive to try.

Throughout this essay we have been concerned to trace the emergence of those political rights of citizenship in Canada normally vested in the citizens of liberal democracies. Rather than focusing on the details of a particular act, we have examined the broad sweep of policy that, over more than a century, governed entry into and participation in the national community of political citizens. In particular, we have sought clues which indicate how the national government conceived of Canadian citizenship and used it as a tool to build a Canadian political nationality and support the institutions of government in a new nation. By exploring this problem, we have tried to direct attention to the deliberate nation-building, citizen-creating activities of the state.

It seems clear that these activities have not been informed by any consistent notion of a Canadian citizenship nor any regular patterns institutionalizing political rights. At times the national government has asserted a national policy: at others it has backed away, leaving considerable initiative to the provinces. Rights have been expanded, but they have also been deliberately restricted. All these developments show the impact of short-term political expediency at work, as politicians, ever sensitive to the electoral winds, struggled for supremacy. By treating basic political rights, and the procedures that implemented them, as a political football, politicians have signalled to the electorate that the basis of Canadian citizenship itself remained at issue. The triumph of pragmatism over principle, however vital it may have been for the political survival of the polity, has not provided any foundation for consensus on the essential elements of a national political community.

It may be that Cartier's conviction that racial unity was "utopian" and "impossible" became a self-fulfilling prophecy. It may be that Macdonald's commitment to a British identity led him to reject the notion of a distinct Canadian citizenship. It may be that popular opinion convinced most politicians that political rights were not a winning issue. Whatever the case, this continuing ambivalence has perpetuated a set of conflicts about the essence of Canadianness that lies at the heart of the political system. Canadians divide between anglophone and francophone, old and new, immigrant and aboriginal, partly because there is no common meeting ground, no agreement on what constitutes a Canadian. The debates over citizenship in the postwar period revealed little movement from the positions taken in the 1860's, and the subsequent decline in the salience of the British connection has only seemed to aggravate tensions between English and French-speaking Canadians. The vacuum created by the end of the Empire forced anglophone Canadians to think again about who they were. The conflict engendered by the decision of the Pearson government to adopt a national flag demonstrated how divided the Canadian community was and how little agreement there was about the future of the national identiy.[28] Certainly, native peoples have never been incorporated in common definitions of the community, and their enfranchisement in 1960 only marked the beginning of their struggle to redefine themselves within the broader political nationality.

The absence of any standard of Canadianness, rooted either in long historical tradition or proclaimed in ringing declarations of nationhood, has increased the opportunity for parochial political elites to engage in province-building. All provincial governments have attempted to use their governmental resources to create a provincial community and engender a sense of loyalty to it. In no small part the identities and loyalties so created have been set against those due the national community, and they have been mobilized by provincial governments in their jurisdictional and fiscal conflicts with the national government. The cases of Quebec and Alberta have perhaps received the most attention of late, but even have-not provinces such as Newfoundland and Labrador have played this game aggressively. This syndrome has characterized the long history of provincial variations in basic political rights. A distinctive Canadian citizenship might have constrained provincial politicians; its lack has proved costly to nation-builders in Ottawa who have sought to strengthen the entire community.

With the Constitution Act of 1982, the long acceptance of piecemeal development through pragmatic response may have ended. Indeed, for many Canadians, the attraction of an entrenched Charter of Rights was its promise to spell out the norms and rights of a common citizenship. The Supreme Court and not Parliament will now decide the limits and obligations of our political rights and will do so in a way that creates a uniform national citizenship.[29] Certainly, this should make it extremely difficult for national politicians to tamper with the franchise (thought not, with immigration or naturalization policies) in the manner of the past. The Charter will set a positive standard against which all Canadians will begin to measure themselves and their governments. Provincial governments are unlikely to be exempted from this development. They will increasingly be expected to justify deviations from national norms in a fashion consistent with the standards of a common political nationality. In the new Constitution, the national government may have created its most useful tool yet for developing a Canadian citizenship.

But the lessons of our history ought to make us cautious about these possibilities. After all, the Charter of Rights is qualified by "reasonable limits prescribed by law," limits with which Canadians have had much experience. It is also modified by the capacity of determined provincial governments to opt out of its protections. The tensions between individual and collective rights on language have been perpetuated and are bound to remain in conflict, for they derive from one of the basic divisions in our society. To resist the nation-building potential of the new constitutional amendments, Quebec provincial politicians denied its legitimacy and frustrated its operation in that province. The Charter also sets aboriginal peoples apart, but their position has been left ambiguous and undefined. Indeed, it seems a parody of all previous Canadian experience to leave the basic political rights of one section of the population, a poor and marginal one at that, to an indefinite number of federal-provincial conferences peopled by a constantly shifting set of politicans, most of whom have at least one eye fixed on the next election. Still, Cartier's 1865 remonstrations should command our attention. If the new Charter marks an important development, it is no less true that Canadians have some distance to go before basic agreement is reached on what constitutes Canadian political citizenship.

NOTES

1. P. B. Waite, ed., *The Confederation Debates in the Province of Canada/1865* (Toronto: McClelland and Stewart, 1963), p. 50.
2. The authors wish to thank Professor C. Sharman for his extremely helpful comments on the concept of citizenship.
3. James H. Kettner, *The Development of American Citizenship, 1608–1870* (Chapel Hill, NC, University of North Carolina Press, 1978), p. 28.
4. W. L. Morton, "The Extension of the Franchise in Canada: A Study in Democratic Nationalism," Canadian Historical Association, *Report* (1943): 72-81.
5. John Garner, *The Franchise and Politics in British North America, 1755–1867* (Toronto: University of Toronto Press, 1969), p. 10. The comment, though made of the pre-Confederation period, is an apt account of the period after 1867 as well.

6. Hutterites, Mennonites, and Doukhobors were barred briefly just after the First World War; Jewish refugees were excluded during the 1930's and 1940's. Order in Council P.C. 1204, 6 June 1919; Irving Abella and Harold Troper, *None Is Too Many: Canada and the Jews of Europe, 1933–1948* (Toronto: University of Toronto Press, 1982).
7. Mildred A. Schwartz, "Citizenship in Canada and the United States," *Transactions of the Royal Society of Canada,* series 4, 14 (1976): 86.
8. John Porter, in *Canadian Social Structure: A Statistical Profile* (Toronto: McClelland and Stewart, 1967), Table D3, suggests that no more than 2 per cent of the population were non-white, aboriginal peoples excepted.
9. In 1946, twenty years' continuous residence was accepted in lieu of the language requirement. 10 Geo VI, c. 15, s. 10.
10. Norman Ward notes that it was not until 1881 that Manitoba completely abolished dual representation, though it persisted via the Senate rather longer, and in Quebec legislative counsellors could always be senators. *The Canadian House of Commons: Representation* (Toronto: University of Toronto Press, 1950), p. 65.
11. Ibid. p. 213.
12. Alan C. Cairns, "The Governments and Societies of Canadian Federalism," *Canadian Journal of Political Science* 10, no. 4(1977).
13. Garner, *The Franchise and Politics, passim.*
14. Ward, *Canadian House of Commons,* p. 218.
15. Gordon Stewart, "John A. Macdonald's Greatest Triumph," *Canadian Historical Review* 63, no. 1 (1982): 3.
16. Conrad Black, *Duplessis* (Toronto: McClelland and Stewart, 1977), pp. 224–25.
17. It was not always thus in Quebec. Garner, *The Franchise and Politics,* pp. 156–57, reports women voting in the first three decades of the nineteenth century. They were not disenfranchised until 1834, though the Colonial Office disallowed that act. The legal disenfranchisement of women did not occur until 1849.
18. Quoted in Ward, *Canadian House of Commons,* p. 228.
19. Ibid., p. 204.
20. C. F. Lee, "The Road to Enfranchisement: Chinese and Japanese in British Columbia," *BC Studies* 30 (Summer 1976): 44–76.
21. Ward, *Canadian House of Commons*, p. 236.
22. Since then two changes have been made in the qualifications required for political citizenship: the voting age has been lowered to eighteen, and the special political status of non-citizen British subjects has been withdrawn.
23. The courts have already used the charter to extend the right to vote. In British Columbia, a probationer has had a provincial disqualification declared *ultra vires.*
24. A. I. Silver, *The French-Canadian Idea of Confederation, 1864–1900* (Toronto: University of Toronto Press, 1982), p. 119.
25. Ibid., p. 170.
26. W. Peter Ward, *The Japanese in Canada* (Ottawa: Canadian Historical Association, 1982).
27. Their success in having "existing aboriginal treaty rights" entrenched in the constitution marks a major step forward in this effort.
28. For a moving testimony of the views of ordinary Canadians, see the selection of letters written to Mr. Pearson reprinted in John Matheson, *Canada's Flag: A Search for a Country* (Boston: G. K. Hall, 1980), ch. 9.
29. The courts will, of course, operate in a piecemeal fashion deciding the cases brought before them. The point is that different actors and different procedures will now have a considerable nationalizing impact on the system.

5

National Political Parties and the Growth of the National Political Community

DAVID E. SMITH

Political parties in democratic states seem always to be unpopular. In Canada the indictment against them is long and has included, among other charges, fidelity to the "interests," betrayal of the powerless, and abdication of intellectual purpose. Another old complaint recently refurbished is their failure to integrate the country's diverse parts. There are no national parties any more, it is said, and cited as proof is the dismal record of the Liberals in the West since 1958 and the Progressive Conservatives in Quebec for much longer. A more charitable view of their performance suggests the fault lies not solely with the parties but also with the tradition of counting votes so that victory goes to the candidate first past the post. Parties, it is claimed, cannot be expected to act as guardians of national integration without some reform to the plurality electoral system.

It is this last criticism—of parties as nation-building or nation-maintaining institutions—that provides the text for this paper, for it is the one that most obviously touches on the theme of the Canadian political community. The interests the parties represent, those they ignore, and the extent to which both have changed during Canada's history are subsidiary though not unrelated concerns of the main topic.

Critics and reformers agree that political parties are of fundamental importance as institutional linkages, and that the diversities of Canada's federal society are today imperfectly reflected in Parliament through the medium of the major parties. The same premise explains the proliferation of schemes to reform the Senate of Canada: both the upper chamber and the electoral system for the lower house operate so as to exclude representation of territorially-based interests from the national forum. Criticism of the Senate extends back to Confederation; criticism of the electoral system does not, but taken together, the old and the new complaints signal another outbreak of political morbidity in Canada.

Neither patriation of the constitution nor entrenchment of a charter of rights has checked the institutional introspection to which Canadians seem disposed. Continued demand for constitutional change has become a salient feature of Canada's politics and one which may reveal more about the health of our government than any projected or realized reform.[1] An evaluation of the impact of recent constitutional changes on the operation of existing institutions must of course await the passage of time, although it is striking how little speculation is to be found in the political science literature. The possibility, for instance, of a new, "popular" constitution based on rights guaranteed in the Charter and open to citizens through access to the courts has yet to be explored either for what it will mean for traditional representative institutions or for its effect on political parties.

Absence of discussion is all the more remarkable since these are topics of wide interest in American political debate and the controversies of that country are never far removed from Canadian attention. On the contrary, Canadian opinion about the efficacy of its neighbour's governmental structures is cyclical, and in recent years it has been mostly favourable. Generous praise for the United States Supreme Court and its expansion and defence of civil liberties is now matched by admiration for the representative capacity of the republic's legislative and executive institutions. The two houses of Congress and the chief executive, each with its own distinctive electoral base—district, state, and nation—and the accommodative character of the political parties who operate these institutions contrast sharply (and invidiously in the minds of critics) with Canada's inadequate mechanisms for territorial representation.

Whether such commendation is justified is not of concern here, although it should be noted that Americans who must work with and live under these institutions are less enamoured of their virtues and more envious of other systems, particularly that at Westminster.[2] What Canadians need always to remember is that politics is not only about rights, or representation, or about both of these. Its object is this and much more; for instance, it is about the policies the system produces, about the character and quality of debate that accompanies the creation of policy, and about the calibre and choice of political leaders it offers. These are considerations that must weigh in any judgment of the performance of a political system. And these too are considerations that must enter into an evaluation of the contribution of political parties. The roles that parties play are several, diverse, and mutable. There is no single measure by which to gauge performance and where one criterion, say representation, is used, then the conclusion, be it favourable or unfavourable, is suspect.

One cannot spend time studying American politics without soon coming to wonder at the foresight of the American founding fathers who devised so sensitive and balanced a system of representation, while equally being puzzled at the ineptitude of the Fathers of Confederation in designing representative institutions to promote the federal principle. So striking a contrast forces the conclusion that the Canadian founders did not grant representation the same primacy as their American counterparts, and a century later, in a world where political debate ranges over questions of how to realize one-man-one-vote-one-value and how to guarantee minority representation, their handiwork seems singularly flawed. Such criticism is irrelevant, however, since it applies the "retroactive Stakhanovite" test, which is the "setting of unobtainable or unrealistic norms for people of the past."[3] It is as well inapt, for as partisans themselves, the Fathers of Confederation were alive to matters of representation. Nonetheless, what they sought first from federation were practical results: relief from debt, new railways, and enlarged financial and credit capacity. The legitimacy of the new federal state rested on these and other purposes of government successfully achieved.

If the American experiment can be called "representational federalism," then its Canadian equivalent could be labelled "purposive federalism."[4] At the outset at least, the measure of Canadian federalism lay in the needs that required satisfying and in the capacity of institutions to do the job. And it was the same standard that became the measure of political parties.

In 1867 Cartier's new political nationality remained inchoate, waiting to be formed out of the successful pursuit of an agreed set of national priorities. Samuel Beer has said of revolutionary America that its "federalism presuppose[d] its nationalism."[5] That sequence was reversed in Canada, and thus the burden of creating a nation fell directly on institutional performance. It was a heavy responsibility to place on human arrangements and may well be the origin of the Canadian penchant for proposing structural reform. The burden was manageable, however, for the very reason it existed: the imperial framework in which Canadian development took place. The imperial tie made unification of the three British North American colonies possible in 1867 just as it made the Northwest attainable. Thus, the reasons customarily given for the new start constituted necessary but not satisfying conditions for the achievement of a new political community. The fragment societies, as depicted in the literature of new world development, were still fragmented societies when viewed from British North America; the pulse they shared in common originated at the heart of Empire. But though the source of life was distant, it was certain, and it allowed a political pace and attitude very different from that found in the United States.

Particularly when compared to Americans, Canadians are used to thinking of their development as less coherent, less dynamic. Impenetrable geography, scattered population, and divided culture condition our view of ourselves and award the prize for incentive and determination to the United States. There growth was welcomed; here it threatened: or, in Robin W. Winks' epigram, in the first, "More meant Safer"; in the second, "More meant Weaker."[6] But the balance has not always tilted in favour of the American experiment. Following the revolution, established authority could not be taken for granted; there was an urgency in the need to build and grow. Removed from the protective umbrella of the British Empire and exposed to threats from Indians and foreign powers, the United States could not be confident of its future. Leonard D. White's masterful history of the Federalist period makes clear how the uncertainties of the age drove Americans, struggling with a new constitution, to assert authority over the hinterland, organize federal-state relations, and mould their central institutions. As an example of the last, he cites how "the crisis in foreign affairs which developed in 1783 brought about conferences with such frequency that by the end of the year the Cabinet as an institution for consultation and advice was firmly established."[7]

With the exception of the American threat itself, the Maritime and Canadian colonies lay safe in the fastness of the north, where development suffered from no comparable pressure. The colonies matured slowly: the evolution that preceded the achievement of responsible government at the centre and to the east early in the nineteenth century was paralleled after Confederation by more decades of federal tutelage over the prairie provinces. By contrast, the speed and scope of American expansion were breathtaking, especially when viewed against the obstacles of environment and primitive technology.

In Canada, the pace was measured because there was less need to hurry. The leaders of the new Confederation were the old colonial leaders. The political forum and the political rules remained unchanged from pre-Confederation days; the difference was the size of the stage on which politics was to be played. Moreover, the symbolic content of Confederation produced no conflict, for the symbols were imperial. Familiarity helps explain the easy transition from colony to dominion, and it also explains the low temperature of national rhetoric. As well, the transition was aided by an absence of alternatives. The imperial government, who wanted Confederation, promoted it through the Crown's representatives and discouraged those who resisted: "the [Maritime] Antis were branded, though most unjustly, with disloyalty."[8]

Precedent not experiment more often informed political action in

Canada. After 1867 three levels of sovereign power guided Canadian development, although in the Macdonald scheme, with faith in dual representation, disallowance, and central appointments, the federal and provincial sovereignties meshed in a quite unfederal way. The new federal elite carried on the negotiating process begun at Charlottetown, both to consolidate its gains and to enlarge them. Charles Tupper's view that the "character and success of the Dominion demands the *immediate* removal of the Nova Scotia difficulty . . . at any personal, party or pecuniary sacrifice" anticipated Macdonald's conviction that Joseph Howe must be induced to enter the cabinet: "Being a representative man, our Parliament would accept the fact of his coming into the Administration as sufficient evidence of the pacification of the province."[9] In the same spirit of acquisition, the centre reached out to embrace the North-West, British Columbia, and Prince Edward Island. From the perspective of critics like Edward Blake and Sir Richard Cartwright, the bargains struck were "insane," coercive, and, always, materialistic.[10] But Macdonald realized what his critics seemed ever ready to ignore: "the prospect of getting something new" was the one sure basis for expansion, and thus the bargains were essential if Canada was to fasten together the territories that would make it a transcontinental state.[11]

The sense of Canadian community had to be created, and in the first instance responsibility lay with the federal government. Students of American history have cited as evidence of an emerging common consciousness in pre-revolutionary America the exchange of information through the newspapers of the thirteen colonies.[12] But excluding Quebec, imperialism's theistic view made certain that the British Isles would remain the source of Canadian consciousness, to be challenged only gradually by the achievements, and the failures too, of the federal government and the political parties that composed it. For the Conservatives building the C.P.R. and for the Liberals settling the West fall in the first category, while for both parties the First World War, because of its human toll and national disruption, falls in the second. An event that was both failure and achievement was the 1885 Rebellion. Sir John Willison wrote that "there are few more ugly incidents in Canadian history than the erection of the Regina scaffold into a political platform," and the subsequent division of the country's electorate proved a heavy price to pay—not only by the Conservative party.[13] But there were countervailing forces of unity as well: "When the North-West Rebellion broke out," George F. G. Stanley has said, "maritimers were compelled to look at their country, Canada, for the first time in national rather than in regional terms." This was true less because of passions for or against the Métis in Maritime hearts and more the result of "political parties . . . being organized on a national as well as provincial basis, and maritimers . . . were forced to view the rebellion from a national perspective.''[14]

At the outset, then, Confederation invoked few new principles, but it promised benefits. First among these was economic development. Absence of large-scale private enterprise, unless heavily subsidized by government, and a geography that discouraged foreseeable returns on development capital induced federal authorities to play an active role from the start. Through control of such levers as credit, immigration, and settlement, Ottawa could direct the economy along the route it wished to see developed, and that route lay westward. There is endless literature on the effects of federal policies—land, tariff, freight rates, and retention of natural resources—on the West's view of itself and its place in Confederation, all of it however a footnote to Vernon Fowke's tart comment that the policies were ''national only in the sense that they were decisions of the national government.''[15] But in the West at least, the growth that was believed thwarted was a function of realized expansion. In the Maritimes, it was a different story. There the costs of building a national community appeared unrelieved by any advantage. It was, as the Antis had predicted, a tale of ''taxation without remuneration.''[16] Political rancour fed economic grievance. The creation of two large prairie provinces in 1905 and the generous extension of boundaries to Ontario, Quebec, and Manitoba in 1912 heralded no compensation for the three Maritime provinces. Indeed, not only would greater wealth now accrue to the exchequers of the enlarged provinces, but also their members could speak with a stronger voice in Parliament because of the increased numbers. To be deprived of ''*adequate* representation'' in return for contributing not only capital to build the nation but also ''sons and daughters'' to help bind east and west through ''bonds of sympathy'' was gall indeed.[17]

Notwithstanding the mixed motives and conflict of interests, each step in the rounding out of Confederation helped mobilize a national electorate. In the new provinces created after 1867, indigenous rivalries ebbed as political energy was diverted into Liberal and Conservative organizational channels. Realignment might take a decade, or two, but provoked by federal policy or in emulation of provincial reaction elsewhere, voters in the new provinces were incorporated for federal electoral purposes.[18] The mechanics for defining that national body of electors was an important stimulus as well to political consciousness.

The Liberals never tired of accusing Macdonald of violating the ''rep by pop'' principle when he was negotiating the entry of new provinces into Confederation, for after 1867, each province that entered received more MPs than it was entitled to under the representation formula found in section 51 of the British North America Act. And they attributed this "fraud" (Cartwright's word) to Macdonald's desire to balance western Tory victories against Ontario Tory losses. While there was a good deal of cant in the Grit protestations, there was also, as George Eliot would say, a "mustard-seed" of principle, one which was to divide, take root, and become a hardy perennial of controversy during the episodic debate over the franchise from 1880 until 1920. The event was small—were local or federally appointed officials to compile the federal voters' list?—but the issue was great: no less, in W. L. Morton's words, than "the nature of the Canadian union."[19] Liberal speakers in the 1885 debate swept by the details of how to compile the list and struck at the principle that underlay the Conservative proposal for federal registrars. The Tories, Laurier charged, were mistakenly treating "this country as a single community"; when, for the Liberals, political reality was quite different: "Only in the provincial legislatures are individuals represented as such. In the federal parliament it is the provinces which are represented by provincial delegations."[20] The arguments were repeated in 1898, though with different partisan emphasis now that the Liberals were in power, and again in 1917 with the restoration of a federal franchise. In the last instance, the debate focused on the inequities of the War-time Elections Act, although W. F. A. Turgeon, attorney-general of Saskatchewan, complained bitterly about a manipulated franchise which guaranteed that the members of Parliament from a province "would not represent sentiment and ideas in that Province."[21]

In none of these debates, save the last perhaps, and then in a very specific way, was the issue in dispute the extension of the franchise. None of the reforms gave the vote to larger numbers of the previously unenfranchised, and thus what happened in Canada was very unlike what happened in Great Britain, where the franchise bills of the nineteenth century, by mobilizing different classes of male voters, introduced a new kind of democracy. The issue fought in Canada was whether there was a single national community represented in the House of Commons. To that question the Liberals of the day answered "no" and the Conservatives "yes." The debate over the franchise was important for Canadian history and for the growth of a national political community because it provided a rare opportunity for politicians to express their sense of the Canadian nation. A country needs such debates, and Canada has witnessed fewer than it deserves. Disengagement from empire and the maintenance of a binational state have diverted attention, often desirably, from these potentially disruptive subjects. The constitutional debate of 1980–82 was a singular modern parallel to the old franchise question, especially where it touched on the federal government's proposal to introduce a referendum into the amending process.

That a Liberal government a century after the first franchise debate should propose a national referendum and that modern-day Conservatives should oppose it reveals the long journey the old parties have made since setting off at Confederation. The Canadian equivalent of the British experience of progressively incorporating new classes of voters came with the arrival of the flood of immigrants after 1896. The vast majority of these people went to the prairie provinces, and there the old parties made their plea for new supporters. The pleas were directed not to class but to religious and ethnic values—the Liberals spoke of toleration of diversity, the Conservatives of king and country. The Liberals, whose active solicitation the immigrants had answered, were the champions by far in securing new allegiances, and, as a result, the Prairies provided them with the votes necessary to ensure a majority, with only occasional respites, until the Diefenbaker landslide. Indeed, in the last quarter-century, the Liberals success at winning the newly enfranchised ethnic vote, now located in Ontario and Quebec, was a major reason for their rejuvenation in the 1960's.

The immigrants liberalized as well as nationalized the Liberal Party. On the prairies, the old separate school question with French Catholic and English Protestant combatants was transformed into a "national" issue by the presence of large numbers of recently arrived Europeans, many of whom were Catholic, but all of whom had to be "Canadianized." What that process implied was far from clear, but it did suggest a vital role for the schools. It was not fated that the Liberals should be the immigrants' champion, nor were they especially fitted by experience to play that role. But as the governing party, who in pursuit of economic development had sought immigrants abroad, the job was theirs. And it was not surprising that they should use the opportunity to weld these massive numbers of voters and potential voters to their cause.

The task was speeded and its outcome made more certain by the mechanisms then available. No public policy exhortations to promote bilingualism or multiculturalism were necessary since the means lay in freely dispensed patronage by which the party governed the public service and used it for its own ends. The interpenetration of party and bureaucracy assured a berth for party organization at public expense and opened the door of public recognition to the "non-English," which a merit policy of recruitment would have kept shut. Here, and through myriad other contacts with the immigrants, the Liberals moulded the social structure of the West in a unique way: unique in Canada because it did not happen in other sections of the country where the social structure had set before the formation of parties and unique in North America because in the United States government did not play a direct role in fostering immigration. Not in power when the first great waves of immigrants arrived, the Conservative Party never rivalled the Liberals even after the election of 1911, while their actions during and after the First World War on the franchise and naturalization permanently disabled them in appeals for immigrant voter support.

The party-bureaucratic symbiosis provided a particularly effective institutionalized link between governor and governed, especially since as a federal state Canada possessed multiple bureaucracies so that when electoral storms at Ottawa proved damaging, there was always, somewhere, a provincial refuge. In the years before the Great War, a mobilizable party organization, entrenched in the bureaucracy at both levels of government, made integrative electoral strategies possible. And with the prairie immigrant and Quebec voters united in the Liberal party, Tory Ontario faced a formidable challenge.

The fiftieth anniversary of Confederation marked the apotheosis of party life. Union government in 1917 signalled the collapse of the old political order and not, as some hoped, the start of a new one. The first and most obvious casualty of coalition was the Liberal Party. But its split was not fatal; instead, subsequent elections revealed that the Conservative Party was the real victim. That story as well as the appearance of the Progressives, their influence on the electoral fortunes of the old parties, and the social and economic changes which the war accelerated and which in time transformed Canada into an urbanized and industrialized polity have all been discussed many times. What needs to be noted is how events in postwar Canada modified the conditions that had influenced the growth of the political community since Confederation.

The conditions may be summarized as follows. During the first half of Confederation, development occurred as a result of what has been called purposive federalism, carried out under imperial aegis by an active federal government. Federal political parties grew in tandem with the expansion of the Dominion, the Conservatives promoting Canada as a multiple of its parts, the Liberals viewing it as the sum only. In sequence, the Conservatives and then the Liberals, each lodged within the bureaucracy, asserted their dominance over the political system of the day, but with the arrival of large numbers of immigrants, the Liberals obtained an almost permanent competitive edge through their political mobilization of the "non-English" voter in the prairie provinces.

The prosecution of the First World War has been interpreted as a rite of passage to national maturity. By any measure its effects were great, and none more so than on Canadian-imperial relations. In the name of Empire thousands in the West had been disenfranchised, while in the name of Empire thousands in Quebec had been provoked to resist, even riot against, military conscription for overseas service. The war, in short, had been divisive. The symbolic content of Confederation which had eased the transition from colony to dominion fifty years before was less unanimously accepted after the war. Laurier had been sensitive to words and symbols and their implication for status even at the time of the Queen's Jubilees, but his successor as party leader, W. L. Mackenzie King, was to make a career out of gauging such intangibles. As Blair Neatby has said, in King's mind "foreign policy was an aspect of domestic policy."[22]

The theistic perspective of empire had ended; the pluralism of the imperial war cabinet and the imperial delegation at the Treaty of Versailles but, most of all, the cautious suspicions of one man, Mackenzie King, saw to that. The unwinding of the imperial relationship has continued right down to agreement in 1981 on an amending formula, and at each step the Liberal Party has identified itself with the growth of Canadian autonomy. Whether this was a wise course to follow, whether it threw Canada even more certainly than before into American arms are important but irrelevant questions here. What is germane is that Canada has gained a set of national symbols (constitution, flag, anthem, external personality) through the efforts of a political party and, more particularly, through the efforts of a handful of that party's leaders. And the Conservatives—Meighen, Drew, Diefenbaker—resisted. The importance of international relations in defining an identity, as well as boundaries, for a people is not lost in modern third world countries nor on separatist movements in first world countries. But Canadians, and especially their Liberal Party leaders in this century, have been peculiarly alive to this fact.

The eclipse of empire coincided with the passing of the federalist period of economic expansion. The twenties opened with the consolidation and nationalization of all major railroads except for the C.P.R. and with the government refusing to take responsibility for marketing wheat, the country's major export commodity. The dynamic of development was already shifting into the hands of the provinces as they contemplated the exploitation of their natural resources. At the same time, demands for social welfare expenditure, though still muted, revealed pressure for development in a similar direction. The purposes of the Dominion were becoming purposes to be met in right of the provinces as the phenomenon of province-building emerged. Economic depression and prairie drought in the 1930's reversed this trend, and war and reconstruction in the next decade prolonged the reversal. But by the 1950's, fiscal complexity and accelerated provincial activity testified to the different relationship then existing between the two levels of government than in the first half of Confederation.

As the party normally in power from the mid-point of the Depression onward, the Liberals could be expected to preach fiscal restraint. But for at least half of this period, their orthodoxy in fiscal matters and their preference for private economic activity profoundly affected the national economic community: there was no economic nationalism to parallel the Liberals' political nationalism. The old political parties are said to be non-ideological, and this may be true, for scant debate over doctrine is heard within or between them. But party leaders have views, some of which can only be ascribed to ideology, and given the leaders' pre-eminence in the Liberal and Conservative parties, these views can be as determining as those of any party doctrine. On the matter of the economy and the right road for governments to follow, the contrast between King and R. B. Bennett, for example, is striking, mostly for the greater willingness of the Conservative leader to countenance government intervention.

In Canada, where all governments have traditionally assumed a prominent economic role, the difference between the old parties may be more one of degree than of kind, but the difference is significant and not only for what governments themselves do. The economy has, as Beer has said, a private as well as a public face. Government's actions condition the actions of business, labour, farm, and a host of functional associations. The incidence of their activity will shift between public and private spheres as government expands or contracts its activity. Similarly, the non-public economic realm will adjust as the locus of economic activity shifts between levels of government. Those adjustments will have a consequence for the integration of the national community as interests and concerns twist from a horizontal national plane to a vertical provincial one—redirecting pressure, stimulating new elites, improving or undermining government's capacity to satisfy wants. Province-building, then, is not an economic phenomenon alone. For the political parties, it has been a significant cause of their decentralization. Economic objectives cut across partisan loyalties, pitching provincial governments and parties of whatever stripe against the federal government which almost always wears the same stripe. In federal-provincial conflict, partisanship has proved an inadequate countervailing power.

Political parties have been indirect casualties of this alteration in federal-provincial relations: their traditional organization, based in the provinces but co-ordinated during national elections to serve federal objectives, was disrupted by the long-term expansion of provincial power and activity. But they were also the victims of direct reform. Until the second decade of this century, the interpenetration of party and bureaucracy and the use of patronage ensured a secure and loyal constituency of party workers, and voters too. The Borden government introduced major civil service reforms which have been strengthened several times since, all aimed to separate that which had been so entwined. Competitive examination and the merit principle permanently expelled partisanship from the public service, as outrage at rare examples of its unregenerate survival still testifies. As a method of democratizing as well as professionalizing government, the reforms have much to recommend them. Their effect on parties, however, cannot be ignored, for they deprived them of both the security and purpose that accompanied their emergence and growth. And, coupled with the transformation in federal-provincial relations, they set the old party system adrift from its traditional moorings constructed during Confederation's first half-century.

That parties should now be excluded from areas where their performance was once central—federal-provincial relations and public policy—indicates the magnitude of political change that has occurred in Canada. It also explains the reason for the discontent, even disillusion, that surrounds their operation. They seem to be reduced to legions whose sole purpose is to sustain their leaders: the loyalty question bedevils both old parties—the Liberals, where it invariably obtains, appear impervious to dissent, and the Progressive Conservatives, where it habitually falters, appear immune to agreement. Complaints about party discipline are hardly new; what provides fresh piquancy are signs of federal strain on all sides. Not only does the party system apparently fail as a channel of incorporation, but also nothing appears to have replaced it. Federal and provincial governments, including their public servants and regulatory agencies, seem to be permanently in dispute. It is this absence of ameliorating bodies that explains the unusually strong appeal of institutional reform today.

Elections to the House of Commons, it is said, fail to translate voter preferences into legislative power; the plurality system of counting votes blunts expression of popular discontent and excludes bodies of opinion. Again, the phenomenon is not new, but the distortion, revealed at repeated general elections in the form of a fragmented national electorate, has become so longstanding a criticism of the political system as to sharpen the contrast between parliamentary ideal and reality. The composition of the Senate, where provinces are unequally represented but where party organization finds refuge in the large contingents from Ontario and Quebec, is a permanent reminder that accommodation of Canadian diversity must occur elsewhere than in the upper chamber.

The Charter of Rights is one possibility. Classes of interests which once looked to Parliament and to parties as their advocates will now be expected to find expression outside these traditional channels. Although political parties may be deprived of one more activity, the nation-maintaining effect of the Charter should be welcomed. The standardization of rights provides an important and symbolic claim on government which all Canadians share. But the Charter's influence is not solely of a nationalizing nature, if the opinion of one justice of the Supreme Court of Canada is to be believed: "Senior provincial courts will become de facto courts of the last resort for all cases except those involving the Charter of Rights and federal-provincial contests."[23] What this will mean in terms of province-building remains unclear, although it is obvious that the Charter is not an outright restraint on this feature of Canadian political evolution.

The future of the party system is no more certain. Political parties which helped unify the country through their federal-provincial structure have disappeared. Their modern organizational impact is found in provisions devised to promote intraparty democracy in the formulation of policy and the selection of leaders. But taken together, their impact—on party members and, more importantly, on political adherents who though not formal members witness the debates through the mass media—is reshaping the national political community. To adopt R. MacGregor Burns's useful term, a national "followership" for each leadership candidate is formed,[24] and in each instance ideology, doctrine, or policy, but not territory, is stressed in the quest for delegates who, when assembled, stand as virtual representatives of nationwide bodies of opinion.

The disintegrative effect of leadership conventions on traditional party structures is evident with each recourse to that selection. Their integrative effect on the political system has yet to be studied, though clearly it should not be ignored. Like other institutions and processes, the effect of political parties remains recursive: shaped and moulded by Macdonald and Laurier to achieve Confederation and hold it secure, political parties now provide the stage and even the choice of script by which new leaders bid for national prominence. As instruments to achieve governmental power, they rank still as primary influences on the national political community.

NOTES

1. On the significance of continuity in political claims, see Murray Edelman, *The Symbolic Uses of Politics* (Urbana: University of Illinois Press, 1964), p. 166.
2. See Nelson W. Polsby, *The Consequences of Party Reform* (New York: Oxford

University Press, 1983); and review by Seymour Martin Lipset, *New Republic,* 28 March 1983, pp. 29–30.

3. Naomi Bliven, *New Yorker,* 17 May 1982, p. 137.
4. The term is found in Samuel H. Beer, "Federalism, Nationalism and Democracy in America," *American Political Science Review* 72 (March 1978): 15.
5. Ibid., p. 12.
6. *The Relevance of Canadian History: U.S. and Imperial Perspectives,* the 1977 Joanne Goodman Lectures, The University of Western Ontario (Toronto: Macmillan, 1979), p. 14.
7. Leonard D. White, *The Federalists: A Study in Administrative History* (New York: Macmillan, 1956), p. 40.
8. William M. Baker, *Timothy Warren Anglin, 1822–96, Irish Catholic Canadian* (Toronto: University of Toronto Press, 1977), p. 105.
9. Tupper to Macdonald, 2 May 1868, and Macdonald to Tupper, 28 January 1869, in E. M. Saunders, ed., *The Life and Letters of the Rt. Hon. Sir Charles Tupper, Bart., KCMG.* (Toronto: Cassels and Co., 1916), 1:166, 191.
10. Sir Richard Cartwright, *Reminiscences* (Toronto: William Briggs, 1912), p. 179; Joseph Schull, *Edward Blake: The Man of the Other Way, 1833–1881* (Toronto: Macmillan, 1975), pp. 164–65.
11. On the relationship between benefits and territorial change, see Karl Deutsch, "The Price of Integration," in Phillip E. Jacob and James V. Toscano, eds., *The Integration of Political Communities* (Philadelphia: Lippincott, 1964), p. 173; see also, Preston King, *Federalism and Federation* (Baltimore: Johns Hopkins University Press, 1982), p. 35.
12. Richard L. Merritt, *Symbols of American Community, 1735–1775* (New Haven: Yale University Press, 1966).
13. Sir John Willison, *Reminiscences: Political and Personal* (Toronto: McClelland and Stewart, 1919), p. 146.
14. George G. F. Stanley, "New Brunswick and Nova Scotia and the North-West Rebellion, 1885," in John E. Foster, ed., *The Developing West: Essays on Canadian History in Honor of Lewis H. Thomas* (Edmonton: University of Alberta Press, 1983), pp. 93–94, 95.
15. Review of W. A. Macintosh, *The Economic Background of Dominion-Provincial Relations: A Study Prepared for the Royal Commission on Dominion-Provincial Relations,* Appendix 3, (Ottawa: King's Printer, 1939), in *Canadian Journal of Economics and Political Science* 7 (1941); 75 ff.
16. Edgar McInnis, "Two North-American Federations: A Comparison," in R. Flenley, ed., *Essays in Canadian History* (Toronto: Macmillan, 1939), pp. 114 ff.
17. "Memorandum on Representation of the Maritime Provinces," Canadian Sessional Papers, 1914, No. 118a; pp. 1–3 in R. MacGregor Dawson, ed., *Constitutional Issues in Canada, 1900–1931* (London: Oxford University Press, 1933), pp. 173–75.
18. R. O. MacFarlane, "Manitoba Politics and Parties after Confederation," Canadian Historical Association, *Report* (1940): 45 and 55.
19. W. L. Morton, "The Extension of the Franchise in Canada: A Study in Democratic Nationalism," Canadian Historical Association, *Report* (1943): 77.
20. Ibid., p. 78. See also Edward Blake, *House of Commons Debates* (1885), pp. 1180–92.
21. Turgeon to Laurier, 12 September 1917, Turgeon Papers, Box 30, pp. 179–80, Saskatchewan Archives Board.
22. H. Blair Neatby, *William Lyon Mackenzie King, 1932–1939: The Prism of Unity* (Toronto: University of Toronto Press, 1976), p. 172.
23. *Star-Phoenix* (Saskatoon), 19 April 1983, A7.
24. R. MacGregor Burns, *The Vineyard of Liberty* (New York: Knopf, 1982).

6

Leadership Conventions and the Development of the National Political Community in Canada

JOHN C. COURTNEY

To fashion a more "representative" and "democratic" leadership selection process, Canadian parties early in the twentieth century abandoned the parliamentary caucus in favour of the leadership convention as the body responsible for choosing party leaders. Has the change made the development of a strong national political community in Canada any less problematic? The question cannot be answered easily, or with any measure of certainty. The widespread support for leadership conventions has been derived from, among other things, the commonly held view that they have played a positive role in nation-building.[1] Yet there may well be other previously unexplored dimensions to leadership conventions which, taken together, yield a less favourable verdict on this uniquely Canadian institution and its contribution to the national political community.

The switch from the parliamentary caucus to a leadership convention as the means for choosing party leaders has not helped the parliamentary parties to become more truly "national" bodies. The first national leadership conventions were seen as ways of compensating for the respective parties' lamentable regional weaknesses in parliament, and since then conventions have been justified principally on representational grounds. That the Liberal parliamentary membership in 1919 was drawn overwhelmingly from the province of Quebec and that the Conservative caucus in 1927 was composed almost entirely of MPs from Ontario, British Columbia, and Nova Scotia distressed the politicians of the day. Understandably, they were attracted to an institution which overcame their representational concerns by ensuring an equal number of participants from every constituency in the country.

But as the 1979 and 1980 elections reminded Canadians, problems have persisted with respect to the distribution of regional support within the parliamentary parties. Could one of the myriad reasons for this be that by having opted for leadership conventions, Canadian parties unwittingly reduced the importance of regional representation? The incentives for a parliamentary party to represent the interests of regions with few MPs in its caucus were strong when the parliamentary party was the only legitimate ''national'' institution acting on a party's behalf.[2] But parliamentarians now have less cause to seek to redress weaknesses resulting from the regional imbalances of their caucuses when they know that from time to time the public's attention will be riveted on a larger party forum structured so as to guarantee representation for all regions. The implications could be profound for caucus deliberations and policy decisions, as well as for leaders bent on accommodative moves with respect to areas of regional party weakness.

As befits a country preoccupied with regionalism, the representational imbalances that conventions were originally designed to correct were of a regional nature. It was thought that the representational strength of a leadership convention would derive from its capacity to bring party supporters together in a way no longer available to the parliamentary parties.[3] The move to improve regional participation in leadership selection meant a sharp reduction in the relative numerical importance of the parliamentary party, although less so in the early years than later. The first conventions accorded more than twice the weight to the parliamentary party than the recent ones, as a comparison of the proportionate strength of the parliamentary caucuses of 1919 and 1984 in the conventions of those years bears out. The 85 Liberal MPs in 1919 accounted for 7.5 per cent of the first national leadership convention, whereas the 145 Liberal MPs constituted less than 4 per cent of the total number of delegates eligible to attend the 1984 convention. The increase in the number of delegates per constituency (from three in 1919 to a current seven for the Liberals, and from four in 1927 to a current six for the Conservatives), coupled with the absolute growth in the number of constituencies, explains part of the change. But an equally important cause is to be found in the vastly expanded list of delegate categories.

Fortuitous or not, the early categories of delegates were designed to reinforce the pre-eminent position of the parliamentarians and their provincial counterparts. With the exception of those named by their constituencies, all other delegates were, *ex officio,* members of the federal and provincial legislative wings of the parties: senators, federal and provincial members, defeated candidates, and provincial leaders. Of those, the MPs in particular wielded considerable influence when it came to deciding who would attend from their constituency and how they would vote. Chubby Power's account of this relationship between MPs and delegates in earlier Liberal conventions describes a deferential political structure that was to pass from the scene by the mid-1960s: "Very often the constituency delegates are the choice of the federal member of Parliament and reflect his views and vote as he directs. . . . This in a sense indirectly perpetuates the old custom of selecting the party leader by members of the parliamentary caucus."[4]

The primacy of the parliamentarian was gradually eroded as new categories of convention delegates were added: national and provincial executives, university clubs, women's associations and youth clubs, until now no fewer than eighteen categories of delegates, for example, attended the 1983 PC convention. (See Appendix A.) In admittedly varying degrees, each of these groups has its own responsibilities, membership, interests, and authority structure, which means that the views of its members will not always match those of the parliamentarians. In his analysis of a party's reciprocal deference structure, Samuel Eldersveld has shown that as a party's membership and its subcoalitional system becomes more heterogeneous, centralized control over the membership becomes "not only difficult but unwise."[5] Modern national leadership conventions in Canada fit Eldersveld's description. The growth in the variety of groups (the heterogeneous subcoalitions) entitled to delegate status at national conventions has had the effect of dispersing power within the parties, of making the membership less deferential to its parliamentary party, and of lessening the control of the parliamentary wing over the direction of the party's affairs. The 1966–67 struggle within the Conservative party over John Diefenbaker's leadership served as the first (and to date, the classic) instance of these altered intraparty relationships.

As the new sections of the parties have grown in number and have taken on a life of their own, their standing in the political subsystem has become increasingly legitimate and powerful. Nowhere is this truer than of the youth and campus sections of the parties. Not only do they now select approximately one-third of all convention delegates in their own right (see Appendices B and C), but by their parties' constitutions their members also participate in the selection of delegates in other categories. In the Conservative party, for example, an eighteen to twenty-nine year-old female university student is entitled to vote in party elections for four different categories of delegates (constituency youth, constituency senior, university, and women's association), whereas a male, thirty years of age or older, is entitled to vote for one category of delegate only (constituency senior). For its part, the Liberal constitution guarantees constituency representation to women and youth, but to no other groups. One practical expression of those guarantees occurred at the time of the intended 1980

Liberal leadership convention (cancelled after the defeat of the Clark government and the calling of the 1980 election), when one of the handful of constituency parties to elect its seven delegates and seven alternates chosen only four males over the age of twenty-five in its total delegation of fourteen.[6]

For its part, the NDP treats representation at national conventions differently from the Liberals and Conservatives. This may well stem from the view of the labour/farmer movements at the time they created the CCF in the 1930s: loyalty and service counted heavily in measuring one's commitment to the socialist cause. For the NDP, membership in the party or in one of its affiliated organizations (principally trade unions) is an obvious way of establishing an individual's credentials as a socialist, particularly if that membership is a longstanding one. Accordingly, representation at national conventions is based not on an equal number of delegates from every constituency, but on the actual number of members in a constituency party or in an affiliated organization. (See Appendix D). Such a principle has important implications for the party and the political system. The formula rewards areas of organizational strength, which for the most part are also the areas of the party's electoral strength. But by the same token, it reinforces the party's organizational and electoral weaknesses. At the NDP's last national leadership convention (1975), 86 per cent of the 1,168 constituency delegates were from the four provinces in which the party has traditionally enjoyed its greatest measure of electoral and organizational strength—Ontario, Manitoba, Saskatchewan, and British Columbia. For their part, the Quebec constituency delegates (35 in all, which was less than one delegate for every two constituencies in the province) accounted for barely 2 per cent of the convention total. The Atlantic provinces fared even less well. Such evidence suggests that the NDP has forfeited at least one opportunity to establish a more "national" presence in the Canadian political community through its maintenance of what amounts to a "bonus" system of alloting delegates and its failure to require delegate selection in equal numbers from all federal constituencies.

Canadian political parties have long prided themselves on their "openness." It is no doubt a mark of a healthy liberal democracy that parties have permitted relatively unrestricted access to the publicly announced meetings called for the express purpose of choosing constituency delegates. That they should have survived the exercise suggests an even greater measure of health on their part, for as became painfully obvious from the process of selecting delegates for the 1983 Conservative convention, for example, open parties are also vulnerable parties. Openness at the local level invites mischief, which, in turn, can have the effect of bringing the party, and beyond it the larger political system, into disrepute. But while the Conservatives' experience in 1983 with "Tiny Tories," "Mission members," "Campus Clubs," and other instant supporters may have introduced new twists into the political game of packing meetings, the general practice is not new. It has enjoyed a venerable history in both of the older Canadian parties.[7] Nonetheless, it is clear that the loose rules which permit abuse at the local level during the delegate selection stage deserve to be corrected in much the same way as the various national convention committees have adopted consistently tighter regulations over the past two decades with respect to the candidates' campaigns and the convention procedures.[8] The parties could go a long way toward ending the unsavoury practices that mark some delegate selection meetings by adopting stiffer constitutional requirements regarding residency, age, and length of party membership.

As troublesome as the abuse of rules may be, of greater interest are the implications of open delegate selection in the context of modern national leadership conventions. Canadian leadership conventions can be divided conveniently into two distinct categories: those up to, and including, the Liberal convention of 1958, and those beginning with, and following, the Conservative convention of 1967.[9] Compared to the most recent five conventions, the former were markedly smaller in size, had substantially fewer candidates, and required fewer ballots to decide the winner. The eight national conventions held up to 1958 averaged 1,424 delegates, four candidates, and 1.6 ballots per convention, whereas the five held since 1967 have averaged 2,838 delegates, nine candidates and four ballots per convention.[10] Moreover, leadership selection in Canada since 1967 has been marked by demanding and expensive preconvention campaigns, keen competition for delegate support, extensive media coverage, and a growing use of direct mail solicitations, computer technology, survey research, and sophisticated electronic gadgetry.

Among other things, the shift from the old to the new variety of convention is bound to have affected the role and influence of different political actors. The member of Parliament, for example, is likely to have become a good deal less influential in the delegate selection process than was once the case, given the energy, skills, and resources of candidate organizers and the relatively easy access that this new group has to the vastly increased variety and number of delegates. The world of Chubby Power has been displaced by networks of extraparliamentary professionals: experts in media communications and surveys, advisers on policy and organization, and technicians and managers for constituency delegate selection meetings and convention floor logistics. Clearly, no serious candidate would stand a chance of winning without them.

Whether the change has helped parties to select and to inform a group of delegates who are any more representative of the party and the nation than was previously the case is debatable. By having created larger and more open conventions and delegate selection meetings, parties certainly have widened the circle of political activists involved in leadership selection, a move that has been justified on democratic grounds. If it were simply a matter of access and numbers, there would be no cause for concern, for certainly no parliamentary caucus could support a claim to being as "democratic" and "representative" as a convention of three thousand delegates chosen in hundreds of meetings across the country. But democracy and representation are about more than numbers and openness; they involve no less the concepts of political responsibility, authority, and accountability.[11]

Delegates in the older system may have been a good deal fewer in number and more deferential to the parliamentarians than is now the case, but that was not without value to the political system. Parliamentarians were (and still are) the principal group in the party with a continuing obligation to protect both the party's and the nation's interests within the larger political context of electoral accountability. In the past, it was in their interest to select delegates according to those obligations. The new organizational experts, for their part, have special skills which are important to a candidate's campaign, and their energies are understandably so directed. But their actions, together with those of the delegates for whose selection and enlightenment they are partially responsible, are performed in response to different authoritative patterns and without the ultimate obligation of electoral accountability. In assessing the change to more "open" nominating conventions and procedures in the United States, Jeane Kirkpatrick, in her exhaustive study of the 1972 Democratic and Republican nominating conventions, concluded that

> participatory politics poses a special pitfall for political parties: the danger of mistaking those who turn out to participate in party governance for "the people," for the voters to whom the party is answerable on election day. The Democratic experience of 1972 . . . illustrates the errors of concluding that "open" processes and thousands of meetings will produce a convention in which "the people" are represented. Herein lies the reason that conventions based on "open" participatory politics may turn out (as in 1972) to be less representative of party rank and file (and other voters) than conventions peopled by labor leaders, political "bosses," and public officials.[12]

There is much relevance to the Canadian situation in such a statement.

Public officials have public responsibilities in the national political community; most candidate enthusiasts do not. Moreover, such political institutions as cabinets, shadow cabinets, and parliamentary caucuses are unmatched for the opportunities they provide their members to judge a colleague's leadership potential *and* his likely contributions to the party's national well-being should he stand for the leadership. However unintentional it may have been, the effect of having increased significantly the quantity and variety of the "rank and file" at conventions has been to discount the value of the parliamentarian's experience and judgment and to enhance the role of the media and of candidate organizers as sources of information for the delegates. This has been a not entirely adequate substitution, for the work of the candidate's organization is by definition promotional, and the natural inclination of the media is to concentrate on personal qualities and images at the expense of critical assessments of policies and professional capacities.[13] Understandably, these developments have prompted concern among members themselves.[14]

The move away from the parliamentary caucus to a convention as the means of choosing party leaders has dramatically altered the recruitment patterns and career routes of party leaders. Party conventions have been instrumental in opening up the competition to outsiders—to provincial premiers, public servants, and, in some cases, others who had not previously been identified with party politics at either the federal or provincial levels. Accordingly, those with little or no experience in national politics have a proven chance of gaining their party's leadership and, in the process, of beating others whose service to their party and whose career in Parliament had been considerably longer. Some MPs who spent years apprenticing on the backbenches and in cabinet or shadow cabinet positions have paid a heavy price for having endured the rigours of parliamentary life when they finally tried to gain their party's leadership. Seemingly at the pinnacle of their careers, they have found that the relative newcomer, the fresh face of the outsider, was too much for a majority of the convention delegates to resist.

This tendency to choose outsiders as party leaders leaves the parliamentary parties in a position of some uncertainty. Caucus membership and a solid, sustained parliamentary performance cannot be seen as having great value when, for example, an MP can forsake the Commons and yet remain among the most widely touted of his party's prospective leaders years after his withdrawal from parliament. For many years, this was the case with both John Turner and Donald Macdonald. In some instances, a caucus may have to accept as its leader someone other than the one whom the majority of its members would have preferred, which could lead to a difficult and testy relationship between a newly chosen leader and his parliamentary caucus and greater intraparty discord than would otherwise be the case.[15] It is, after all, the MPs—not the delegates—who the morning after the convention have to begin working for the months and years ahead with the leader chosen. By definition, the MPs' interests in party leadership are more long-term and wide-ranging than the delegates'. They extend beyond the immediate policy and electoral concerns common to all party activists to include the larger parliamentary, managerial, and organizational skills of the leader.[16] In still other instances, a leader may invoke on his own behalf the fact that he was chosen by the party's membership in convention, arguing successfully in the face of a threatened parliamentary revolt that the body to which he is ultimately responsible, and the body which is the party's only legitimate basis of authority for leadership selection *and* removal, is the extraparliamentary party meeting in convention. Mackenzie King was known to have silenced caucus critics of his leadership by claiming that what the parliamentary group had not created it could not destroy.[17] The origins of the leadership review provisions of party constitutions could be traced to this argument. Together, these examples suggest that the value of a parliamentary career and the legitimacy and authority which previously marked the parliamentary group as an important national institution have been adversely affected by the introduction of leadership conventions.

At the conventions themselves, each delegate casts a secret, individual vote. Ballots are held in rapid succession; the candidate with the lowest number of votes on a ballot is dropped; no new nominations are permitted once voting has begun; and candidates eliminated or withdrawing from the contest are not allowed to address the delegates or to have a statement read on their behalf with instructions to their supporters. The winner is the first candidate to gain a clear majority of the votes cast.[18] The combined effect of these rules is to produce an unorchestrated and individualized selection process whose analogue, as Krause and LeDuc have noted, is not the American nominating convention with its state primaries and caucuses held to choose delegates and its open convention floor voting by state delegations. Rather it is the more familiar one of voting in federal or provincial elections.[19] That a leadership candidate must win by a majority, not simply a plurality of the vote, and that successive ballots may be needed in order to produce that majority make it obvious that there are important differences between a general election and a leadership convention. But on balance, the analogy is an apt one.

Among other things, it implies that Canadians have successfully adapted a nonparliamentary institution to their political system principally by altering it to conform to electoral practices with which they were familiar. If the measure of its success is orderly leadership transitions and (given the absence of any substantial literature or body of opinion critical of leadership conventions) seeming widespread public acceptance of the institution itself, then the judgment appears to be correct. Other benefits claimed on its behalf seem only to gild the lily: party conventions accord well with Canadian values and political culture; they contribute a nationalizing influence to the Canadian political system; delegates represent the Canadian political mainstream; and the secret ballot equalizes all delegates regardless of province or status within the party.[20] There is doubtless truth in all of these assertions, even though empirical evidence is not always offered in their support. Arguably, the national leadership convention is seen as the most important extragovernmental political institution in Canada.

But, as this paper has suggested, the assessment of leadership conventions should not be entirely one-sided. The structure and design of one institution will invariably affect those of another with which it is closely connected. In the case of a leadership convention, the status it has been accorded as a national political institution has come to a considerable extent at the expense of the parliamentary party. As is evident from the changed political recruitment patterns, leadership career routes and intraparty authority and deference structures, the parliamentary party no longer occupies the key position that it once did in the political system. The place that the parliamentary party once occupied for the purposes of leadership selection has been filled by an institution designed initially to put into operation within American political parties the doctrine of separation of powers. In their 150-year history, American nominating conventions have reinforced the distinctiveness of the authority and power of the president, in effect stressing the independence of his office from Congress. It would be difficult to conclude that in Canada forces similar to those in the United States have not been at work: the symbolic and authoritative importance of choosing a "national" leader of a "national" party in a "national" convention can only contribute to the separateness of that leader's office from those of his parliamentary colleagues.

On a more practical level, one consequence of the substantial increase over the past few years in the number of delegates attending national conventions has been to bring into the selection process of both the Liberal and Conservative parties large numbers of relatively young party activists who, for the most part, have had little or no prior experience in politics. Figures from the Conservative party illustrate the point: the share of all convention delegates under the age of thirty has climbed dramatically from 19 per cent in 1967, through 25 per cent in 1976, to 31 per cent in 1983, and the share of delegates reporting less than five years' experience in politics jumped from 11 per cent in 1967 to 31 per cent in 1976.[21]

This increase in the number of relatively inexperienced and relatively unknown political activists participating in leadership conventions in Canada has been matched in the United States by the Democratic party in its post-1968 reform phase. There the group has been labelled part of "the new presidential elite," a term used to describe the large number of convention delegates selecting and voting more independently of the regular party structure than was previously the case. The new elite was responsible, for example, for the selection of George McGovern in 1972.[22] Whether there is a Canadian equivalent in the form of a "new prime ministerial elite" is not at all certain, although it should be recalled that according to survey research, those delegates who were the youngest and the least politically experienced of their convention tipped the scales in favour of Pierre Trudeau in 1968, Joe Clark in 1976, and Brian Mulroney in 1983.[23]

What is striking about the representational aspect of national leadership conventions in Canada is that the original reason for holding conventions (to compensate for the regional weaknesses of the caucuses) was eventually displaced by the organizational imperatives of the parties themselves. While these do not necessarily work at cross-purposes, they do reflect different streams of representational thought: the geographic/demographic, on the one hand, and the political/organizational, on the other. The first gives more obvious expression to the federal and regional dimensions of an important national political institution, whereas the second relates more to the particular internal requirements of the party. When Canada initially adopted its form of leadership conventions directly from turn-of-the-century American politics, one of the several features it did not import was the American formula for involving state party organizations in the deliberations and voting at presidential nominating conventions. Until the introduction of the intraparty convention reforms of the past decade, American *national parties* for presidential elections could be described largely as the products of the deals struck by *state party* organizers—mayors, governors, and bosses, who could effectively deliver votes in return for policy and material rewards and concessions.[24] Canadian parties have never accepted the American practice of political notables bartering large blocs of votes at national conventions. Part of the obligation they have assumed in consequence is that of maintaining a *national* existence through an institution which grants sizeable representation to all segments of the party's *organization* but which, apart from certain categories of party executives and the provincial legislative contingents, structurally minimizes the provincial and regional dimension of Canadian politics. Whatever strength leadership conventions may have as national institutions in Canada derives, in a curiously unCanadian fashion, from the nonfederal structure of the conventions themselves.

APPENDIX A

Categories of Delegates Eligible to Attend Progressive Conservative Leadership Conventions

a) Progressive Conservative Privy Councillors.
b) Progressive Conservative members of the Senate.
c) Progressive Conservative members of Parliament and official candidates in the last federal election unless a new candidate has been nominated, in which case the new candidate shall be the qualified voting delegate under this article.
d) Progressive Conservative members who are elected members of a provincial or territorial legislature or who are leaders of a provincial or territorial Progressive Conservative Party duly recognized by the National Executive.
e) Past federal Progressive Conservative Party Leaders.
f) Past presidents of the Association.
g) Honorary officers of the Association, not to exceed five (5) in number.
h) Presidents in each province and territory of the recognized Progressive Conservative associations, Progressive Conservative Women's organization, and Progressive Conservative Youth organizations.
i) All members of the National Executive of the Association.
j) All members of the Board of Directors of PC Canada Fund, not to exceed fifteen (15) in number and all provincial and territorial fundraising chairmen, not to exceed fifteen (15) in number.
k) Ten (10) members of the Policy Advisory Council.
l) Fifteen (15) members of the National Campaign Committee.
m) Six (6) constituency delegates from each federal constituency; elected by the general membership of the federal constituency association after due notice of a meeting to select delegates; one (1) of whom shall, in the normal case, be the constituency association president; and, of the senior (nonyouth) delegates at least one (1) of whom must be a woman (elected by the Women's Association(s), in the constituency where such exists); at least one (1) of whom must be a man; at least two (2) of whom must be persons under the age of thirty (30) and elected by the constituency Progressive Conservative Youth organization recognized in accordance with Article 3 Sub-section 1 n) or if such an organization does not exist, by those members of the constituency association under the age of thirty (30).
   Each constituency should also elect six (6) alternate delegates using the same guidelines as to age and sex and designate these as to their priority as voting delegate substitutes.
n) Three (3) delegates and three (3) alternate delegates to be elected by each Progressive Conservative post-secondary campus organization recognized at least sixty (60) days prior to any meeting of the Association or any leadership convention.
o) Delegates-at-large to be appointed by the recognized Progressive Conservative association of each province equal in number to one half (1/2) the number

of federal constituencies in the province; provided that there shall not be less than five (5) such delegates for each province and provided that at least twenty (20) per cent of such delegates must be under age thirty (30) who shall be recommended by the duly recognized Progressive Conservative Youth organizations in each province and provided that one half (1/2) of such delegates-at-large shall be of each sex (except that where a fraction occurs the next highest number shall apply and alternate between men and women).

p) Two (2) delegates-at-large to be appointed by the Progressive Conservative Association of the Yukon and two (2) delegates-at-large from the Northwest Territories; one each to be appointed by the Progressive Conservative constituency associations in the Northwest Territories.

q) The National Executive of the Youth Federation and the National Progressive Conservative Women's Caucus (Women's Caucus), to a total of not more than ten (10) delegates from each organization.

r) Two (2) delegates and two (2) alternate delegates from each duly recognized Progressive Conservative organization in existence for at least one (1) year having a membership over one hundred (100) which promotes the principles and policies of the Progressive Conservative Party and is independent of and unrelated to constituency associations; such delegates and alternate delegates to be elected by the general membership of the Progressive Conservative organization after due notice of a meeting (on the same basis as a constituency association) to select delegates and alternate delegates.

Source: Article 3, Constitution of the Progressive Conservative Association of Canada (as amended 29 January 1983).

APPENDIX B

Total Potential Delegate Registration—Progressive Conservative Convention*
June 9–11, 1983

	TOTAL	NWT	YUKON	BC	ALTA	SASK	MAN	ONT	QUE	NB	NS	PEI	NFLD
Privy Councillors	19(A)	—	—	4	1	—	—	8	3	—	—	1	1
Senators	24	—	—	—	1	1	3	5	5	2	3	2	2
M.P./Official Candidates	283	2	1	28	22(B)	14	14	95	75	10	11	4	7
M.L.A.	370	4	8	—	73	54	22	70	—	38	37	21	43
Provincial Leaders	9	—	1	—	1	1	1	1	—	1	1	1	1
Past Party Leader	1	—	—	—	—	—	—	1	—	—	—	—	—
Past National Presidents	6	—	—	—	—	—	—	2	2	1	—	—	1
Honourary Officer	1	—	—	—	—	—	—	—	—	—	—	1	—
Presidents of Prov. Assoc.	12	1	1	1	1	1	1	1	1	1	1	1	—
Pres. Prov. Women's Assoc.	9	—	—	1	1	1	1	1	1	1	1	1	1
Pres. Prov. Youth Assoc.	12	—	1	1	1	1	1	1	1	1	1	1	—
Delegates-at-Large	151	2	2	14	12	7	7	2	1	1	1	1	1
National Executive	56	2	3	7	5	4	3	48	38	5	6	5	5
PC Canada Fund (Directors)	15)							9	6	4	4	4	5
Policy Advisory Committee	10)												

National Campaign Comm.	15)	TO BE DISTRIBUTED AMONG THE PROVINCES AND TERRITORIES FROM THE NATIONAL TOTALS											
PC Canada Fund (Prov.)	15)												
Youth Executive	10)												
NPCWC Executive	10)												
Senior Constituency Delegates	1128	8	4	112	84	56	56	380	300	40	44	16	28
Youth Constituency Delegates	564	4	2	56	42	28	28	190	150	20	22	8	14
Campus Delegates	408	0	0	21	24	6	15	72	168	12	24	3	63
Independent Club—Delegates	12	—	—	—	2	—	2	8	—	—	—	—	—
TOTAL DELEGATES	3140												
Senior Constituency Alternates	1128	8	4	112	84	56	56	380	300	40	44	16	28
Youth Constituency Alternates	564	4	2	56	42	28	28	190	150	20	22	8	14
Alternates-at-Large	151	2	2	14	12	7	7	48	38	5	6	5	5
Campus Alternates	408	—	—	21	24	6	15	72	168	12	24	3	63
TOTAL ALTERNATES	2251												

(A) One Privy Councillor is not presently residing in Canada.
(B) 2 people will be representing Calgary North: the sitting Member and the nominated candidate.

* As of 6 April 1983
Source: PC Party, Ottawa

APPENDIX C

Total Potential Delegate Registration—Liberal Convention*
June 14–16, 1984

	TOTAL	NWT	YUKON	BC	ALTA	SASK	MAN	ONT	QUE	NB	NS	PEI	NFLD
Privy Council	36	—	—	2	1	1	1	16	9	1	—	1	4
Senate	64	1	1	4	2	4	3	16	16	6	6	2	3
Senate (retired)	13	—	—	2	—	—	—	5	2	2	1	—	1
Members of Parliament	145	1	—	—	—	—	2	51	72	7	5	2	5
Defeated Candidates	114	1	1	24	17	11	11	36	1	3	5	2	2
Newly nominated candidates	8	—	—	1	1	—	—	5	—	—	1	—	—
Provincial Liberal leaders	12	1	1	1	1	1	1	1	1	1	1	1	1
National Executive LPC	26	1	1	4	3	3	1	3	3	2	3	1	1
National Executive WLC	21	1	1	3	2	1	2	4	2	1	2	1	1
National Executive NYC	17	—	1	1	1	3	1	4	2	1	1	1	1
Four members provincial executives	48	4	4	4	4	4	4	4	4	4	4	4	4
Youth delegates	201	2	1	20	15	10	10	67	53	7	8	3	5
Women's Liberal clubs	340	4	—	30	4	22	2	66	88	84	26	14	—
Provincial women's Liberal assoc.	22	2	2	2	2	2	2	2	—	2	2	2	2
Standing committees	91	6	4	10	8	8	9	18	9	6	6	5	6
Riding presidents	276	1	1	28	21	14	14	94	73	10	9	4	7
Seven riding delegates	1974	14	7	196	147	98	98	665	525	70	77	28	49
Provincial assemblies	183	6	4	14	19	16	14	31	30	15	13	8	13
Total Delegate	3595	45	29	346	248	198	175	1088	890	222	170	79	105
Riding Alternatives	1974	14	7	196	147	98	98	665	525	70	77	28	49
Grand Total	5569	59	36	542	395	296	273	1753	1415	292	247	107	154

* as of 13 June 1984.
Source: Liberal Party, Ottawa

APPENDIX D

Representation at NDP Conventions

1. Every delegate to a Convention shall be an individual member in good standing of the Party.
2. All members of the Council of the federal party shall be delegates to a Convention.
3. (1) Each federal constituency association shall be entitled to one delegate for 50 members or less, one delegate for each additional 50 members or major fraction thereof up to a total of 200 members, and one delegate for each additional 100 members or major fraction thereof.
   (2) The provincial parties shall advise the federal party as to the number of individual members in good standing in each federal constituency association within the province. For purposes of representation, membership in good standing shall be calculated as at the end of the previous membership year, or as at 60 days prior to the convention, whichever is the greater.
4. Each affiliated local group or organization, and each affiliated local, lodge or branch of a group or organization, whose affiliation fees are not more than 90 days in arrears, shall be entitled to one delegate for the first 1,000 members or major fraction thereof.
5. Central bodies composed of affiliated organizations, and not eligible for direct affiliation to the Party, which officially undertake to accept and abide by the constitution and the principles of the Party and have been recognized by the Council of the federal party, shall be entitled to representation as follows: one delegate from each such central local body and two delegates from each such central national and provincial body.
6. All members of the party caucus in the federal Parliament shall be delegates to a Convention.
7. The Young New Democrats shall be entitled to representation on the basis of two delegates from each chartered provincial Young New Democrat section.

Source: Article 6, Constitution of the New Democratic Party.

NOTES

1. See John C. Courtney, *The Selection of National Party Leaders in Canada* (Toronto: Macmillan, 1973), ch. 9.
2. Sir Wilfrid Laurier's reaction to the Conservative government's handling of the Manitoba Schools Question in the 1890's and Edward Blake's insistence on Laurier succeeding him as Liberal leader in 1887 are examples of the accommodative moves that parties and leaders made with, among other things, electoral benefits in view.
3. See Courtney, *Selection of National Party Leaders,* ch. 4.

4. C. G. Power, *A Party Politician: The Memoirs of Chubby Power,* ed. Norman Ward (Toronto: Macmillan, 1966), pp. 371–72.
5. Samuel J. Eldersveld, *Political Parties: A Behavioral Analysis* (Chicago: Rand McNally, 1964), p. 9.
6. Saskatoon-East Liberal Association. Theoretically, all Liberal constituency delegates could be women under the age of twenty-five; unlike the Conservative constitution, the Liberal one guarantees no constituency representation to men or to nonyouth members.
7. For earlier illustrations of packed delegate selection meetings, see Courtney, *Selection of National Party Leaders,* pp. 91–94.
8. For their 1983 convention, for example, the Progressive Conservative Convention Committee adopted a seven-page set of regulations and eight standard forms governing Candidate Qualifications, Campaign Conduct, Nomination and Candidate Speeches, Withdrawal as a Candidate, and Ineligibility for Subsequent Ballots. PC Party, "Regulations for the Leadership Convention of the Progressive Conservative Party of Canada, June 8–11, 1983" (Ottawa, March 1983).
9. D. V. Smiley, "The National Party Leadership Convention in Canada," *Canadian Journal of Political Science* 1 (December 1968): 373–97; and Robert Krause and Lawrence LeDuc, "Voting Behaviour and Electoral Strategies in the Progressive Conservative Leadership Convention of 1976," *Canadian Journal of Political Science* [*CJPS*] 12 (March 1979): 97–135.
10. The conventions were in 1919, 1948, 1958, 1968, and 1984 (Liberal) and 1927, 1938, 1942, 1948, 1956, 1967, 1976, and 1983 (Conservative). The number of delegates refers to potential not actual figures.
11. See the excellent work by Hannah Fenichel Pitkin, *The Concept of Representation* (Berkeley and Los Angeles: University of California Press, 1967), pp. 38–39, 58.
12. Jeane Kirkpatrick, *The New Presidential Elite: Men and Women in National Politics* (New York: Russell Sage Foundation and The Twentieth Century Fund, 1976), p. 330.
13. See the important work of Doris A. Graber, "Personal Qualities in Presidential Images: The Contribution of the Press," *Midwest Journal of Political Science* 16 (February 1972): 46–76. On media coverage of leaders during a Canadian election campaign, see Frederick J. Fletcher, "The Mass Media in the 1974 Canadian Election," in *Canada at the Polls: The General Election of 1974,* ed. Howard R. Penniman (Washington: American Enterprise Institute for Public Policy Research, 1975), esp. pp. 266–71.
14. At the time of Mr. Trudeau's announced retirement in November 1979 and the calling of the soon-to-be-aborted leadership convention, Monique Bégin complained that many Liberal MPs were discouraged by the process of leadership selection. They felt that they had no effective part to play in the choice of a new leader. See "Liberal MPs Want Leadership Role, Bégin says," *Globe and Mail* (30 November 1979), p. 9.
15. Some of Joe Clark's difficulties with his parliamentary party might well have been foreshadowed by his absence of strong parliamentary support going into the 1976 PC leadership convention. Only three Conservative MPs had worked actively on his campaign. See David L. Humphreys, *Joe Clark: A Portrait* (Ottawa: Deneau and Greenberg, 1976), p. 216. It was widely believed after the 1976 convention that more Conservative MPs supported Claude Wagner than Joe Clark on the final ballot. Clark's subsequent troubles with his caucus (up to the defection of Jack Horner) would tend to confirm that impression.
16. In one study of the 1967 Conservative convention, it was found that leading participants in the party (such members of the party elite as candidates' organizers and those closest to the candidates) tended to cite affective reasons (such as friendship for the candidate) rather than policy reasons for supporting an individual on the first ballot; for other delegates, policy agreement was cited as the first reason. As the party elite category would undoubtedly include MPs, one can infer a marked difference between reasons for support between MPs and other delegates. See George C. Perlin, *The Tory*

Syndrome: Leadership Politics in the Progressive Conservative Party (Montreal: McGill-Queen's University Press, 1980), Tables 3 and 20.

17. John W. Lederle, "The Liberal Convention of 1919 and the Selection of Mackenzie King," *Dalhouse Review* 27 (April 1947): 86. John Diefenbaker seems to have subscribed to the same principle: see Courtney, *Selection of National Party Leaders,* p. 129.
18. Rules vary slightly from party to party and from convention to convention. For their 1983 convention, for example, the Conservatives closed nominations seventeen days before the convention and ruled that any candidate receiving fewer than seventy-five votes on any ballot and the candidate with the fewest votes on any ballot would be eliminated. PC Party, "Regulations."
19. Krause and LeDuc, "Voting Behaviour," p. 101ff.
20. These typical claims are taken from Courtney, *Selection of National Party Leaders,* pp. 234–35; Smiley, "National Party Leadership Convention," p. 397; Lawrence LeDuc, "Party Decision-making: Some Empirical Observations on the Leadership Selection Process," *CJPS* 4 (March 1971): 117; and Ronald G. Landes, *The Canadian Polity: A Comparative Approach* (Scarborough: Prentice-Hall 1983), p. 275.
21. Figures from Courtney, *Selection of National Party Leaders,* Tables 5–2 and 5–10; and Krause and LeDuc, "Voting Behaviour," p. 123.
22. See Kirkpatrick, *The New Presidential Elite,* esp. ch. 1.
23. See LeDuc, "Party Decision-making," pp. 115–16, and Krause and LeDuc, "Voting Behaviour," pp. 123–25.
24. For an analysis of Canadian and American (largely prereform) leadership selection, see Carl Baar and Ellen Baar, "Party and Convention Organization and Leadership Selection in Canada and the United States," in Donald R. Matthews, ed., *Perspectives on Presidential Selection,* (Washington, DC: The Brookings Institution, 1973), pp. 49–84. For the post-1968 developments in the American party system, see Nelson W. Polsby, *Consequences of Party Reform* (Toronto: Oxford, 1982).

7

Ceremonial Politics: Federal-Provincial Meetings Before the Second World War

CHRISTOPHER ARMSTRONG

> A constitutional conference composed of the Prime Minister of Canada and the first ministers of the Provinces shall be convened by the Prime Minister within one year after this Part [concerning aboriginal rights] comes into force. (*The Constitution Act, 1982*, s. 37 (1))

> A constitutional conference composed of the Prime Minister of Canada and the first ministers of the Provinces shall be convened by the Prime Minister within fifteen years to review the provisions of this Part [concerning the amending formula]. (*The Constitution Act, 1982*, s. 49)

When the premier of Quebec suggested to the prime minister in 1887 that there ought to be a meeting of first ministers to review the first twenty years of the operation of the Canadian federal system, Sir John A. Macdonald brusquely declined to attend, remarking that such a gathering would serve "no good purpose."[1] Honoré Mercier and Oliver Mowat of Ontario went ahead anyway and organized an interprovincial conference, although Macdonald did his best to dissuade other premiers from attending. After the conference had passed a series of resolutions calling for sweeping changes in the British North America Act to decentralize the federal system, he refused even to receive a delegation of premiers to present these. Times have obviously changed. Not only have federal-provincial conferences become as familiar and nearly as frequent as the change of seasons, but the conference of first ministers has been enshrined in the new Canadian constitution with vital responsibilities.

This paper examines the sixteen interprovincial and dominion-provincial conferences which took place between 1887 and 1941* in an effort to understand how an institution once without any formal standing in the constitutional scheme of things began to move towards a central place. Was it, perhaps, because the conferences came almost at once to be recognized as forum for the negotiation of vital changes? No. In fact, it turns out that these conferences were almost entirely ceremonial affairs at which little of substance was achieved. But that, paradoxically, had its own significance, for as Murray Edelman points out in *The Symbolic Uses of Politics* the choice of a setting may be as critical as the event itself, especially when what is at stake is:

> 1) the importance of impressing a large audience, as distinct from the need to convince an individual through logical demonstration;
> 2) the intention of legitimizing a series of future acts (whose content is still unknown) and thereby maximizing the chance of acquiescence in them and compliance with the rules they embody;
> 3) the need to establish or reinforce a particular definition of self in a public official.[2]

Analysis of the conferences of first ministers prior to World War II reveals that the participants took account of all three.

Establishing a particular type of self-definition was particularly important to the premiers of the provinces and led them to press for the convocation of the early interprovincial conferences. The Fathers of Confederation might have envisaged the provinces as no more than "large municipal corporations,"[3] but the premiers showed no inclination to accept a role as glorified mayors. Instead, they sought to portray themselves as statesmen with broad national concerns who yet reflected the diversity of the regional interests within the Canadian polity. They supplied the impetus for the calling of the interprovincial conferences in 1887, 1902, 1906, 1910, 1913, and 1926 so that they might focus the limelight upon themselves. In time, federal politicians grasped the fact that these gatherings might be made to serve their purposes, too. Beginning in 1918 there began to be held dominion-provincial conferences at which federal ministers joined their provincial counterparts around the table. The conferences proved to be ideal occasions for the announcement of important changes in the relations between the Dominion and the provinces, changes which had already been decided upon in advance by Ottawa, so that the discussions which went on proved little more than window-dressing. Public opinion was the target, and a ceremonial occasion was better adapted to impressing that large audience than convincing individuals through logi-

---

*See Appendix A for a list of these conferences.

cal demonstration (which might be done in private). Gradually, prime ministers like R. B. Bennett and Mackenzie King also recognized that the holding of such conferences might be either a substitute for action or a means of legitimizing actions already planned to which the provinces would not consent. A skillfully orchestrated meeting which broke up in disagreement could provide an excuse for the prime minister to act unilaterally to deal with pressing national problems. Thus, ceremony served a useful purpose, and in the course of time it began to be accepted that a conference of first ministers was the proper forum for discussions of the highest constitutional significance. After World War II there remained no question that the dominion-provincial conference must pronounce upon key changes in the Canadian federal system.

Honoré Mercier and Oliver Mowat sought to convene an Interprovincial Conference in 1887 because they were both committed adherents of the "compact theory" of Confederation. They disliked the highly centralized form of federalism favoured by Macdonald, in which the provinces were thoroughly dominated by the central government. Macdonald had once even remarked that he hoped to see the provinces "absorbed in the General Power" altogether during his lifetime; Mowat and Mercier would have none of that. Instead they adopted the view summarized by the *Globe* as follows:

> The Confederation had its origin in a bargain between certain Provinces, in which the Provinces agree to unite for certain purposes and to separate or continue separated for others. . . .The Dominion was the creation of these Provinces . . . .The Dominion being non-existent at the time the bargain was made was plainly not a party to the bargain. It cannot, then, be a party to the revision of the bargain.[4]

However dubious this view historically,[5] its virtue, as Mowat and Mercier were quick to grasp, was that it granted the provincial premiers a crucial role in defining the nature of Canadian federalism. Since Macdonald, who knew full well the intentions of the Fathers of Confederation, was certain to resist decentralization, it was desirable to have some means of impressing the broader audience of politically aware citizens of the rightness of their case, and a ceremonial occasion was well-suited to this purpose.

The Fathers of Confederation saw no need to include any provision for formal intergovernmental gatherings in the B.N.A. Act because they believed that they had provided a permanent body to represent regional (as distinct from provincial) interests in Ottawa.[6] But the Senate failed to function as expected because its members proved loyal to the political parties which had procured their appointment rather than to the interests of their native provinces. Meanwhile, Macdonald's determination to enforce strong central control over the provincial governments through the office of the lieutenant-governor and the use of the power of disallowance had created mounting friction with the premiers. In summoning the interprovincial conference, Mercier complained that

> The centralizing tendencies, manifested of late years by the Federal Government and favoured by the obscurity—in some respects—of the British North America Act, 1867, have aroused legitimate fears with regard to the maintenance of our local institutions and render it imperative that there should be an understanding between the Provincial Governments with a view to the organization of a system of common defence.[7]

Macdonald succeeded in using his influence to persuade the Conservative premiers of Prince Edward Island and British Columbia not to attend the 1887 interprovincial conference, although he did not deter John Norquay of Manitoba, angry about the C.P.R.'s monopoly. When the five other premiers gathered in Quebec City, Mercier did his best to try to establish the legitimacy of the gathering by immediately harking back to the Quebec Conference of 1864 at which the original terms of union had been hammered out by the representatives of the British North American colonies. The interprovincial conference of 1887, said Mercier, was

> the first which has been held since 1864, which was attended by the distinguished statesmen from Upper and Lower Canada, New Brunswick and Nova Scotia, and whose resolutions served, in some respects as the basis of the Union Act of 1867. . . . You, as well as ourselves, feel that it is not out of place nor opposed to the general interests of Canada, still less of the Provinces, to convene after a lapse of twenty years representatives from the Governments of all [sic] of the Provinces for the purpose of examining certain questions, as amicable solution of which the past few years has shown to be necessary.[8]

The Quebec premier thus sought at the very outset to demonstrate the propriety of this gathering, all the more important in light of Macdonald's refusal to play any part and of his efforts to abort it.

The major concern of most of the premiers who attended the 1887 conference was, as Macdonald well understood, to put pressure upon Ottawa to amend the B.N.A. Act to increase the subsidies paid to the provinces by tying them to current population levels rather than those of 1860. But they were also quite prepared to go along with Oliver Mowat, a strong proponent of the compact theory and of wider provincial powers, so they readily endorsed sixteen other resolutions calling for such things as the abolition of the federal power of disallowance, the appointment of half the senators by the provinces, and an end to parliamentary declarations that particular undertakings were "for the general advantage of Canada" and hence under federal jurisdiction.[9] Macdonald, as we have seen, refused even to receive a delegation to submit these resolutions.[10] To the end of his life, he rejected this new conception of federalism. Yet events had begun to pass him by. The federal power of disallowance came to be much less freely used, and the courts upheld provincial claims to jurisdiction over ever broader areas. And eventually politicians of all parties began to be heard mouthing the slogans of provincial rights and expressing their endorsement of the compact theory.[11]

When he won power in 1896, Sir Wilfrid Laurier was much indebted to a number of powerful Liberal premiers (including Mowat), and he came to recognize that interprovincial conferences might have their uses in permitting the ventilation of provincial grievances. When one premier or another approached him requesting a subsidy, moreover, he could deftly turn him aside with the suggestion that this could be considered only as part of a general revision of the financial terms of Confederation.[12] In 1902 Premier S. N. Parent of Quebec finally took the initiative and called a second conference. When the delegates gathered in Quebec City, Parent welcomed them with a speech which once more emphasized the propriety and legitimacy of the premiers gathering to discuss important constitutional issues:

> The question of amendments to the Union Act is not now submitted for the first time to the attention of the public men of this country. . . . It was especially at the time of the meeting of the distinguished men who formed part of the Interprovincial Conference held here in 1887 that it gave rise to the most earnest debate and that the claims of the Provinces were most clearly formulated.[13]

This effort to establish the historical role of the conference of premiers was all the more necessary because Premier George Ross of Ontario was absent owing to a series of crucial by-elections and the new premier of British Columbia, E. G. Prior, had not made the long journey from

Victoria. Ross did, however, send along a memorandum endorsing the idea of increased provincial subsidies, and the conference quickly approved the idea proposed in 1887 of tying the annual per capita grant to the current population rather than the 1860 figures.[14] Early in 1903 all the premiers waited upon Laurier to submit their demands. He was encouraging but remained adamant that the subsidy question should be settled once and for all. He received the resolutions but failed to act upon them.[15]

Laurier resented those premiers who assumed that once the conference had framed its resolutions, their demands would be met automatically:

> Some of the Premiers write as if they were claiming the payment of a debt for money advanced or loaned. The truth of the matter is that whilst for my part I am disposed to consider favourably the application made by the Provinces, I never could see my way to grant the request as formulated, and I see very serious objections to such a course.

As for any other changes in the constitution, the prime minister insisted that

> Pour moi, la question se resume simplement a celle-ci . . . : est-il opportun de changer la constitution sur la demande de quelques provinces seulement? Et n'est-il pas préférable d'affirmer le principe que pour être accordée, cette demande devrait être unanime de la part des provinces?[16]

By 1906, all the provincial legislatures had approved the resolutions of the 1902 conference regarding a subsidy increase, except British Columbia which sought an even greater increase. Lomer Gouin of Quebec took the steps to call another interprovincial conference to endorse the demands made in 1887 and 1902.[17] Laurier gave way at last in the face of these repeated requests and agreed to the amendment of the B.N.A. Act. To his regret, however, he was unable to persuade the British Parliament to declare this a "final and unalterable" settlement of all provincial demands.[18]

Although the 1906 conference had resolved that the premiers of Ontario and Quebec should call their counterparts together each year to "consider matters of common interest,"[19] another interprovincial conference was not held until 1910. The Maritime provinces had become concerned that they would lose more seats in the House of Commons owing to the growth of the western provinces. Laurier cannily suggested that the premiers should try to come to an agreement on this issue and submit it to the government. But this proved impossible owing to Quebec's resistance to any decrease in the proportion of MPs which it elected to the Commons. After only a single day, the conference broke up.[20]

The prospects for agreement seemed brighter at the next meeting in 1913. All the provinces needed additional federal subsidies, and the new Conservative prime minister, Robert Borden, was known to be beholden to such powerful Conservative premiers as Sir James Whitney of Ontario, Sir Richard McBride of British Columbia, and Sir Rodmond Roblin of Manitoba. The delegates quickly passed a resolution calling for Ottawa to grant them an annual 10 per cent share of the customs and excise revenues.[21] Borden, however, proved unenthusiastic when this was presented to him, returning a "non-committal answer saying they should not come oftener than once in ten years for [an] increase."[22] Once again the premiers failed to agree on the question of Maritime representation, and they were forced to resolve, lamely, "That this Conference expresses the opinion that not representing the Provinces for the purposes of this matter of representation, it declines to take any action in regard to it."[23]

By World War I, the premiers had not succeeded in establishing the interprovincial conference as a key body for making national decisions. True, many politicians paid lip-service to the compact theory, and Laurier and Borden had not expressed any open hostility to these gatherings as Macdonald had done. But neither had they shown any inclination to leap into action in response to the conferences' resolutions. The subsidy increase granted in 1907 had, after all, been proposed twenty years earlier at the first such meeting and twice subsequently endorsed. That the conference had secured no monopoly over constitutional change was quite evident from the way in which two important constitutional amendments were introduced during the war.

The failure of the provinces to agree upon a solution to the problem of Maritime representation in 1910 and 1913 left it open to the federal government to act. In 1915 it prepared an amendment to the B.N.A. Act guaranteeing every province a minimum number of MPs equal to its Senate delegation. The provinces were not consulted, but with unanimous approval from the Parliament of Canada, Britain quickly acted to insert the amendment into the constitution. Likewise, in 1916, an amendment was passed extending the life of Parliament for one year. In neither case did any of the premiers raise any objection to this method of altering the constitution.[24]

The most important development in intergovernmental relations during the war occurred in 1918. The Borden administration was desirous of provincial co-operation in dealing with certain economic and social problems, particularly increasing food production and arranging programmes for demobilized soldiers. As a result, it was decided to hold the first dominion-provincial conference at which delegates from both levels of government would sit together in February 1918. In fact, though, the federal authorities viewed this as little more than an opportunity to announce new policies to the provinces. Federal Agriculture Minister T. A. Crerar actually suggested to the prime minister that the premiers be invited without revealing what was to be discussed. Otherwise, he thought, they might "come with more or less provincial ideas as to details, which might tend to have the conference get away from the main issue involved."[25] Although Borden rejected this idea, he gave the conference little time or attention, merely recording in his diary: "Went to Provincial Conf[eren]ce at 11 and addressed them for ½ hour. Then to office." Otherwise, he left the conduct of the meetings to Crerar and General S. C. Mewburn, the Minister of Militia and Defence.[26]

A second dominion-provincial conference was scheduled for November 1918, by which time Borden had departed for the peace conference in Europe, leaving Sir Thomas White in charge. Most of the business of that conference also seems to have consisted of the premiers listening to statements from federal ministers concerning policies such as land settlement and the employment of returning soldiers. About the only issue which the provinces raised to which much time was devoted was the matter of the return of the lands and natural resources in western Canada to provincial control. Efforts by the premiers to persuade Ottawa to abandon the income taxes imposed in 1917 or to increase subsidies to the provinces fell upon deaf ears.[27]

While the summoning of these dominion-provincial conferences had a symbolic significance, a recognition that the premiers had the right to sit down and consult with Ottawa on certain questions, the practical import of the meetings may be gathered from the fact that no such conferences were held until the fourth year of the war. The federal government really did not seek consultation but a forum in which to announce policies already decided upon. Provincial co-operation was deemed desirable but by no means essential. Thus, the first half-century of Confederation ended without the provincial leaders having attained any formal right to pronounce upon vital constitutional issues. Even the B.N.A. Act could be amended without any reference to the provinces.

The postwar era saw little change. Not until 1926 was another meeting of premiers convened, once more an interprovincial conference on prewar lines. This came about largely at the instance of Premier J. D. Stewart of Prince Edward Island, who was seeking an increase in the subsidy. Believing that Alberta was near to settling with Ottawa upon the return of its lands and natural resources, he considered the moment opportune to open the whole issue of federal grants to the provinces. He approached Howard Ferguson of Ontario and L. A. Taschereau of Quebec and asked them to call the premiers together.[28] Although Taschereau was cool to the idea, Ferguson and a number of other premiers proved enthusiastic, and the delegates gathered in Ottawa in June, though there was no representative from Alberta present owing to a provincial election.[29]

This reversion to the prewar practice of meeting without representatives of the Dominion present indicates the rather halting development of the conference as a national institution. John Bracken of Manitoba, however, considered this format preferable. He recalled that when the federal finance minister and his provincial counterparts had met in the fall of 1924 to discuss duplication of taxation,

> nothing was accomplished, largely because the Provinces had not arrived at a basis of agreement amongst themselves and the Dominion took the attitude that until the Provinces had agreed on general principles there was no cause for it to be concerned. I feel that if the Provinces could come to an agreement with reference to some problems and then discuss those upon which they were agreed with the Federal authorities, a great deal more would be accomplished.[30]

Federal officials were also content to be absent because they feared the conference would develop into "a united raid on the Treasury in which the smaller Provinces particularly would join with enthusiasm."[31] In fact, after some discussion, the premiers merely passed a rather tepid resolution expressing

> sympathy with those Provinces, which by reason of conditions peculiar to them, have not progressed as anticipated, and urge[d] upon the Federal Government that it should favourably consider affording relief to each of such Provinces in a form that will ameliorate these conditions.[32]

By the time the premiers left Ottawa, a chain of events was already underway which would lead the King government to decide unilaterally to adjust the subsidies. By 1925 three well-established Liberal administrations in the three Maritime provinces had been displaced by Conservative ones. In the federal election that autumn, the Tories carried twenty-three of the twenty-nine seats in the region, and a "Maritime rights" movement had been formed to protest the disadvantages suffered from national policies.[33] Although Mackenzie King was able to cling to power, he decided in April 1926 to try and placate the angry Maritimers by appointing a royal commission to study the grievances and recommend remedies. Working with extraordinary speed, Sir Andrew Duncan and his colleagues submitted a report in September recommending hefty subsidy increases. Fresh from his victory in the 1926 election, King agreed to implement the recommendations.[34]

Officially, however, the subsidy increases were granted only on a temporary basis, reserving a final arrangement until after a dominion-provincial conference in the fall of 1927. Thus, as in other subsequent instances, the conference was to be used as a means of ratifying a decision already taken, giving it an official, ceremonial imprint. The prime minister nonetheless took the gathering seriously, even rearranging the tables in the Railway Committee Room of the Parliament Buildings for the opening session himself.[35] What King was seeking was approval of his policies, on the tacit understanding that the western provinces would shortly receive their lands and natural resources back without having to give up the subsidies which they had always received in lieu of them. In order to leave as little as possible to chance, he suggested to Liberal Premier James Gardiner of Saskatchewan that he come to Ottawa a few days ahead of time as "I think it might be well for some of us who share kindred views of Government to talk over in advance some of the matters which are likely to create differences of view at the Conference itself."[36] Gardiner applauded the idea and suggested that the Liberal party opposition leaders in Manitoba and Alberta should be invited to the briefing, too. But King shied away from that idea which was likely to offend the non-Liberal premiers by derogating from their status. Such a gathering of Grits might, as he delicately put it, "suggest some political intention to which the press of the country might take exception," but he promised to try and see each of the provincial Liberal leaders individually in the weeks before the conference.[37] Open partisanship had thus come to be seen as inappropriate to the character of a gathering concerned with the nation's well-being.

Behind the scenes, of course, the political manoeuvring was intense. Conservative Howard Ferguson took steps to try and forge a coalition of premiers beforehand to oppose King if necessary. He suggested to Gardiner

> that there might be a great saving of time, and it would perhaps expediate [sic] the solution of a great many questions if the Provinces were to confer together and ascertain upon what questions they hold common views. It would appear we might clear away a lot of unnecessary discussion if we first hold a conference amongst ourselves.

Gardiner steered clear of any involvement, arguing

> that it would scarcely be proper for us to assume that there will be sufficient difference of opinion as between the Dominion and the Provinces to warrant our holding a conference of Provincial Governments in advance of the Conference between the Provincial Governments and the Federal Government.[38]

And the Saskatchewan premier warned Mackenzie King that "Mr. Ferguson appears to be putting forth every effort to organize any opposition that there may be to any attitude which your Government may decide to take with regard to matters under discussion." The prime minister responded with an interesting view of the essential nature of federal-provincial relations in Canada behind all the window-dressing:

> I think you are quite right in asserting that a lineup on the part of the provinces of Canada against the Federal Treasury is not to be desired either in the public interest or in the interests of the provinces themselves.[39]

The eve of the conference found King in a pessimistic frame of mind. He thought Finance Minister J. A. Robb was not well prepared to deal with the subsidy issue: "I look to see him make a fiasco of phases of it. The truth is we are not in good shape for a Conference."[40] In the event, however, the week-long meeting passed off amicably enough. Neither the Maritimers nor the westerners were disposed to make waves after having been promised better terms. The obvious stumbling block was Ontario, but Howard Ferguson soon made it clear that he (and L. A. Taschereau of Quebec) were more interested in settling their longstanding dispute with Ottawa over the ownership of waterpowers on navigable rivers by referring it to the courts. When it became evident that King was willing to concede this item, Ferguson raised no objections, remarking grandly that

> He did not . . . intend to cavil about small things. He regarded it as supremely important to bring about a situation which would be satisfactory to all provinces. . . . The big problem was to promote satisfaction and prosperity by giving fresh inspiration to those who needed help. . . . The expenditure of a few hundred thousand dollars was nothing if optimism, harmony and industry could be inspired.[41]

The only real discussion at the 1927 conference revolved around the issue of constitutional amendment. In 1925, Parliament had passed a resolution calling for reform of the Senate to be discussed at a dominion-provincial conference. In 1926 the imperial conference had approved the Balfour Declaration on the equality of the members of the Commonwealth. Justice Minister Ernest Lapointe therefore concluded that amendment of the constitution should be taken up with the provinces. He wanted the B.N.A. Act formally patriated, contending that "our self-respect as a nation demanded our right to amend ourselves." The federal cabinet concluded, however, that this was too dangerous an issue to raise, since it was likely to unite in opposition the imperialistic Ferguson with Taschereau, who considered that Britain could still provide significant protection for French-Canadian rights. Thus, it was decided to discuss only Senate reform and a formula for approving constitutional amendments in Canada (rendering formal patriation unnecessary).[42]

Senate reform was briefly discussed, then dropped, but the amending formula proved controversial. Lapointe opened the discussion by formally conceding the provincial claim to an important role:

> the B.N.A. Act is an agreement between different parties and . . . no substantial change should be made without consulting the contracting parties. The B.N.A. Act is the charter of the provinces in which powers have been fixed and determined between the Dominion and the provinces. Consequently the provinces have the right to be consulted about establishing a new procedure to amend it.

The justice minister suggested dividing the provisions of the act into three separate categories. Some crucial sections like 92 (10), 92 (12), 93, and 133 would require unanimous provincial consent. Matters affecting only federal jurisdiction might be changed by Parliament alone, while the remaining sections would need the approval of six of nine provincial legislatures.[43]

Ferguson led a strong attack upon the idea. Who, he asked, wanted an amending formula except the editorialists at the Manitoba *Free Press?* He claimed that the constitution had already undergone thirty-three changes since 1867. "The new method would be much more troublesome. There lurks the danger of raising one province against another." Ferguson hinted darkly that this was all part of the King government's efforts to destroy the British connection by emphasizing Canadian autonomy. Taschereau joined in the attack:

> The Fathers of Confederation have stated that changes should be made not by a majority but by consent of all. . . . Quebec is composed

of French people with a different code. Even with a fixed constitution rights have been infringed upon, so we must be very careful to open the door for other changes. Why not let it remain? Quebec is unanimously against a change. If the majority can decide on an amendment there is no security in our charter. If, on the other hand, we require unanimity there are also difficulties ahead. On some questions Quebec would be alone and would be pointed out as a barrier to the progress of other provinces. I do not want my province to be in such a position.

The three Maritime premiers also expressed opposition to the change.[44]

With support for Lapointe's plan coming only from the four Liberal and farmer governments in western Canada, progress was clearly impossible. As Mackenzie King had declared at the conference's opening session, "This is a conference, not a cabinet or a convention."[45] No decisions could be taken in the absence of a broad consensus, and for the federal Liberal party, there was little profit in pressing ahead against the opposition of the powerful Liberal premier of Quebec. Thus, the 1927 dominion-provincial conference, like its predecessors, proved to be an almost entirely ceremonial affair, devoted to ratifying decisions taken in advance. Yet, viewed as part of the historical development of the conference as an institution, it was not without its significance. For the first time federal and provincial first ministers sat down together to discuss issues of national importance. And Lapointe's statement formally conceded the claims which proponents of the compact theory of Confederation had been making for so long about the right of the provinces to be consulted on changes in the constitution. Perhaps a measure of the new sense that this kind of meeting was one where crucial decisions might one day be taken lies in the pre-conference manoeuvring. Ferguson sought to achieve a consensus amongst the provinces on certain issues that crossed party lines, while King was warning his men not to be inveigled into a Tory trap. Some real flesh had begun to cling to the institutional bones.

The promise of consultation with the provinces about any significant constitutional change became a reality at the next dominion-provincial conference in 1931. As a consequence of the Balfour Declaration, the Statute of Westminster was drafted in 1929 to provide a formal statement of the equality and independence of the self-governing members of the British Commonwealth. But the draft Statute threatened to create certain problems for the Canadian federal system because it appeared to permit the modification of any British enactments which applied to Canada (including the B.N.A. Act) without any reference to the provinces. The division of jurisdiction between the two levels of government might thus be altered unilaterally. When the Canadian parliament discussed the statute in the spring of 1930, the problem was raised by the Conservative opposition, but the King government did nothing.[46] Before the imperial conference met in October 1930 to ratify the statute, however, Mackenzie King was replaced by R. B. Bennett. Ferguson, his fellow Conservative, promptly registered a strong protest against this failure to consult the premiers. In a lengthy brief, he elaborated the compact theory of Confederation as justification,[47] a position supported by Taschereau, who argued that

> Confederation was a contract entered into by the various Canadian provinces after lengthy discussion and on terms acceptable to the contracting parties. I fail to see how such a contract can be altered without the concurrence of all parties thereto.[48]

Although federal officials were most unhappy about the doctrine that changing the B.N.A. Act should require unanimous provincial consent,[49] Bennett proved sympathetic to the idea of a conference, called for April 1931.[50] Secretary of State C. H. Cahan even proposed that the premiers try to agree upon an amending formula but he does not seem to have received much support.[51] The prime minister preferred to seek an amendment to the Statute of Westminster which would simply preserve the status quo. At the conference all the premiers expressed willingness to accept this plan, although Taschereau, facing a summer election, was

> very nervous lest he might do something which would give his political opponent, [Conservative leader Camilien] Houde, a chance to say something in the campaign against him. He, therefore, reserved consideration for his whole cabinet. However, he had no criticism of the form of the amendment, but was very careful lest any stand he might take might be misinterpreted.[52]

In order to secure an agreement, Bennett promised that

> to meet the position of Quebec, which he appreciated, he was willing to make a declaration that in future no amendments to the British North America Act would be made by the present government until an opportunity had been given the Provinces to discuss the amendment and the practice that has heretofore prevailed would not be relied upon.[53]

By 1931, both major parties were committed to the proposition that there should be "discussion" or "consultation" with the provincial governments about constitutional amendments, which meant, of course, that the dominion-provincial conference was likely to become the central forum for such negotiations. Although the 1931 conference was designed simply to make certain that the status quo was preserved, it was clear that one version of the compact theory of Confederation had become accepted dogma. The provinces and their premiers had to be involved in the process (though they lacked a formal veto), and a future gathering was promised to try and work out an amending formula and permit patriation while reconciling "the two essential features of reasonable elasticity of change and the preservation of provincial rights."[54] Still, the actual achievements of such conferences to that date were pretty slim, a fact that did not escape the editorialists at the Ottawa *Morning Journal:*

> Just what the conference is going to do or say we don't profess to know, and we doubt whether many will care or long remember anything they may do. A half dozen constitutional lawyers will say it's important, and a few pedants will write frightfully dull articles about it. . . . The man in the street won't know or care or be interested at all. . . . He knows instinctively that this gathering doesn't matter a tinker's curse. . . . For every person who is interested [in the conference] there are at least a thousand who want to see the *Canadiens* win the Stanley Cup.[55]

So far as concrete achievements were concerned over the next few years, this assessment proved quite correct. Just as the 1931 meeting had merely agreed to preserve the status quo, the conferences held in 1932, 1933, and 1934 functioned as podiums for the announcement of federal policy initiatives decided upon in advance. The depression crisis placed great strains upon the federal system as upon much else. The problem was brutally simple: how to find the money needed to provide relief to the growing number of unemployed? Municipal and provincial politicians bore the constitutional responsibility to aid those out of work, but the federal government had a broader and more lucrative tax base. What would the Bennett government do?

In 1930, $20,000,000 had been set aside to fund shared-cost programmes with the provinces. As unemployment worsened, the pressure to increase these sums intensified. In April 1932, provincial officials were summoned to the capital to hear that the federal government was dropping its support for relief works to devote all the funds to more economical direct relief payments. Many of the premiers did not even bother to make the journey to Ottawa, perhaps because they calculated that there was no likelihood of persuading the prime minister to change his mind. If so, they proved correct, and the conference quickly broke up.[56]

By the end of 1932, however, the financial straits of the four western provinces had become a serious cause of concern. If they defaulted on their debts, many people believed that this might do irreparable harm to Canada's credit rating abroad. Even though it was realized that it would do little to cure the present unemployment situation, there began to be talk in Ottawa about a national unemployment insurance scheme. The difficulty was that this would require a constitutional amendment, so R. B. Bennett decided to call the premiers together to discuss the idea.[57] At a meeting summoned for 17 January 1933, they were asked to consider

> The relative legislative jurisdiction of the Dominion and Provinces respecting Old Age Pensions, Unemployment and Social Insurance. If dealt with as national problems, what amendment, if any, is necessary to the British North America Act, and what steps should be taken to effect such an amendment?[58]

Before the conference met, George S. Henry of Ontario, who had succeeded Ferguson, enquired of the prime minister whether or not other private interests such as business groups, insurers, and municipal leaders might be represented at the gathering.[59] The enquiry is significant because it demonstrates that the form of the conferences still remained fluid. During the 1920's there had been several occasions on which private groups had joined with federal and provincial politicians as well as civil servants to discuss social questions.[60] This time Bennett ruled out the idea on the grounds that the focus of the conference concerned constitutional issues in which only the ten governments had a direct interest.[61] But during the 1930's there continued to be suggestions that municipal officials should be given a hearing on relief problems. In 1935, for instance, a number of mayors gathered in Ottawa and applied to make representations to the conference. Mackenzie King was quick to point out that hearing one delegation might open doors to a multitude of others. Premier W. M. Lea of Prince Edward Island agreed:

> There is no doubt that if a precedent of that kind is established other delegations will demand the same right, and various boards of trade and other bodies would be bringing here all kinds of minor matters that cannot be dealt with by this conference, because we have not the time. I thought it was only matters of interest as between the provinces that were to be considered by the conference.

King proposed that the rules of the conference be modelled upon those of imperial conferences, which would rule out such activities, although he and the premiers might meet informally with the mayors outside of the formal conference sessions.[62] As in the case of other important institutions like Parliament itself, the question of who was entitled to be summoned to a dominion-provincial conference was one which was only settled as historical precedents developed.[63]

The 1933 conference devoted itself to a quick review of the bleak national unemployment situation before turning to the question of an insurance programme. Bennett opened this discussion by at once demanding to know whether the provinces were now ready to surrender jurisdiction to the federal Parliament and how large a financial contribution they would make for being relieved of the burden of unemployment. Taken aback by this bluntness, the premiers asked him to explain the scheme he had in mind in more detail. Bennett refused. He replied that his questions must be answered before the discussion could proceed further. While the three prairie premiers seemed amenable, the Ontario and Quebec leaders would have none of it. Taschereau repeatedly demanded a further explanation of Ottawa's plans. Ontario Attorney-General W. H. Price argued that no constitutional amendment would be necessary if each province passed enabling legislation for a national plan.[64] This position was in keeping with Ontario's conservative attitude towards constitutional change, which had been evident in both 1927 and 1931. As one provincial civil servant put it,

> I would recommend that the Ontario administration adhere to the policy of provincial rights, thus following the example of every Ontario administration since Confederation. "Hands off the B.N.A. Act" will simplify most of the problems on the agenda. Any indication that Ontario might join with the Dominion in a petition to amend the B.N.A. Act would probably result in the sacrifice of provincial rights and in the result create more problems than it solved.[65]

The failure of the provinces to agree obviously irritated the prime minister. Although he had admitted to the premiers that he "thought all forms of social insurance were largely incompatible with the spirit of freedom," he maintained that by signing the Treaty of Versailles and joining the International Labor Organization, Canada had obligated itself to introduce such programmes.

> As matters stood, however, the peculiar character of our constitution, the distribution of the responsibility between the Dominion and the

> Provinces left the Dominion without the power to carry out these obligations. . . .The question before the Conference was: were the Provinces prepared to enable the Dominion to discharge its obligations?

But the premiers of Ontario and Quebec remained obdurate, and after some further inconclusive discussion, a subcommittee of provincial delegates was set up to see if some common provincial position could be hammered out. Meanwhile, the first ministers turned their attention to the problems of duplicate taxation.[66]

This committee failed to reach any agreement. Its chairman, Price of Ontario, reported back that after a number of meetings, some provinces were not prepared to declare themselves in favour even of the *principle* of unemployment insurance. Placing the blame upon the federal government's tactics, he added,

> as no plan has been made which could be a basis of consideration, and as the subject is a very large one with conditions varying as they do, I think the consensus of view is that we would like to have more information and go more fully into the question before making up our minds as to whether it is wanted or not. With such a plan outlined we could come to a conclusion on the method and the basis of contribution.

Bennett brusquely rejected this recommendation, turning back the resolution on the grounds that it was not "a responsive answer" to the question on the agenda, and the issue was simply dropped.[67]

Thus, the 1933 dominion-provincial conference achieved nothing with regard to the major issue before it, not even resolving upon some kind of noncommittal formula as a means of saving face. But this seems to have been exactly what R. B. Bennett desired. As one journalist wrote privately, "On unemployment insurance, without doubt, he hoped that Taschereau and the others representing the provinces would balk at the transference of jurisdiction, thus enabling him to drop the policy without unpleasant political consequences."[68] One Ontario civil servant had noted sourly before the meeting that the federal authorities would then be in a position to blame the premiers for having "knowingly and deliberately declined to permit the Dominion to save mankind."[69] The editorialists at the Vancouver *Sun*[70] were thus wrong to complain about "the excessive degree of nothingness which has been accomplished by the Interprovincial Conference at Ottawa." That was the whole point of the gathering, which was, as many others had been both before and since, purely ceremonial. The function of the conference was to be, not to do.

Yet the problems created by the economic crisis were inescapable and their constitutional implications obvious. Near the end of 1933 the newly elected premier of British Columbia, T. D. Pattullo, complained that

> The provinces have limited jurisdiction which is not sufficient, nor has the Dominion sufficient authority unless plenary power such as might be justified in actual war is exercised. It seems to me that some extraordinary measures will necessarily have to be adopted to meet the present situation.[71]

The Bennett government could not ignore the ever-increasing likelihood that one of the western provinces might default on its debt. A powerful faction within the cabinet was insistent that "there be no more loans unless the provinces accept federal supervision and control."[72] In the spring of 1933 the prime minister sternly reproved each of the four western premiers:

> no convincing evidence has been adduced to show that every possible effort is being made by the legislature and government of your province to adjust your affairs and work into a position of self-reliance. On the contrary, intimation has come from your government that you anticipate making further requests for aid.

Unless provincial budgets were balanced, the premiers could expect no further aid on previous terms, and for more loans to be granted if this was not achieved,

> I must state that the only alternative I can propose . . . is that the finances of your government be supervised . . . by a financial controller, who may be nominated by your government but must be satisfactory to the government of Canada. It will become the duty of such controller . . . to supervise all proposed expenditures and thus ensure that no expenditure can be made and no engagement involving expenditure undertaken without his approval. . . . The necessary steps by way of legislative and executive action will have to be taken by the province to give the controller the necessary powers, and to continue them so long as the loans to the Dominion remain unpaid or until the government of the Dominion indicates that the services of the controller are no longer required.[73]

Bennett failed to carry out this threat, but as the year dragged on without economic recovery, the concerns of federal officials increased. In December 1933, the western premiers met and agreed to press the prime minister to increase the level of assistance and to start a new federal public works programme.[74] The refusal to surrender authority apparently convinced Bennett that he must try to force the premiers' hand. To do so, he decided to convene another dominion-provincial conference in January 1934.[75] Like the one a year earlier, this meeting was not intended to reach any agreement but rather to lay the groundwork for subsequent unilateral action by Ottawa after the blame for the current situation had been shifted onto provincial shoulders so far as possible.

The conference devoted almost all of its time to discussing the problem of unemployment relief.[76] After listening to a catalogue of woes from the premiers, Bennett suddenly went on the attack:

> The provinces were jealous of their provincial position and were not prepared to surrender administrative control over any commission which the Dominion might set up to administer relief measures. Without their consent no federal commission to control unemployment and relief measures would be any use. . . .If relief payments were not uniform or effectively controlled that was the fault of the provinces.

To reduce costs, Bennett suggested that the three Maritime provinces should unite since "three separate governments and so small a population was anomalous." Likewise, "It must be admitted that the cost of government in the west was too high. Four separate executive governments was too many." In a statement particularly surprising from an adoptive Calgarian, Bennett went on,

> It had also been suggested that the west should discontinue some of its services—services which were suitable and within the means of the old established communities but which were sometimes difficult to justify in the new ones. An example was old age pensions. He admitted that these had been authorized by federal legislation passed in connection with a political crisis and that the provinces had been coaxed to accept them, but they did impose a tremendous burden for the future on the provinces. There should be some more effective means to control fraud before the Dominion granted further assistance.

Ontario and Quebec did not escape the lash of the prime minister's tongue: "The two central provinces . . . should not be receiving any assistance from the Dominion in connection with direct relief. They were rich and powerful enough to look after themselves." The premiers, said Bennett, must take the initiative:

> Criticism has often been advanced, especially in certain newspapers, that there were too many governments in this Dominion. Any reform along this line, however, could not be forced by the Dominion on the provinces—it must be voluntary. The provinces came in on their own and would have to go out the same way.

Aside from the historical inaccuracy of these last remarks, at least insofar as the prairie provinces were concerned,[77] this extraordinary diatribe was guaranteed to prevent any concessions from the provincial leaders.

The conference simply concluded its business by passing a resolution endorsing the continuation of the existing cost-sharing agreements regarding direct relief until conditions improved.[78] Thus, Bennett stuck to his earlier strategy of blaming the premiers for having "knowingly and deliberately declined to permit the Dominion to save mankind."[79] Like the 1933 meeting, therefore, the first dominion-provincial conference of 1934 was a purely ceremonial affair, orchestrated by a prime minister who had to face the electorate himself before long and was trying to portray his government in the most favourable light. Even had the premiers evidenced much disposition to agree to fundamental constitutional changes, Bennett's methods made certain that nothing significant would occur.

The federal ministers had by now convinced themselves that provincial relief programmes were riddled with waste, their rolls filled with people not really entitled to such assistance. The prime minister later admitted that he would have cut back Ottawa's 33 per cent contribution to direct relief costs sooner had it not been that Conservative governments were facing elections in both Ontario and Saskatchewan on 19 June 1934.[80] One week before election day, Labour Minister W. A. Gordon warned the provinces that the matching grants would end on 15 July.[81] Provincial protests led the deadline to be extended to 15 August, but meanwhile grants were reduced to 25 per cent. The premiers were summoned to Ottawa for the second dominion-provincial conference of the year on 30 July.[82]

Bennett and Gordon had apparently succeeded in persuading their cabinet colleagues that "There is manifest now amongst the provinces an organized effort which is almost Dominion-wide to cast the burden of relief on the Federal Government."[83] The cry of provincial rights could no longer be allowed to conceal a "racket" in which the aged, the infirm, and the handicapped were being loaded onto the relief rolls. The only way to discipline the provinces was to impose a "means" test upon them and unilaterally decide upon a fixed sum of money to be granted to each.

When the conference met, Bennett took the floor to announce this new policy, which he claimed had been forced upon him by the unwillingness of the premiers to surrender any of their constitutional jurisdiction to Ottawa. The provincial politicians were naturally dismayed; they tried to draw the prime minister into a discussion of the principles involved, but he refused. After some fruitless wrangling, the premiers were ordered to appear one by one in the office of the finance minister.[84] There they were received by a group of senior ministers, made their requests, and were told how much money they would receive for relief in the coming months.[85] Bennett proved implacable. In the words of Ontario's new Liberal premier Mitchell Hepburn he told the provinces, "Here's your alimony. Now it's up to you to bring up the children." From the prime minister's point of view, it was simply a matter of placing

> relief upon a proper basis. It is the constitutional responsibility of the provinces to deal with relief. That has never been questioned. We now propose to have no division of authority but to leave it to the provinces to carry out their duty, giving them assistance based upon necessity and means.[86]

Once again, Bennett had indicated that he regarded the dominion-provincial conference not as a forum for the give-and-take of negotiation but as a place in which federal decisions could be announced. At the same time supposed provincial failings could be mercilessly exposed to public scrutiny. Naturally, as Grant Dexter noted in the Manitoba *Free Press*,[87]

> The immediate consequence of this new deal has been to stir up the deepest resentment on the part of the provincial governments. To be told that they are solely responsible for a problem that, patently, is beyond their financial capacity to cope with, to be put off like poor relations with cash handouts conceived in a niggardly, ungenerous way, has been exasperating in the extreme. . . . Had it not been for the all-impressing, inescapable necessity of getting money from Ottawa, there would have been an eruption of temper early in August which would have startled the country.

When the premiers tried to stall by suggesting a discussion of the principles of constitutional change, R. B. Bennett refused to listen. That, he said, could be discussed at another conference in the fall of 1934. And he duly wrote to the premiers a few weeks later inviting them to such a gathering. The invitation made it clear that he conceived it in the same spirit as the two earlier dominion-provincial conferences that year. The discussion would centre upon whether "the provinces were prepared to surrender their exclusive jurisdiction over legislation dealing with such social problems as old age pensions, unemployment and social insurance, hours and conditions of work, minimum wages, and so forth, to the Dominion parliament?" Faced with that prospect, none of the premiers evinced any enthusiasm for such a gathering. Meanwhile, Bennett went ahead and brought in his "New Deal" legislation, which merely asserted federal jurisdiction over unemployment insurance, wages, and hours.[88]

In the spring of 1935 the House of Commons established a Select Committee to consider amendment procedures for the B.N.A. Act. But the provinces made it clear that they now considered a dominion-provincial conference the only appropriate forum for such discussions. Although invited to appear, none of the provincial attorneys-general agreed to do so, and the committee itself recommended that another conference be held to devise an amending formula.[89] When Mackenzie King recaptured power in the fall of 1935, he quickly called a meeting for December, expecting it to serve several purposes. First of all, he intended to use the gathering, as Bennett had done, to announce changes in the federal policies on funding relief, but also he planned to begin working towards certain constitutional amendments.

By 1935, seven of the nine provincial governments were in the hands of the Liberals (Manitoba being controlled by the Progressives and Alberta by Social Credit), and the King government proposed to pay some of its political debts to these friendly premiers by increasing the block grants for relief by about 40 per cent.[90] This announcement was naturally received with enthusiasm. Yet the western provinces were still teetering on the brink of bankruptcy, and federal officials were concerned to strengthen their borrowing capacity. Much attention had come to be focused upon the idea of a national loan council on Australian lines which would supervise provincial borrowing in return for a federal guarantee which might permit markedly lower interest rates. Deputy Minister of Finance W. C. Clark believed that "If all governmental bodies must pay the price for the profligacy or unorthodoxy of any one body, it would seem that some form of control over all, by all, should be established."[91] Yet this would require a constitutional amendment since it derogated from provincial powers, and that, in turn, brought up the whole matter of an amending formula for the B.N.A. Act.

The conference, therefore, broke up into subconferences to discuss the separate issues, but it soon became clear that there were serious differences of opinion on the loan council. As usual, Ontario and Quebec were not at all as enthusiastic about the idea as the less well-off provinces. Mitchell Hepburn (who served as his own provincial treasurer) demanded that any council should be given authority over federal borrowing, too. This was flatly refused by Finance Minister Charles Dunning, who feared that even the hint of debt refunding might harm the country's reputation in New York and London. Hepburn also complained of the plan to have Ottawa retain half the votes on the council and requiring the provinces to make up half the sums lost through any default. "We pay over 40% of all Federal taxation and a lion's share of the other 60%," Hepburn complained. "I do not like the idea." Quebec's treasurer, R. F. Stockwell, supported him, and despite the backing of the western provinces, the committee could only agree to recommend that a further meeting be held.[92]

On the issue of a constitutional amending formula, more progress was made. Ontario and Manitoba presented a detailed proposal which received general approval except from the government of New Brunswick, which clung to an extreme version of the compact theory of Confederation.[93] Yet, solid progress seemed to have been made, and warmed by the prospect of increased federal relief grants, the 1935 dominion-provincial conference adjourned amidst general amity and self-congratulation. Federal Mines Minister T. A. Crerar remained doubtful, however, as to what had actually been done: "On the whole the achievements of the Conference, in my opinion, were not so real as popular opinion seems to be. Everyone, however, remarked on how different it was from the last conference they had with Bennett."[94] Whether or not this new spirit could be translated into substance remained to be seen.

In January 1936, provincial representatives were called together to discuss the loan council further. To meet Hepburn's objections, Charles Dunning now proposed to set up a separate loan council for each province to guarantee its debt. All the provinces agreed, provided that they were not compelled to join one. In fact, they were much more interested in obtaining the right to levy an indirect retail sales tax. The federal government consented to introduce a constitutional amendment covering both, and it passed the House of Commons in the spring of 1936. But strong opposition to the tax change developed amongst the Conservatives in the Senate, which eventually turned down the whole proposal.[95] By that time Ottawa's enthusiasm for the loan council scheme had pretty well evaporated, for it was recognized that the provinces were unwilling to surrender real authority. It had to be admitted that an "effective and permanent Loan Council would destroy the federal principle and ineffective control would simply saddle the Dominion with new liabilities."[96]

The chances of agreement on a constitutional amending formula seemed brighter. When provincial and federal representatives met in early 1936, a broad consensus emerged backing the idea of dividing the provisions of the B.N.A. Act into four categories, each with a different amending procedure. Matters solely concerned with federal jurisdiction would be amended by Parliament alone, while changes which affected some but not all provinces would not require the consent of those not involved. A few key provisions concerning religious and educational rights would need the unanimous consent of all ten legislatures, while the remaining powers could be redistributed with the approval of parliament and six of the nine provincial legislatures representing 55 per cent of the nation's population. Despite this general agreement, however, New Brunswick clung obstinately to its insistence on unanimous consent, although the other provinces seem not to have taken its objections very seriously.[97] But the failure to reach agreement meant a loss of momentum, and the federal government seems to have become content to let matters drift as before.

Any impression that beginning in 1935 the dominion-provincial conference became the arena for taking key national decisions is thus largely mistaken. Although the cordiality of the gathering may have contrasted with those under Bennett, the purposes of the conference were much the same: to announce new federal policies in suitable circumstances. The effort to agree upon significant constitutional changes foundered upon the unwillingness of certain provinces to surrender their powers, while Ottawa began to have second thoughts about the whole process. Ceremonial politics remained the order of the day.

Further evidence that the dominion-provincial conference had not yet become an all-important body was soon forthcoming. Mackenzie King could not ignore the social and economic problems of the country. The western provinces still risked bankruptcy; many municipalities had exhausted their financial resources in the fight against unemployment; Canada still lacked any comprehensive national programmes of social insurance. All these facts seemed to point in the direction of a redistribution of constitutional and financial responsibilities amongst the different levels of government. Yet King turned not to the conference of premiers for solutions but to the time-honoured device of a royal commission.

Originally conceived to deal with the financial problems of the western provinces, the Royal Commission on Dominion-Provincial Relations was broadened in 1937 into a full-scale study of the balance of jurisdiction and fiscal capacity.[98] Testimony was collected not only from the provincial governments but from all manner of public and private interest groups as well.[99] Meanwhile, King set himself the task of securing the agreement of each of the premiers *individually* to an amendment to the B.N.A. Act to permit Ottawa to establish a national scheme of unemployment insurance.[100]

Neither the consent of all of the premiers nor the report of the royal commission were received until early 1940.[101] By that time Canada's economic situation had changed markedly owing to the outbreak of war. Prosperity was reviving and with it employment so that the burden of relief was gradually lifting. After his sweeping victory in the 1940 election, Mackenzie King felt little inclination to discuss constitutional issues while the fighting lasted. When Premier John Bracken of Manitoba pressed him to call a dominion-provincial conference to discuss the Rowell-Sirois Report, the prime minister replied,

> With the war in progress it would certainly be felt by many that the government should await developments before seeking to bring the provinces as a whole into conference with the Dominion on matters so all-important as those dealt with in the Commission's report.[102]

Other influences were at work, however. Officials in the Department of Finance and the Bank of Canada were concerned that some of the provinces might yet prove unable to cope with their crushing load of debt. At the same time, skyrocketing government spending seemed to make some rationalization and streamlining of the system of taxation essential.[103] As a result, King was persuaded to send Finance Minister J. L. Ilsley on a tour of provincial capitals to consult the premiers about their willingness to hand over collection of all succession duties and income taxes to Ottawa. Ilsley received a particularly cool response from Hepburn, who had been sparring with King for the previous five years. As a result, the prime minister concluded that there was no use calling a dominion-provincial conference to discuss constitutional and financial questions.[104]

Ilsley and his officials continued to argue, however, that such a meeting would have symbolic value. Even if it failed to reach agreement, the premiers could be warned in no uncertain terms that tax reforms were inevitable because of the war. At last King reluctantly agreed that a conference would

> serve the advantage of enabling our government to state clearly the financial problem as it presents itself to the government at this time in the war. It will lay the groundwork for such action as may shortly become imperative, and it should help to advance the necessary reforms by at least a step.[105]

In other words, the conference would lay the groundwork for the announcement of a decision already taken by the federal authorities.[106]

King recognized, however, that the conference posed certain special problems. For the first time there existed, in the form of the royal commission report, a comprehensive proposal for financial and constitutional change. But the prime minister was determined not to tie himself too tightly to the recommendations for he gradually became convinced that the meeting would "amount to nothing" in view of the opposition expressed by Hepburn. He drafted his opening statement with the aim of constructing "a mattress that would make it easy for the trapeze performers as they dropped to the ground one by one. I have never believed that the Conference could succeed at this time of the war." Ilsley agreed. All he wanted was to have the premiers' view of the report "properly stated and the whole break up without too much friction."[107] This would open the way for immediate tax changes without ruling out the possibility of returning to the recommendations as a part of postwar reconstruction.

By the time the premiers arrived in Ottawa on 14 January 1941, it was clear that there were three factions. Bracken of Manitoba, W. J. Patterson of Saskatchewan, A. S. Macmillan of Nova Scotia, and Thane Campbell of Prince Edward Island approved of the report's recommendations. Adelard Godbout of Quebec and J. B. McNair of New Brunswick were cordial but noncommittal, while Hepburn had rallied T. D. Pattullo of British Columbia and William Aberhart of Alberta to oppose the changes. Expecting little agreement, the federal government took pains to emphasize the ritualistic aspect:

> It was decided . . . to surround the Conference with all the dignity possible, especially in its opening session. It was arranged that this opening session would be held in the House of Commons chamber, with all the members of the Federal Government who were in Ottawa and with the Provincial delegates and their advisors on the floor of the chamber. In addition, many Members of Parliament were present. The result was that practically every seat in the House of Commons was occupied. The general public had the galleries. In this setting, the Prime Minister sat at the head of the Clerk's Table and the nine premiers were seated around it in order of their precedence.[108]

As Edelman suggests in *The Symbolic Uses of Politics,* the setting itself had become evidence of the significance of the event. To further emphasize the point, it was decided to make a verbatim transcript of the entire proceedings to be published. Such transcripts had often been made in the past by the federal authorities for their own purposes, but to that date the published records of the conferences (when records were published at all)* had consisted solely of a précis with the exception of the opening and closing statements at the 1935 conference. Bennett's finance minister once defended this practice of meeting *in camera:* "I cannot see how a conference can succeed if it is public. Certainly, it cannot be a conference in the true sense under those conditions and decidedly not one in which concessions can be made." Since agreement was not the aim of the 1941 conference, concessions would not be required. Mackenzie King did, however, balk at the idea of a recording of the conference being made for posterity. He expressed his opposition to "dramatizing situations of the kind,"[109] by which he meant that the stump oratory of a William Aberhart or a Mitchell Hepburn was likely to make more compelling listening than his own pedantic dronings.

Nonetheless, when the conference opened, King himself could not avoid sitting through a stinging denunciation by Hepburn, who complained that his meddling with the constitution in wartime amounted to "national vandalism." The other premiers then said their pieces as predicted, including a long, tedious address by Bracken in favour of the Rowell-Sirois recommendations. King then announced that the premiers would meet *in camera* with Ernest Lapointe and T. A. Crerar the following morning to settle an agenda.[110] This meeting, which one observer called "the god-damnedest circus and exhibition you can imagine," reached no agreement because Hepburn, backed up by Aberhart and Pattullo, refused to agree to the creation of a series of committees to deal in detail with the royal commission's report.[111] When the conference reconvened in the afternoon, therefore, King simply called upon his finance minister to read a prepared statement warning of the need for drastic changes in the tax system to finance the war effort. Hepburn insisted upon replying, and each of the other premiers then had his say, followed by a number of federal ministers who took the floor to rebut criticisms. By six o'clock in the evening, it was clear that further discussion was fruitless, and King insisted upon adjourning the conference despite pleas from several provincial leaders to keep on talking in the hope of arriving at some consensus.[112]

King had achieved what he had set out to do, and as usual he concluded that the results had been most satisfactory:

> Far from being a failure the conference has resulted in achieving beyond expectation the principal aim for which it was called, namely the avoidance of any excuse for protest on the part of the provincial

*See the notes to Appendix A.

> governments once the Dominion government begins, as it will be obliged very soon to do, to invade fields of taxation which up to the present have been monopolized in whole or in part by some of the provinces.
>
> We have now been told that we have the power to tax where we please, and have been invited to go as far as we believe the war effort demands. You can imagine what would have happened some months hence had no conference been called and what by custom had become provincial fields of taxation had been invaded in any way by the federal government.[113]

Thus, this ceremonial gathering had served a real purpose, and within a few months Finance Minister Ilsley would introduce a budget which did just that, offering the provinces compensation if they would sign Wartime Tax Agreements.[114]

By the time of the Second World War, the conference of first ministers had evolved into an institution of some significance, but this had been a gradual process then not completed. Beginning with the first meeting in 1887, all of the interprovincial conferences up to 1926 were aimed at reinforcing the stature and legitimacy of the premiers (or in Edelman's words designed "to establish or reinforce a particular definition of self in a public official"). By meeting in Quebec City in 1887 and 1902, the premiers had attempted to demonstrate their rightful role as "Fathers of Re-Confederation" by harking back to the Quebec conference of 1864. Thus, they aimed at "legitimizing a series of future acts . . . and thereby maximizing the chance of acquiescence in them and of compliance with the rules they embody." This choice of setting acknowledged the need, again in Edelman's terms, of impressing the public rather than a single individual, in this case the prime minister, through logical demonstration. This attention to ceremony was not, then, incidental, but a means to the very purpose which the premiers sought to achieve.

In practical terms the interprovincial conferences held in 1887, 1902, 1906, 1910, 1913, and 1926 produced very little beyond a revision in the subsidy arrangements. These gatherings could do little more than attempt to provide evidence of the importance and unanimity of the premiers. When the latter was sorely lacking, as in 1910, the meetings quickly adjourned. Sir Wilfrid Laurier was a shrewd enough politician to recognize that these conferences might be made to serve *his* purposes, too. He let the premiers understand that he might attend to their demands but only after providing them with a clear sense of exactly what he was prepared to concede. And he insisted that the provincial leaders be unanimous (or almost so). They could present their requests and the federal authorities might grant them as a matter of grace-and-favour.

When the provinces failed to agree, as in 1910 and 1913 about the parliamentary representation of the Maritime provinces, the initiative reverted to the federal government, which did not hesitate to act unilaterally. If the demands of the premiers seemed too extravagant, as in requesting that 10 per cent of all customs and excise revenues be added to the subsidy in 1913, the federal government could simply ignore them. The crucial weakness of the interprovincial conference as an institution lay in the absence of the federal representatives from the negotiating table. This reduced the provinces to supplicants for Ottawa's favours. To this day the same problem plagues the annual premiers' conference in the summer, which is usually treated more as a pleasant holiday than as a serious business meeting.

Beginning in 1918 federal ministers did take their seats with the premiers (except in 1926), but the results were less dramatic than might have been expected. Just as Laurier had recognized that periodic conferences might have their uses in relieving provincial discontent, the Ottawa men realized that a dominion-provincial conference made a perfect backdrop against which to announce decisions already taken. Sometimes there was some preliminary discussion with the provinces, as in 1931, but more often the federal cabinet simply made up its mind what it wanted to do, then proclaimed it, as at the two conferences in 1918, in 1927, the meeting in July 1934, and in 1935. Lastly, there were the gatherings which ostensibly had a purpose, but which were, in reality, intended to achieve nothing. Their advantage lay in shifting the blame for inaction off federal shoulders and putting in place the groundwork for subsequent unilateral action by Ottawa. The conferences of 1933, January 1934, and 1941 would fit into this category.

Only on the issue of constitutional amendment was there much real intergovernmental negotiation in 1927, 1931, and 1935. The gradual acceptance of the compact theory of Confederation implied consultation with the provinces, and the dominion-provincial conference was the obvious vehicle. Beginning in 1927 the King government made some efforts to develop an amending formula for the B.N.A. Act, and in 1936 agreement was almost reached. But such conferences were not well adapted to the generation of comprehensive proposals concerning the restructuring of the federal system. In 1937 Mackenzie King turned that task over to a royal commission instead. The circumstances of 1941, however, rendered agreement improbable: three of the premiers were opposed to the commission's recommendations, and the prime minister had little enthusiasm for pursuing the matter. Thus, the wartime conference provided the illusion of consultation rather than the reality.

By that time, though, fairly regular meetings of the first ministers had become an accepted fact, reinforced by the solemnity and sense of purpose which surrounded them. Key national issues were *supposed* to be addressed at such conferences. And after 1945 they did become important forums for the discussion of national issues and the reshaping of the federal system. Moreover, their ceremonial aspect diminished markedly, and real negotiations began to take place. The 1945 Reconstruction Conference, for instance, saw the presentation of the first comprehensive set of constitutional proposals generated by the federal bureaucracy and of formal responses by the provinces.[115] That proved to be the beginning of a lengthy series of intergovernmental negotiations which gradually brought about important changes in the distribution of jurisdiction, such as federal old age pensions and tax-sharing agreements.

Ironically, however, the process which produced the new constitutional arrangements of 1982 really commenced with one final purely ceremonial gathering. In November 1967, the Confederation of Tomorrow Conference was convened by Premier John Robarts of Ontario, atop a bank tower in Toronto, to "examine Confederation as it is today, to take stock of 100 years, to examine the areas of agreement and disagreement and to explore what can be done to ensure a strong and united Canada."[116] As with Mercier's and Mowat's initiative in 1887, this meeting was strongly opposed by federal officials, who viewed it as a derogation of their authority. But the premiers went ahead anyway, each stating their views as weightily as possible to confirm their images as far-sighted statesmen of a re-Confederation. Thereafter commenced a decade and a half of hard bargaining before the agreement of November 1981 was finally arrived at.

The process by which ceremonial institutions like these conferences acquired real authority in the course of time is one familiar to historians. There are some striking parallels, for instance, with the rise of the English Parliament in the thirteenth century. Then, powerful barons were determined to curb the powers of the monarch. In 1215, they tried to bind the feckless King John to a written agreement, but he quickly made it clear that he had no intention of abiding by the Great Charter he had been forced to sign at Runnymede. During the long reign of Henry III (1216–72), however, Parliament developed into a body which compelled the king to attend to the views of his most powerful subjects or face open revolt. When Henry failed to comply with the Provisions of Oxford, passed by Parliament in 1258 to create a formal supervisory council, the result was civil war. Gradually, Parliament became the institution through which the barony made its collective wishes known and enforced its will.[117]

In Canada, the provincial barons had never to resort to open warfare to establish the conference of first ministers as the proper forum for the discussion of critical national issues. Seeking some institutional arrangement to express their views, they hit upon the interprovincial conference in the 1880's. Although largely ceremonial at first, in the course of time these conferences of first ministers did become the place for making some important decisions. Discerning whether such gatherings will remain so important under the new constitutional amending formula, which requires the approval of parliament and the assemblies of at least seven provinces with 50 per cent of the total population, is, happily, a task which falls to political scientists rather than historians.

APPENDIX A

Interprovincial and Dominion-Provincial Conferences 1887–1941

Meetings between federal and provincial representatives have occurred right from the time of Confederation. For instance, in 1871 representatives of all the provinces met with federal officials at Ottawa to discuss immigration. This list, however, includes only those conferences at which most of the provinces were represented by their first ministers, no private parties were present and which were styled as interprovincial or dominion-provincial conferences.[1]

Interprovincial Conference, Quebec, 20–28 October 1887
Interprovincial Conference, Quebec, 18–20 December 1902[2]
Interprovincial Conference, 8–13 October 1906[3]
Interprovincial Conference, 9 December 1910
Interprovincial Conference, 27–29 October 1913
Dominion-Provincial Conference, 13–16 February 1918[4]
Dominion-Provincial Conference, 19 November–4 December 1918
Interprovincial Conference, 7–9 June 1926[5]
Dominion-Provincial Conference, 3–10 November 1927
Dominion-Provincial Conference, 7–8 April 1931[6]
Dominion-Provincial Conference, 10 April 1932[7]
Dominion-Provincial Conference, 17–19 January 1933[8]
Dominion-Provincial Conference, 17–19 January 1934[9]
Dominion-Provincial Conference, 30–31 July 1934[10]
Dominion-Provincial Conference, 9–13 December 1935[11]
Dominion-Provincial Conference, 14–15 January 1941

NOTES TO APPENDIX A

1. On the 1871 conference, see V. C. Fowke, *Canadian Agricultural Policy, The Historical Pattern* (Toronto: University of Toronto Press, 1946; reprint, 1978), p. 155; the official records of some but by no means all of these gatherings were published in two volumes in 1951, entitled *Dominion-Provincial and Interprovincial Conferences from*

1887 to 1926/Conférences Fédérales-Provinciales et Conférences Interprovinciales de 1887 à 1926, and *Dominion-Provincial Conferences, November 3–10, 1927, December 9–13, 1935, January 14–15, 1941/Conférences Fédérales-Provinciales, Du 3 au 10 novembre 1927, Du 9 au 13 décembre 1935, Les 14 et 15 janvier 1941* (Ottawa: King's Printer, 1951). The first volume omits any record of the first conference of 1918, and the second omits the conferences between 1931 and 1934.

2. This conference reconvened in Ottawa on 27 January 1903 with all the premiers present to ratify its resolutions and present them to the federal cabinet. See Ontario, *Sessional Papers*, 1903, no.4. All subsequent conferences were held in Ottawa.
3. This meeting and the one in 1910 are referred to in the table of contents of the official compilation (see above, n.1) as "Dominion-Provincial Conferences" although the page headings read "Interprovincial Conference." Laurier officially convened the 1906 conference and made an address of welcome before withdrawing. There were some joint discussions between federal and provincial delegates, apparently on the issue of sharing the costs of the administration of justice, but the main discussions of the subsidy question were conducted by the premiers alone and the resolutions submitted to the federal government as in 1902. The federal government does not appear to have been formally involved at all in the 1910 conference.
4. The printed agenda of the conference is headed *Conference, Dominion and Provincial Governments, Canada, February, 1918* (Ottawa, 13 February 1918). A copy may be found in the Sir George Foster Papers, vol. 44, Public Archives of Canada [hereafter PAC]. See also "Minutes of the Conference of Dominion and Provincial Governments, February, 1918, Confidential," in Sir Robert Borden Papers, OC 529, ibid.
5. Between 1918 and 1926 there were three gatherings referred to as Dominion-Provincial Conferences which are not discussed in this paper. In April 1920 there was a meeting of a "Dominion-Provincial Commission appointed to consider the subject of Uniformity of Labour Laws." All the provinces except P.E.I. were represented, but the delegates included many private parties. The federal delegation under Labour Minister G. D. Robertson included his deputy minister as well as Tom Moore of the T.L.C. and a representative of the C.M.A. and the Employers' Association. A copy of the "Summary Report, Proceedings and Discussions" of the commission may be found in Sir Robert Borden Papers, RLB 3002. In September 1922, the federal government called a meeting of federal and provincial ministers to discuss unemployment. Only Ontario and Nova Scotia were represented by their premiers, and Mackenzie King withdrew after giving the opening address. See "Report of Proceedings of Unemployment Conference, held at Ottawa, September 5–6–7, 1922" in R. B. Bennett Papers, 12531–825, PAC. In November 1924, there was a conference on taxation called by the federal finance minister. Only P.E.I. was represented by its premier, and B.C. and Saskatchewan sent no representatives. See Attorney-General's Records, 1927, no. 2981 for "Minutes of Conference on Taxation Between Representatives of the Dominion and the Provinces, Held at Ottawa, November 11, 1924," mimeo, Archives of Ontario.
6. See the typed transcript, "Report of the Dominion-Provincial Conference, 1931" in R. B. Bennett Papers, 115899–923, and "Dominion-Provincial Conference, 1931, Minutes of Meetings," Department of External Affairs Records, RG 25, vol. 760, PAC.
7. No formal records seem to have been kept of this meeting. It was attended by only four premiers (from Nova Scotia, New Brunswick, Quebec, and Alberta) with the other provinces being represented by ministers or officials. See *Globe*, 11 April 1932.
8. "Minutes of Meetings of Dominion-Provincial Conference, January 17th–19th, 1933, Ottawa," R. B. Bennett Papers, 346894–955, and "Resolutions of the Dominion-Provincial Conference, January 17–19, 1933," ibid., 116160.
9. *Report of the Dominion-Provincial Conference, 1934* (Ottawa: King's Printer, 1934). See also "Minutes of the Dominion-Provincial Conference, 1934," R. B. Bennett Papers, vol. 181.
10. "Dominion-Provincial Meeting on Relief, July 30–31, 1934, notes by Dominion Commissioner of Unemployment Relief Harry Hereford" and Memorandum re.

"Dominion-Provincial Meeting on Relief, July 31, 1934" by Harry Hereford, R. B. Bennett Papers, vol. 182.

11. There are minutes of a number of the subconferences in which most of the business was done to be found in Dominion-Provincial Conference Records, RG 47, vols. 60, 62, 65, PAC.

NOTES

1. Macdonald to Mercier, 4 October 1887, John A. Macdonald Papers, vol. 576B, Public Archives of Canada [hereafter PAC].
2. Murray Edelman, *The Symbolic Uses of Politics* (Urbana, ILL: University of Illinois Press, 1967), p. 98.
3. The phrase was used by delegate E. B. Chandler of New Brunswick at the Quebec conference in 1864.
4. On the compact theory, see Ramsay Cook, *Provincial Autonomy, Minority Rights and the Compact Theory, 1867–1921,* Studies of the Royal Commission on Bilingualism and Biculturalism, 4 (Ottawa: Queen's Printer, 1969); Macdonald expressed his views in a letter to Brown Chamberlin, 26 October 1868, reprinted in Joseph Pope, ed., *Correspondence of Sir John Macdonald* (Toronto: Doubleday, 1921), p. 75. The *Globe,* 9 March 1888 is quoted in Cook, *Provincial Autonomy,* p. 41; the irrelevance of the federal government is naturally emphasized because of Macdonald's recent refusal to attend the 1887 conference.
5. The classic dissection (and refutation) of the compact theory is Norman McL. Rogers, "The Compact Theory of Confederation," *Proceedings of the Canadian Political Science Association* (1931), pp. 205–30.
6. The Quebec Conference of 1864 spent a full week on the Senate, more time than on any other issue. See G. P. Browne, comp., *Documents on the Confederation of British North America, A Compilation based on Sir Joseph Pope's Confederation Documents supplements by Other Official Material* (Toronto: McClelland and Stewart, 1969) and also Christopher Armstrong, *The Politics of Federalism: Ontario's Relations with the Federal Government, 1867–1942* (Toronto: University of Toronto Press, 1981), pp. 9–12.
7. Mercier to Oliver Mowat, 8 March 1887, Attorney-General's Records, 1887, no. 1232, Provincial Archives of Ontario [hereafter PAO].
8. *Dominion-Provincial and Interprovincial Conferences from 1887 to 1926/Conférences Fédérales-Provinciales et Conférences Interprovinciales de 1887 à 1926* (Ottawa: King's Printer, 1951), p. 11.
9. J. C. Morrison, "Oliver Mowat and the Development of Provincial Rights in Ontario: A Study in Dominion-Provincial Relations, 1867–1896," in *Three History Theses* (Toronto: Ontario Department of Public Records and Archives, 1961), pp. 265–77; *Conferences from 1887 to 1926,* 20–25.
10. Macdonald to Oliver Mowat, 3 December 1888, in Pope, *Correspondence of Macdonald,* p. 433.
11. Cook, *Provincial Autonomy,* p. 44, notes, "After 1896 provincial rights and the compact theory attained a position close to motherhood in the scale of Canadian political values. It would be difficult to find a prominent politician who was not willing to pay at least lip-service to the principle of provincial rights and its theoretical underpinning, the compact theory." On disallowance, see G. V. La Forest, *Disallowance and Reservation of Provincial Legislation* (Ottawa: Queen's Printer, 1955), pp. 53–57.

12. See, for instance, Laurier to George W. Ross, 22 January 1902, personal, 61597–8, Sir Wilfrid Laurier Papers, PAC.
13. *Conferences from 1887 to 1926,* p. 33.
14. Ibid., pp. 38–44.
15. Ontario, *Sessional Papers,* 1903, no. 4.
16. Laurier to G. H. Murray, 23 November 1905, private, 103575; Laurier to Onésiphore Turgeon, 19 September 1906, confidential, 113785, Laurier Papers, PAC.
17. Lomer Gouin to Laurier, 1 August 1905, 100298 ibid.; *Conferences from 1887 to 1926,* pp. 53–63.
18. J. A. Maxwell, *Federal Subsidies to Provincial Governments in Canada* (Cambridge, MA: Harvard University Press, 1938), pp. 109–14.
19. *Conferences from 1887 to 1926,* p. 63.
20. Ibid., p. 67.
21. Ibid., pp. 71–91; R. C. Brown, *Robert Laird Borden, A Biography,* vol. 1, *1854–1914* (Toronto: Macmillan, 1975), pp. 184–87.
22. Sir Robert Borden, diary, typescript, 28 October 1913, Sir Robert Borden Papers, PAC.
23. *Conferences from 1887 to 1926,* p. 83.
24. Paul Gérin-Lajoie, *Constitutional Amendment in Canada* (Toronto: University of Toronto Press, 1950), pp. 84–91.
25. *Conference, Dominion and Provincial Governments, Canada, February, 1918* (Ottawa: 13 February 1918), Sir George E. Foster Papers, vol. 44, PAC; T. A. Crerar to Borden, 2 February 1918, 57896, Borden Papers, ibid.
26. Diary, 15 February 1918 ibid; OC 529, minutes of the Conference of Dominion and Provincial Governments, February 1918, confidential.
27. *Conferences from 1887 to 1926,* pp. 95–103.
28. Stewart to Taschereau, 13 March 1926, 118747, W. L. Mackenzie King Papers, PAC.
29. Taschereau to King, 2 April 1926, personal, 118759 ibid; Ferguson to Taschereau, 17 March 1926, 118746; *Conferences from 1887 to 1926,* pp. 107–14.
30. Bracken to Ferguson, 16 April 1926, Howard Ferguson Papers, PAO.
31. Memorandum to Mr. King re. Proposal Provincial Conference, 26 March 1926, 118756–7, King Papers.
32. *Conferences from 1887 to 1926,* p. 110.
33. Ernest R. Forbes, *Maritime Rights, The Maritime Rights Movement 1919–1927, A Study in Canadian Regionalism* (Montreal: McGill-Queen's University Press, 1979), pp. 124–57.
34. Ibid., pp. 158–81.
35. W. L. M. King, diary, 3 November 1927, King Papers.
36. King to Gardiner, 30 August 1927, personal and confidential, 121728–31, ibid.
37. Gardiner to King, 6 September 1927, personal and confidential, 121735–6 and reply, 26 September 1927, pp. 121737–8, ibid.
38. Ibid., Ferguson to Gardiner, 23 September 1927, 121740–1 and reply, 28 September 1927, 121742–3, ibid.
39. Ibid., Gardiner to King, 1 October 1927, personal, 121757–8 and reply, 4 October 1927, 121759, ibid.
40. Diary, 1 November 1927, ibid.
41. "Précis of Discussions, Dominion-Provincial Conference, November 3 to 10, 1927," in *Dominion-Provincial Conferences, November 3–10, 1927, December 9–13, 1935, January 14–15, 1941/Conférences Fédérales-Provinciales, Du 3 au 10 novembre, 1927, Du 9 au 13 décembre, 1935, Les 14 et 15 janvier, 1941* (Ottawa: King's Printer, 1951), pp. 2–38; Ferguson's speech is précised on p. 25.
42. "Amendment of the British North America Act, The Prime Minister's office," 1927, by Norman McLeod Rogers, 388226–81 R. B. Bennett Papers, PAC; the quotation is from ibid.; W. L. M. King, diary, 27 October 1927, King Papers.
43. "Précis of Discussions, Dominion-Provincial Conference, 1927," 16298–312, which is actually a verbatim transcript, Bennett Papers.

44. Ibid.
45. *Conferences, 1927, 1935, 1941,* "Précis . . . 1927," p. 9.
46. Gérin-Lajoie, *Constitutional Amendment,* pp. 93–104.
47. *Amendment of the Canadian Constitution, Statement and Protest by the Prime Minister of the Province of Ontario* (Toronto: King's Printer, 1930).
48. Taschereau to Bennett, 19 September 1930, 293939, Bennett Papers.
49. "Dominion Provincial Conference, 1931, Memoranda regarding questions of provincial concern arising out of the recommendations of the Conference on the Operation of Dominion Legislation, 1929, and the Imperial Conference, 1930, for the enactment of the proposed Statute of Westminister, 1931," 7 April 1931, confidential, 116052–159, especially p. 17, ibid.
50. Bennett to George S. Henry, 23 February 1931, 115774–7, ibid.
51. C. H. Cahan to W. H. Price, 23 March 1931, personal, Howard Ferguson Papers.
52. Henry to Ferguson, 10 April 1931, ibid.
53. "Dominion-Provincial Conference, 1931, Minutes of Meetings," External Affairs Records, RG 25, vol. 760, PAC.
54. "Report of the Dominion Provincial Conference, 1931," 115899–923, Bennett Papers.
55. The Toronto *Evening Telegram,* 9 April 1931 appeared to take the same line: "King George is suffering from a bad cold at the time the constitutional cobblers are busy at Ottawa. And the fact that thousands are interested in the King's health to one who cares anything about the Ottawa Conference is a significant indication of the trend of public opinion in Canada."
56. *Globe,* 11 April 1932; only four premiers were present.
57. Memorandum from A. E. Merriam to R. K. Finlayson, 12 December 1932, External Affairs Records, RG 25, vol. 716; Bennett went off to England leaving instructions that his private secretary, Finlayson, and Undersecretary of State O. D. Skelton should draw up the agenda for the conference and submit it to the cabinet for approval.
58. Bennett to Henry, 3 January 1933, George S. Henry Papers. Other agenda items included uniform company law, uniform statistical information, jurisdiction over insurance companies, and regulation of trucks competing with railways on interprovincial routes.
59. Henry to Bennett, 4 January 1933, 347166, Bennett Papers.
60. See Appendix A, n5.
61. Bennett to Henry, 5 January 1933, 347167, Bennett Papers. The government of Saskatchewan also enquired whether only the legal and constitutional aspects of unemployment insurance were to be discussed or whether its minister of labour ought to be present. The federal government replied that while only the former aspects were intended for discussion, the premiers could bring with them any advisors they chose. J. A. Merkley to W. A. Gordon, 23 December 1932, 347158 and R. K. Finlayson to Merkley, 3 January 1933, 347160, ibid.
62. *Conferences, 1927, 1935, 1941,* "Dominion-Provincial Conference, 1935, Report of Proceedings," pp. 27–28. It was agreed, however, that the first ministers would meet informally with the mayors.
63. The commons, for instance, were not invariably summoned to parliament during the thirteenth century.
64. "Minutes of Meetings of Dominion-Provincial Conference, January 17th–19th, 1933, Ottawa," 346894–955, Bennett Papers.
65. Memorandum from R. L. Foster to W. H. Price, 7 January 1933, Attorney-General's Records, 1933, no. 31.
66. "Minutes . . . 1933," 346894–955, Bennett Papers.
67. Ibid., see "Resolutions of Dominion-Provincial Conference, January 17–19, 1933," 116160–2.
68. Grant Dexter to Dafoe, 25 January 1932 [sic, 1933], vol. 6, J. W. Dafoe Papers, PAC.

69. Memorandum from R. L. Foster to Edward Bayly, 11 January 1933, Attorney-General's Records, 1933, no. 31.
70. Ibid., 21 January 1933.
71. Pattullo to King, 17 November 1933, 168264–5, W. L. Mackenzie King Papers.
72. Grant Dexter to Dafoe, 17 January 1934, vol. 7, J. W. Dafoe Papers; Dexter identified these ministers as E. N. Rhodes, C. H. Cahan, E. B. Ryckman, and W. A. Gordon.
73. Bennett to J. T. M. Anderson, 9 March 1933, 165224–5, King Papers; identical letters were sent to John Bracken, J. E. Brownlee, and S. F. Tolmie.
74. Anderson, Brownlee, Bracken and Pattullo to Bennett, 4 December 1933, telegram, 501830–1, Bennett Papers.
75. Bennett to George Henry, 23 December 1933, telegram, 121432, ibid.
76. This account of the conference is derived from "Minutes of the Dominion-Provincial Conference, 1934." vol. 181, ibid.
77. The Prairie provinces, of course, did not come in "on their own" but were created by the federal parliament.
78. *Report of the Dominion Provincial Conference, 1934* (Ottawa: King's Printer, 1934) declared that until unemployment declined "Federal assistance to the Provinces should be continued on the basis of the Provinces dealing with present economic conditions by the distribution of direct relief as provided in the existing agreements between the Dominion and Provinces." The wish was also expressed that "a program of municipal and public works should be undertaken to absorb as large a proportion of the unemployed as possible, and that any such works should be commenced early in the spring in order to be effective in limiting demand for direct relief in the following winter," but without the pledging of federal funds to accomplish this it was obviously no more than a pious wish designed to disguise inactivity.
79. Memorandum from R. L. Foster to Edward Bayly, 11 January 1933, Attorney-General's Records, 1933, no. 31.
80. "Dominion-Provincial Meeting on Relief, July 30–31, 1934," notes by Dominion Unemployment Commissioner Harry Hereford, 121763–82, Bennett Papers.
81. W. A. Gordon to provincial premiers, 12 June 1934, telegram, 485454, ibid.
82. Sir George Perley to provincial premiers, 13 July 1934, 71409, Edgar N. Rhodes Papers, Provincial Archives of Nova Scotia [hereafter PANS].
83. W. A. Gordon to R. B. Bennett, 26 July 1934, 71419, ibid.
84. "Memorandum for the Prime Minister: (The following notes are dictated by General MacNaughton and Mr. Finlayson)," 28 July 1934 vol. 182, Bennett Papers; "Dominion-Provincial Meeting on Relief, July 30–31, 1934," notes by Dominion Unemployment Commissioner Harry Hereford, 121763–82; "Dominion-Provincial Meeting on Relief," 31 July 1934 by Hereford, 121759–60.
85. Memorandum from L. P. D. Tilley to the federal government, 31 July 1934, 71429, Rhodes Papers; John Bracken to R. B. Bennett, 31 July 1934, 71445, ibid; memorandum re Province of Saskatchewan, August 1934, 71476; Taschereau of Quebec insisted on having two weeks to consult his cabinet and municipal officials; see Taschereau to R. B. Bennett, 31 July 1934, 71422, ibid.
86. Hepburn submitted a request but also requested more time to consider; see Memorandum of the province of Ontario, 31 July 1934, Mitchell Hepburn Papers, PAO. The premier is quoted in *Globe,* 1 August 1934. Bennett to W. J. McCully, 6 August 1934, personal, 486476, Bennett Papers.
87. Ibid., 4 September 1934.
88. "Dominion-Provincial Meeting on Relief, July 30–31, 1934," 121763–82, Bennett Papers; Bennett to provincial premiers, 31 August 1934, vol. 182, ibid; *Globe,* 30 October 1934; J. R. H. Wilbur, ed., *The Bennett New Deal: Fraud or Portent?* (Toronto: Copp Clark, 1968).
89. Gérin-Lajoie, *Constitutional Amendment,* pp. 235–43; Canada, House of Commons, Special Committee on the British North America Act, 1935, *Proceedings and Evidence and Report* (Ottawa: King's Printer, 1938).
90. H. Blair Neatby, *William Lyon Mackenzie King,* vol. 3, *1932–1939, The Prism of*

Unity (Toronto: University of Toronto Press, 1976), pp. 148–52.

91. W. C. Clark to Charles Dunning, 7 December 1935, Dominion-Provincial Conference Records, RG 47, vol. 62.
92. *Conferences, 1927, 1935, 1941,* "Dominion-Provincial Conference, 1935, Record of Proceedings,"; Transcript of proceedings of Sub-Conference on Financial Questions, Dominion-Provincial Conference Records, RG 47 vol. 65,; draft minutes of first meeting of Continuing Committee appointed by Sub-Conference on Financial Questions, 13 December 1935, confidential, vol. 62, ibid.
93. "Dominion-Provincial Conference, 1936, Confidential Record of Proceedings of Conference and Sub-Conferences, Ottawa, December 9 to 13, 1935," draft minutes of meetings of committee on constitutional questions, vol. 60, ibid.
94. T. A. Crerar to Dafoe, 17 December 1935, personal, vol. 8, Dafoe Papers.
95. "Proceedings of the Permanent Committee on Financial Questions of the Dominion-Provincial Conference, Ottawa, January 13 & 14, 1936", Dominion-Provincial Conference Records, RG 47, vol. 73; J. H. Perry, *Taxation in Canada* (Toronto: University of Toronto Press, 2d ed., 1953), pp. 163–66.
96. Memorandum from Alexander Skelton re. "Federal-Provincial Finances," 19 March 1936; Dominion-Provincial Conference Records, RG 47, vol. 74; another meeting of ministers was held at the end of 1936 to discuss this matter, with no result; see "The Permanent Committee on Financial Questions of the Dominion-Provincial Conference, Ottawa, December 9, 1936," transcript, 3 vols., vol. 73, ibid., and "Report on the Meetings of the National Finance Committee, Held on December 9th, 10th, and 11th, 1936," attached to Dunning to King, 16 December 1936, 186209–13, W. L. Mackenzie King Papers.
97. Gérin-Lajoie, *Constitutional Amendment,* pp. 245–49; "Dominion-Provincial Conference, 1935, Constitutional Documents for submission to Continuing Committee on Constitutional Questions, Ottawa, January 3, 1936", External Affairs Records, RG 25, vol. 759; W. S. Edwards to O. D. Skelton, 15 February 1936; "Memorandum for Mr. Pickering re. Conference of Attorneys General Held in Ottawa on Monday, March 2, 1926, With Respect to Proposed Amendments to the British North America Act," attached to H. R. L. Henry to T. C. Davis, 4 March 1936, 185695–7, King Papers.
98. Memorandum by W. C. Clark, "Royal Commission on Economic Basis of Confederation," 7 December 1936, confidential, Dominion-Provincial Conference Records, RG 47, vol. 74; T. A. Crerar to Dafoe, 11 January 1937, personal, vol. 10, Dafoe Papers; King to Norman McLarty, 22 March 1937, confidential, 203980, King Papers; J. L. Granatstein, *The Ottawa Men: The Civil Service Mandarins 1935–1957* (Toronto: Oxford University Press, 1982), pp. 59–60.
99. Canada, Royal Commission on Dominion-Provincial Relations, "Evidence," typescript.
100. King to provincial premiers, 5 November 1937, 198234–5, King Papers.
101. King to William Aberhart, 16 January 1940, personal and private, 29958–9, ibid.; Aberhart to King, 22 May 1940, 29965; Alberta was the last holdout after the reservations of New Brunswick and Quebec had been overcome. The release of the *Report* was delayed until 10 May 1940 because there was a federal election under way and King did not want the recommendations to become an issue; see King to John Bracken, 29 January 1940, 30757–8, ibid.
102. King to Bracken, 23 September 1940, 30771, ibid.
103. Graham Towers to King, 15 August 1940, confidential, 43667–72, ibid; "Memorandum on the Report of the Sirois Commission," 11 September 1940, Finance Department Records, RG 19, vol. 2701.
104. A. D. P. Heeney to J. L. Ilsley, 23 September 1940 enclosing "Special Cabinet Committee on Dominion-Provincial Relations Report and Emergency Measures, (Financial and Economic)," 20 September 1940, Secret, ibid.; Grant Dexter to J. W. Dafoe, 17, 25 October 1940, vol. 11, Dafoe Papers.
105. "Report of the Cabinet Sub-Committee Appointed to Consider the Report of the

Royal Commission on Dominion-Provincial Relations,'' n.d. (30 October 1940), Finance Department Records, RG 19, vol. 2701; King to Sir William Mulock, 13 January 1941, 55574–5, King Papers.

106. At least one of the commissioners failed to grasp King's strategy. H. F. Angus wrote, ''I cannot think the P.M. would not have turned the spot-light on himself and the nine provincial premiers if he contemplated proceedings which would make Canada ridiculous or provide him with a grotesque anti-climax. He must have screwed his courage up to the point of risking a public show-down. Can he have done it without any negotiations or understandings?'' Angus to Dafoe, 12 January 1941, personal, vol. 12, Dafoe Papers.
107. King diary, 13 December 1940, quoted in J. W. Pickersgill, *The Mackenzie King Record,* vol. 1, *1939–1944* (Toronto: University of Toronto Press, 1960), p. 159.
108. T. A. Crerar to Dafoe, 16 January 1941, personal and confidential, vol. 12, Dafoe Papers.
109. King diary, 9 January 1941, quoted in Pickersgill, *Mackenzie King Record,* p. 160; Rhodes to P. G. Davies, 26 March 1934, 69253, Rhodes Papers.
110. *Conferences, 1927, 1935, 1941,* ''Dominion-Provincial Conference, Tuesday, January 14, 1941 and Wednesday, January 15, 1941,'' pp. 1–61.
111. Alexander Skelton to Dafoe, 8 February 1941, vol. 12, Dafoe Papers.
112. *Conferences, 1927, 1935, 1941,* ''Conference . . . 1941,'' pp. 69–108.
113. King to A. C. Hardy, 19 January 1941, personal, 49842, King Papers.
114. Armstrong, *Politics of Federalism,* pp. 230–32.
115. Dominion-Provincial Conference on Reconstruction, *Proposals of the Government of Canada* (Ottawa: King's Printer, 1945); Government of Ontario, *Submissions by the Government of Ontario* (Toronto: King's Printer, 1945).
116. Robarts is quoted in Richard Simeon, *Federal-Provincial Diplomacy: The Making of Recent Policy In Canada* (Toronto: University of Toronto Press, 1972), p. 91. Citing Edelman, Simeon notes that the conference was fully staged: ''It was to be a place for discussion, not decision. The agenda was to try to steer clear of contentious issues.''; ibid., p. 92.
117. G. O. Sayles, *The Medieval Foundations of England* (New York: A. S. Barnes and Co., 1961 ed.), chs. 24–25.

III

MANAGING THE POLITICAL COMMUNITY

8

Becoming Canadians: Ottawa's Relations with Maritimers in the First and Twenty-first Years of Confederation

P. B. WAITE

The traditional view of the early years of Confederation is curious. It is well known that New Brunswick history stops utterly after 30 June 1867. Nova Scotia ceases to be of much interest after the Hants by-election and better terms in 1869; it rises briefly above the horizon in 1886, and thereafter it sinks, never to be seen again. Newfoundland history subsists until the autumn election of 1869 when it too goes out of sight, to be seen occasionally in storms, like the Flying Dutchman, a ghost that appears over the sea in bad economic weather. For in 1869 it is time to go west; the Atlantic provinces are consigned to their own devices. By the time Riel has been got safely out of Manitoba in 1870, there is just time to quickly glance at the British Columbians before we head east for the first act of the now famous Prince Edward Island play, "How much did you say the debt allowance was?" Then, after 1 July 1873, Prince Edward Island disappears too, debt allowance, railway and all, and what is left, out there on the Cavendish shore, is the smile of Anne of Green Gables, like the smile of the Cheshire Cat. We have just time to get to Montreal in time for the splendid and latest consignment of correspondence in the Montreal *Herald,* 18 July 1873, on the Pacific Scandal. Thus are we launched into national life.

Everyone knows of course that Confederation began badly; its first year was worse than most people imagine. There was a litany of complaints, and not just Nova Scotia chafed, angry over having been dragooned in: New Brunswick was restless, unhappy, and painfully surprised over the new legislation of 1867–68; Prince Edward Island continued to preen herself on her independence; and Newfoundland had already been inoculated against Confederation by the bitterness of the Nova Scotians and the disappointments of the New Brunswickers.

The first year or, rather, years of Confederation were not easy, not for the dominion government nor for the new provinces. Macdonald's plan for the Northwest Territories, in the act of 1869, was symptomatic of attitudes that had to be refashioned, even partly unlearned. There was more truth than jocularity in the remark of Alexander Campbell, Macdonald's new minister of the interior in 1873, that he was now "Secretary for the Colonies."[1] This perspective—the view from Parliament Hill one might call it—saw the Dominion mainly in terms of the 65 MP's from Quebec and the 82 from Ontario. That there were 19 from Nova Scotia and 15 from New Brunswick was a palpable fact, for there they were, and room had literally to be made for them; the House of Commons chamber had originally been designed for the 130 members of the Legislative Assembly of the Province of Canada; it had now to be stretched to include the 17 MP's that "rep. by pop." added to Ontario, and the 34 from Nova Scotia and New Brunswick. But that stretching of the House of Commons chamber was symptomatic.

The old Province of Canada, though dead, was resurrected. The old officialdom, the officers of the old Legislative Council and of the House of Commons, and the civil service stayed on in Ottawa. Why not? That's where they were already. There would be a few Maritime appointments, but only a few. The new provinces of Ontario and Quebec appointed their own staff; the old civil service of the Province of Canada stayed on with the Dominion of Canada, some five hundred of them, many familiar with the ways of the MP's from Quebec and Ontario. No provision was made to compensate Nova Scotian or New Brunswick civil servants whose offices had been abolished by Confederation; it seems not to have been thought of, or expected. Any Province of Canada employees so affected were pensioned. A debate arose in March 1868 in the Senate on this topic. Senator Holmes of Nova Scotia said he could not consider the officers of the old Legislative Council of the Province of Canada as being proper officers of the Senate. What right, asked his Nova Scotian colleague, W. J. Ritchie, had "most of these employees to be here at all? . . . Why not bring our officials from Fredericton and Halifax at the same time? . . . What would be said if we should come to the House and ask for pensions for the old servants of the Maritime Provinces[?]"[2] The Parliament Hill of 30 June 1867 was nearly the same Parliament Hill 1 July 1867, with scarcely a perceptible shift in thought, deed, or emphasis.

The first session of the Canadian Parliament only made things worse. All the new changes seemed to be dictated by what had previously been done in central Canada, in tariffs, postage, law, systems of administration even, almost all unknown in Nova Scotia and New Brunswick, and some of them distinctly retrograde in character. It was a set of issues that made pro-Confederate New Brunswickers despair and Nova Scotians say venomously, "I told you so."

Prior to 1867 the closest approach the British North American provinces had made to a *Zollverein* was in 1854–66, during the American Reciprocity Treaty. Customs lines between the provinces in natural products were then obliterated by concurrent legislation. The complete interprovincial free trade proposed by Confederation was the system that existed up until March 1866, but now it was expanded to include manufactured goods. After 1 July 1867, te new Dominion of Canada tariff was mainly tariff assimilation to the old Province of Canada model. True, downward revision of the Province of Canada tariff in 1866 had reduced nonpreference, or general rate tariffs, to 15 per cent, a concession to Maritime opinion. It is difficult to gauge the effects of the new Canadian duties technically, since old Province of Canada duties had been largely *ad valorem,* the Maritime ones specific. At the very beginning of the new tariff regime, there was some complacency on both sides, Nova Scotia and New Brunswick turning over their tariff administrations to the Dominion of Canada apparently without much regret. That did not last long. The central Canadian style of administration came as a shock. One has the impression that the old colonial administration in Nova Scotia, and especially in New Brunswick, had been rather easygoing. The new and more rigorous dominion customs-house procedures were mightily resented. These included the retention of the original invoices by the customs department; the actual examination of one package in every ten; the refusal to allow cash discounts as deductions from dutiable value; and even the charging of duty on the casks in which molasses and rum came. Thomas Worthington, the commissioner of customs, replied to complaints about these practices loftily, "Experience has taught us that, in order to be effective, laws for the collection of our revenues can hardly fail to be inquisitorial in their action . . . and exceedingly annoying to those who are subject to their operations."[3]

The first tariff bill brought in by Tilley, the new minister of customs, in 1867 was the act that had been in force in the Province of Canada with only minor alterations.[4] The effect was to produce very extensive changes from old New Brunswick and Nova Scotia tariff structures, especially the latter. Tea, molasses, and sugar would go up to about double the tariff it had been before; flour would be twenty-five cents a barrel, where in New Brunswick it had been free.[5] The duty on spirits was set at eighty cents a gallon for brandy, rum, gin, and whisky. This was not a serious inconvenience for Nova Scotia, where the duty on rum had been forty cents but was raised just prior to Confederation to seventy-five cents. Jones of Halifax proposed that the duty should be sixty-three cents, exactly the excise tax on a gallon of Canadian rye. Most Nova Scotians and New Brunswickers drank rum, not rye, and it seemed sensible to Jones, who was an importer, to make the respective taxes equal. It did not work. Rose's tax was not unreasonable, but he might have avoided rubbing in the five-cent increase on rum. He said that if New Brunswick and Nova Scotia did not like it, they should "accustom themselves to Upper Canada rye."[6]

On 16 December 1867, Finance Minister John Rose brought in the stamp tax—stamps on cheques, promissory notes, and official documents—a tax familiar in the Province of Canada, but unknown in the Maritimes. It was a tax, as E. M. McDonald of Lunenburg observed, that "had cost England half this continent." It seemed to stir up memories in Nova Scotia of the stamp-tax agitation in Halifax of 1765. Nor was Rose very accommodating to objections. The stamp tax, he said, would be in force—he used the word "continue"—and the government "intended putting it in force in the Maritime Provinces at the earliest possible moment."[7]

On top of that was piled postage for newspapers. Nova Scotia and New Brunswick made no charge for the transmission of newspapers through the mail; the Province of Canada did. The Macdonald government's strategy was to reduce existing rates of newspaper postage in Ontario and Quebec while imposing it on New Brunswick and Nova Scotia. In vain did even Charles Tupper urge that it be postponed:

> If ever there ever was a time when it was necessary for the interests of the whole Dominion that just the sort of information which newspapers conveyed, should be disseminated through all the Provinces, it was now. He was most averse from touching upon local or sectional prejudices, but it could not be denied that there was a considerable amount of mutual hostility existing between different portions of the country.[8]

Tupper was joined by D'Arcy McGee. "This tax on the public intelligence," said McGee, "would do the public mind an injury. . . .It was a tax upon a form of knowledge most essential to the people. . . .There was never a time when such knowledge was of greater importance to the country."[9] Brown Chamberlin of the Montreal *Gazette,* MP for Missisquoi, moved that the tax be abolished, whereupon Macdonald threatened to throw over all the proposed post office legislation, thus taking Ontario and Quebec back to its older, and higher, newspaper postage. Two attempts were made to stop newspaper postage and both were defeated, twenty-two to forty, and twenty-three to thirty-six, the last on 20 December, when nearly every Maritime MP had gone home for Christmas.[10] In the Senate, Miller, Bourinot, and Dickey, proGovernment senators from Nova Scotia, opposed newspaper postage; their amendment too was lost.[11]

As Edward Blake pointed out when Parliament resumed in mid-March 1868, Confederation could not be maintained if there existed a permanent feeling of discontent. There was little use "in attempting to prolong such an unwilling Union." Bad as things had been in July 1867, they were now, in 1868, much worse, simply because of the Macdonald government's legislation. No interest required the imposition of the tariff on flour, and, in fact, it was rescinded in May 1868.[12] Senator R. D. Wilmot, who had been a Father of Confederation (having been a delegate to the London Conference), complained in March that instead of being able to go back to New Brunswick and congratulate himself and his fellow citizens on Confederation, he had to admit "the prognostications of its enemies had been fulfilled."[13]

In April 1868 came a series of bills on the assimilation of the criminal law. Macdonald, the minister of justice, did not introduce a code, but following British practice, brought down eleven bills dealing with injuries to property, crimes against persons, criminal procedure, and so on. The bills were based on the common law, of course; but different colonies differed in their views of, and their ameliorations of, the English common law. In the Maritimes, reforms and improvements of old common law penalties had proceeded much further than in the Province of Canada. For example, in England and in the Province of Canada, rape was a capital offence. In Nova Scotia it was not, the change having been made in 1853; in Nova Scotia a jury would not convict if rape were made a capital crime. Senator McCully, another Father of Confederation, objected that by the new bills brought down by Macdonald, men were being sentenced to hard labour for what Nova Scotians would regard as trivial offences. There was not a jail in Nova Scotia, and hardly any in New Brunswick, adapted for such penalties. In fact, Maritime criminal law was much more concise, much less specific; an amendment to postpone application of these wide-ranging changes in criminal law, notably in the Act respecting offences against the Person, was moved in the Senate, and passed, twenty-five to twenty-two, 16 May 1868. Thus, the principal act of criminal law was defeated.[14] In a pique, the government withdrew all the criminal law bills of that session. The Senate earned itself some criticism in central Canada for this action; but far from apologizing, those responsible reiterated their position in 1869, when the Offences against the Person Act again came up. McCully, and Senator J. W. Ritchie (later Justice of the Supreme Court of Nova Scotia), both argued that rape punishable by death was too severe. Nevertheless, this second time it carried in the Senate, twenty-nine to twenty.[15]

Toward the end of 1868, results of this line of action began to show up. In New Brunswick, in York County's by-election in October 1868, J. L. Pickard, a well-known antiConfederate, was elected, replacing Charles Fisher, a Confederate appointed to the bench; in Northumberland, R. L. Hutchinson, another antiConfederate, was elected in December 1868.[16] New Brunswick did not look promising.

Nor was the Intercolonial Railway helping very much. John Bolton, MP for Charlotte, roundly asserted in 1869 that if Confederation had been offered to New Brunswick with the North Shore route attached, it would not have been accepted. He was not the only New Brunswick MP who ascribed the government's insistence on the North Shore route to the political exigencies of Sir George Etienne Cartier.[17] The absurdity of the route recalled to W. H. Chipman, MP for Kings, N.S., the story of the volunteer officer who, practising war manoeuvres in the cabbage garden, tumbled backwards into the cellar. His wife came to get him out; the would-be officer said, "Go away with you, woman, what do you know about war?" Richard Cartwright, still a Conservative at that time, proposed a clever amendment that deplored all discussion about the Intercolonial route, adding that it would only prejudice Canadian credit at home and abroad. This carried one hundred and fourteen to twenty-eight, and the North Shore route stood.[18]

Better terms for Nova Scotia did not pass easily either. Hon. E. B. Wood, treasurer of Ontario, 1867–71, MP for Brant South, boldly asserted that since Ontario paid 60 per cent of the dominion revenue, there was no reason to give in to Nova Scotia. Per capita Ontario paid in twenty-seven cents to the dominion pot and got back six cents; Quebec paid in nine cents and got back six cents; but Nova Scotia, even before better terms, put in five and a half cents and took out eighteen cents, and New Brunswick was much the same. Nova Scotia was doing beautifully as she was. Luther Holton objected strongly to changing the terms of Confederation. "Our Constitution was of the nature of a compact between the Provinces, and could only be violated, disturbed, changed or modified with the consent of all the contracting parties."[19] Better terms did get through the House of Commons by ninety-six to fifty-seven, that is, the government majority plus the Nova Scotians, none of whom had the hardihood to oppose better terms for their own province.

Then, slowly, by fits and starts, things began to get better. The government felt strongly enough to reimpose the flour tariff in 1870; it had Tupper's new name attached to it, "the National Policy," the *quid pro quo* for the tariff on flour being a tariff on coal.[20] Popular disapproval of the 1870 tariff was widespread, but the government backed off only to the tune of 5 per cent in 1871. Nova Scotia had begun to respond. They were still bitter at having been forced into Confederation; but when Tupper entered the cabinet in June 1870, he won his by-election by acclamation. Four months later Colchester was carried by an antiConfederate now willing to support the Ottawa government. By 1871, with the Washington Treaty negotiated by Macdonald, Nova Scotians seemed to think there might be some good in Confederation after all.[21]

What was making the change? Prosperity was, something A. T. Galt, now in 1871 an Independent, was happy to congratulate the government upon.[22] The gradual education in national issues and national questions was another. Political education, not to say ductility, of national parties was a significant part of the process of education. The Liberals had made some effort to establish links with their Nova Scotian and New Brunswick brethren. Alexander Mackenzie visited the Maritimes in the summer of 1870, taking up an acquaintance with A. G. Jones, MP for Halifax, the ablest of the Nova Scotian Liberal contingent in Ottawa. Mackenzie even promised to support the local government in their argument with Ottawa over the provincial building that Ottawa claimed was theirs and which the local government refused to give up. (That was settled by negotiation in 1872.) During the session of 1871 in Ottawa, opposition MP's from Ontario made definite efforts to help ameliorate Nova Scotian bitterness. The local government still remained recalcitrant; not the least of their actions was to disenfranchise, in 1871, all dominion employees from voting in provincial elections. As Wilkins, the Nova Scotia attorney-general delicately put it, "every person who had the smell of Canada upon them." This was aimed especially at the provincial election to take place in May 1871. In fact, it meant that the provincial governments were no longer so confident that antiConfederation was as much use as it had once been. There was feverishness in the shrill call to arms of the *Morning Chronicle* the day after dissolution was announced: the antiConfederates in Nova Scotia were becoming too faint hearted! What was needed was straight, "out and out" antiConfederation:

> No surrender; let each man stick to his post. . . . We have gained much by stubborn and unyielding resistance to Canada. . . . This is no time to speak of "harmony."[23]

But that did not stop the change. A dozen or more Confederates were elected provincially, and in the federal election the following year, Conservatives won ten of twenty-one seats in Nova Scotia, seven of sixteen in New Brunswick. This gain could not be held in the face of the Pacific Scandal, and in 1874 the Conservatives took only three and five respectively. By that time the Mackenzie government was trying its hand at making political accommodation work and, in the process, was finding that the Liberal Nova Scotians provided it with rather green cabinet timber.

Maritimers discovered that central Canadian manufactured goods were in many cases cheaper than American and just as good. Between 1867 and 1874 the central Canadians also discovered there was a Maritime market. By the latter date, over half the agricultural tools used in the Maritimes came from Ontario or Quebec. Manufacturers of heavy equipment, like reapers, had also succeeded in driving the Americans out of the Maritime market, a process that started as early as 1871, the machines arriving by the Gulf of St. Lawrence ports or Portland, Maine. Canadian manufacturers were underselling the Americans by about 25 per cent. A Guelph manufacturer of woollen knit goods said that in fact Confederation had given him the Maritime market. Just as this evidence was being taken by the Mills Committee in 1876, the Intercolonial Railway was being finished. The first through train from Halifax to Quebec left Halifax on 5 July 1876. In 1879 Nova Scotia adopted the National Policy with such enthusiasm, so rapidly did capital and human resources move from staple industries, that between 1880 and 1890 Nova Scotian industry grew more proportionately than Ontario or Quebec.[24]

By the end of the 1880's the problems of Nova Scotia, New Brunswick, and perhaps to a degree even Prince Edward Island, were of quite a different order. The National Policy was a success if judged by the milltowns of St. Stephen or Marysville, New Brunswick, the industrial towns of Amherst, Truro, and New Glasgow in Nova Scotia. The railway policy of the Dominion had had considerable effects. It was noticeable that the Conservative vote tended to follow the dominion railway lines. Railways made good politics; when he was minister of railways, Macdonald had to tell one anxious Nova Scotian MP that the railway the MP was proposing would not carry enough traffic to justify construction. The MP replied with some heat, "Traffic be damned! I wanted the road to carry me back to Parliament."[25]

Nearly all the government railways were in eastern Nova Scotia. If a line were drawn from Moncton to Halifax, east of the line would be found all but one of Nova Scotia's ten senators and the two members of the federal cabinet; and all the railways east of that line were owned and operated by the Dominion and had lower rates. The railways west of the line were company railways. So complained W. C. Bill, the Conservative candidate who lost Kings to Frederick Borden in 1891.[26] The Dominion owned and ran not only the Intercolonial, but the eastern extension, Pictou to the Strait of Canso, and it contracted and built the railway from the Strait of Canso to Sydney. One of Macdonald's very last notes as minister of railways was about a report on the hard-pan problem on the Cape Breton railway.[27]

Not the least part of this process of political accommodation was patronage, in all its many variations. From the Macdonald and the Thompson Papers there emerges the picture of an extensive network of patronage, well defined and highly developed. So much so that one has the impression that Antigonish County, for example, lived by its wharves, breakwaters, and railways. Dominion wharfmasters, Intercolonial railway employees, customs collectors, lighthouse keepers, and postmasters formed part of a well-ramified system of dominion patronage, organization, and administration.

Of all the provinces of Canada, the Maritimes seem to have developed the arts of patronage in the most sincere, unblushing, naked enthusiasm. Nova Scotia had had a fair running start in the practice of it, ever since 1749. There is an interesting perspective about this from J. S. D. Thompson in 1888. Bishop McDonald of St. John's, Newfoundland, was to be in Halifax, and Thompson was asked by Sir John Macdonald and Sir Charles Tupper to write to T. E. Kenny, a Catholic MP in Halifax, to get Kenny to interview the bishop about Newfoundland entering Confederation. Thompson sketched out the advantages of Confederation for Newfoundland and presented them to Kenny as useful arguments to the bishop. What Thompson said was very suggestive of the basis of accommodation that had been arrived at in the Maritime provinces over the previous twenty years. There was, said Thompson, dominion government spending on railways; Newfoundland's resources had been exhausted by 1888 in an ineffective attempt to complete the transNewfoundland railway. Besides railways there were lighthouses, post offices, even militia appropriations. Indeed, said Thompson to Kenny, look at the general position of the smaller provinces in Canada:

> The fear of the smaller provinces in 1867 was that they would be overpowered and disregarded by the larger ones, [but] the result has been that the smaller provinces have obtained a far larger share of consideration (including expenditure) than the larger [provinces], and have more influence than could be claimed on account either of territorial extent or population. The fact that they have always been more troublesome than the larger ones is perhaps one of the reasons.[28]

These arrangements were well known by the late 1880's. Newfoundland's revived interest in Confederation was some kind of a benchmark of the success of Confederation in the three other Atlantic provinces.

The sequence of events in Maritime patronage went like this. A Conservative worthy in, let us say, Pictou County, thought X should have the job of collector of customs in Pugwash. He would recommend X to C. H. Tupper, the Conservative MP, who would in turn mention it to the responsible minister, Mackenzie Bowell. It could go the other way around, that Bowell would ask the Conservative MP in whose riding the vacancy occurred, whom he would recommend. If there were no Conservative MP for the constituency, then the recently defeated Conservative candidate would be approached. As a rule the minister did not need to make too many enquiries, for a cloud of applications would descend upon him the moment the post was known to be open. Indeed, the body of the newly deceased incumbent of the office would be still warm when the letters would be off to Ottawa. With judges, the letters would often arrive before the judge was dead. If Judge Y was very ill, a candidate would write to Sir John Thompson: ''Judge Y's illness is almost certainly mortal,'' the candidate would add cheerfully, ''and please consider me a candidate.''

Thompson's own constituents in Antigonish County ate and drank patronage. The long winters and the halcyon summers seemed only to nourish that delightful preoccupation. Thompson himself was not proud of this unpleasant and important side of his work as MP for Antigonish. His constituency seemed to him greedy, rapacious, impatient, unforgiving, with alarmingly tenacious Scotch memories that kept past rights (and wrongs) clearly in the world of present reality. ''I revolt against Antigonish the more I think of it,'' Thompson grumbled to his wife Annie in 1887.[29]

One day in October 1886, Archie A. McGillivray, an Antigonish constituent, vain, brash and greedy, heard that the Intercolonial Railway stationmaster at Antigonish town had died. ''May his soul rest in peace,'' said Archie piously, ''I hereby apply for the situation . . . and finding that this situation would suit me, I demand it. All I want from you is a decided answer.'' Thompson said no, in a letter written, Archie claimed, ''in that cool faraway tone.'' It made Archie furious. He railed against Thompson's rank ingratitude for all that Archie had done for him over the years in Antigonish County; Thompson's ''dark, ungrateful heart'' would rue the day that he refused the modest exigencies of Archie A. McGillivray.[30]

B. F. Power, another constituent with more brains and more clout than Archie, preferred telegrams. The Antigonish stationmaster died on 11 October 1886; B. F. Power reminded Thompson that very day that the stationmaster was, happily or unhappily, very dead and that B. F. Power's brother Henry was quite available. When the new stationmaster was appointed, it was neither Archie McGillivray nor Power's brother, but D. H. McDonald, promoted from being stationmaster at Tracadie, eighteen miles eastward along the line. B. F. Power kept a watchful eye on D. H. McDonald, however, and two months later came the following telegram:

> If stationmaster here be dismissed for drunkenness you have a right to confer that office on me. I pay all telegrams answer before sixteenth as I will be away state salary.

That was certainly brash enough. Thompson did not ignore it, however; he telegraphed his cousin, David Pottinger, chief superintendent of the Intercolonial Railway at Moncton (1879–92) for information. The pay, said Pottinger, was forty dollars a month; but he added that D. H. McDonald was not in any trouble so far as Pottinger knew.[31] But McDonald was in trouble, and the chief superintendent soon found out.

The Intercolonial Railway rules about drinking by employees were strict and specific. In the rule book of 22 November 1886, Rule No. 59 was that only men of known careful and sober habits were to be employed in the movement of trains. Rule No. 60 was even more specific: any employee drunk on *or* off duty would not be kept on the Intercolonial Railway service.[32] What had actually happened to D. H. McDonald is not altogether clear—it seldom is on such occasions. On the nights of 6 and 7 December he and some friends had something of a party, which included McDonald getting pitched out of a sleigh into an adjacent snowbank, followed by some good-natured but very drunken wrestling in the snowdrifts in front of Antigonish's main hotel. This was not drunkenness, McDonald told Thompson, but only animal energy; all he had had to drink was whisky and milk, taken for strictly medicinal purposes. Whatever McDonald's explanations, he was dismissed for drunkenness. B. F. Power was given the position, even though he could not yet use the telegraph key and would have to learn. It was a clear patronage appointment, and David Pottinger did not altogether relish it. "The usual and proper course," he wrote to his cousin, "would be to promote some experienced person to a station like this, but I suppose we can't."[33]

It can be added that it was also virtually impossible to appoint a man from outside the county to such a position. A Pictou County man, however competent, might even be, *horribile dictu,* a Protestant; in any case being from outside the county, he could not be given an important patronage preferment in Antigonish. The reverse would also be true in Pictou County.

Thompson was less susceptible to patronage pressures outside his own constituency. In his own department, Justice, he preferred to encourage the *esprit de corps* of the civil service. The warden of Dorchester Penitentiary, New Brunswick, as indeed other wardens, had been a patronage appointment when Thompson became minister of justice in 1885. The incumbent in Dorchester, Warden Botsford, was the brother of Senator Amos Botsford (1804–94). Warden Botsford died in April 1887. Within twenty-four hours Thompson had fifteen telegrams about four possible candidates, plus a letter from Sir Charles Tupper. Senator Botsford had his own ideas who should replace his dead brother. The director of penitentiaries, J. G. Moylan, also had a candidate in mind.

Thompson cut all that off. He promoted the deputy-warden, J. B. Forster. Politely, firmly, he told an irate Conservative in Dorchester that promotion of good men to the highest positions in the service was the stuff of which a good service was made. "If these officers find the higher positions disposed of according to political claims, some political advantage may result but the Service will soon be in a useless condition."[34]

Thompson was also concerned to redress the imbalance he observed in Nova Scotian appointments in the inside service. Across the whole inside service, he told Macdonald, Nova Scotia's share of the five hundred or so appointments should have been seventy; she had in 1887 only twenty-six. No Nova Scotian was deputy-minister, none was chief clerk. This argued the more cogently why Thompson should have a free hand in the choice of his deputy-minister, consequent upon the appointment of his former deputy, J. W. Burbidge, to the Exchequer Court of Canada.

> My choice would however be very limited as I could not afford to take a man about whose fitness I could entertain a doubt and I am not at all sanguine that any of the best men would accept. If not I should want to look to Ontario. New Brunswick has far more than her share now.[35]

Tilley and Costigan had clearly been doing their work! Thompson, after inviting Robert Borden of Halifax (who was tempted but said no), appointed Robert Sedgwick of Halifax.

Many of the little Maritime towns, and doubtless others in Quebec, Ontario, and elsewhere, presented curious mixtures of dominion-provincial relations, some seldom explored, or not even known. It was a process of accommodation at its most basic. In Antigonish town, by 1887, there was a small dominion public building, housing the customs office and the post office, but it had room for more than these. It so happened that the postmaster of Antigonish was also the caretaker of the building; besides these offices, he was also sheriff of Antigonish County. The county found the space convenient; it was also cheap since it cost nothing. Thus were accommodated county officials, the registrar of deeds, registrar of probate, and others. The registrar of probate was also a magistrate and did his magistrate's business there, rather to the discomfiture of the other occupants of the building. Since the Municipality of Antigonish County contributed nothing to the building, neither to cost nor upkeep, should not the situation be regularized in some way? It seemed so to Thompson. There was surely no objection, he suggested to Sir Hector Langevin, the minister of public works, to housing municipal officers in dominion public buildings, but they ought to have some regular system of tenure. Otherwise, there would be all kinds of similar demands on dominion public buildings elsewhere.

There was an odd consequence to this. The town of Antigonish discovered that much the best place to hang the town's fire bell was on that dominion building, on the northeast corner. Thompson thought that would do no harm. But the postmaster-caretaker-sheriff thought differently. He objected; he said that the process of hanging that fire bell there on that northeast corner would ruin, positively ruin, his flower garden! It took the bishop and a peremptory telegram from Thompson to get the fire bell placed where the town wanted it.[36]

Such was the infinitude of questions, little and big, that filled so much of the life of Thompson, the conscientious administrator.

At election time the story is more familiar, noticeable from the beginning: the importing of campaign funds from central Canada. Both Nova Scotia and New Brunswick raised roughly half of their own campaign funds, but they seemed to expect, and to get, assistance from outside. This seems to have been especially the case in 1891, where it was known that American money had been imported into both provinces by the Liberals. Both Thompson and young C. H. Tupper found Nova Scotians very canny with their own money; the Halifax merchants and manufacturers never seemed enthusiastic when the time came to dig into their pockets. Senators, who did not have to fight any elections at all, were not very responsive in shelling out money for MP's who did.

In 1891 Maritime money seems to have been channelled, some of it at least, through John Haggart, the postmaster general from Ontario. There were some frank pleas. L. deV. Chipman in Kentville, trying to help W. C. Bill defeat Frederick Borden in Kings County, wrote anxiously that they had raised $1,500 in the Annapolis valley, had got $1,000 more (presumably from Ottawa), but needed a further $2,000. Chipman promised to raise this extra $2,000 himself, provided he were promised the vacant Nova Scotia seat in the senate. Thompson's response was not helpful. F. W. Borden won by 161 votes; Chipman claimed afterward that had Thompson come through with the promise of the senate seat, W. C. Bill would have won by fifty to one hundred votes. Chipman never did get a seat in the Senate.[37] Joseph Pope telegraphed Thompson from Kingston that if more ammunition were needed in Nova Scotia, Thompson could draw up to $2,500 from W. A. Allan of Ottawa. Sir John Macdonald suggested leaving Cumberland to its own devices (where Dickey, Sir Charles Tupper's successor, seemed a certainty) and sending $500 to John McDonald in Victoria, Cape Breton (who won), and $500 to J. N. Freeman in Queens (who did not).[38]

The result of the federal election in 1891 in Nova Scotia surprised everyone, Liberals and Conservatives alike. Thompson won Antigonish by 227 votes, a much bigger majority than either 1885 or 1887. In the province as a whole, the Conservatives took sixteen of twenty-one seats compared to fourteen seats in 1887. In New Brunswick, they took thirteen of sixteen seats. In both provinces it was the best Sir John A. Macdonald's Conservative government had ever done. Even Prince Edward Island, which had given its six seats to the Liberals in 1874 and in 1887, had elected two Conservatives. Indeed, twenty-one seats of the Macdonald government's twenty-seven-seat majority, coming into the new session of 1891, were created by New Brunswick and Nova Scotia. No wonder Sir Richard Cartwright was cross; the Macdonald government, he said, was nothing but a patchwork "made up of the ragged remnants from half a dozen minor provinces, the great majority of whom do not even pretend to be actuated by any principle save . . . a good slice of booty."[39] There was some truth in that. The ragged remnants were New Brunswick and Nova Scotia, joined with Manitoba, British Columbia, and the Northwest Territories. The five together had presented a thirty-four-seat majority to help the Conservative government. There was not a little irony in the fact that by 1891 the shreds and patches of Confederation had won their own victory over the central Canadians who had run things so much their own way only twenty years before.

It was not the end of antiConfederation in the Maritimes or the West. That would come again, like delirium, when the patient ran a fever from economic illness. But it was clear that there were many and widely ramified changes. Even W. S. Fielding, the premier of Nova Scotia, who could not attend a Dominion Day dinner in London in 1892 for fear of hearing speeches that he would have had publicly to disagree with, joined Laurier in Ottawa in 1896. By that time, the process of national accommodation by both political parties was well under way. Perhaps that function, that achievement, has been underestimated.

It is obvious that some of this can be set down in terms of "incentive systems," an expression dear to political scientists. Even mere historians can realize that the party organization by 1888 provided forms of satisfaction familiar enough: power, a sense of national identity, prestige, to say nothing of the ordinary delights of a regular, if modest, salary. In all of this party organizations were shaped by individuals and forces that often went in ways tangential to the apparent or formal purposes of party organization. As Antigonish County showed Thompson, Pictou showed C. H. Tupper, and Kings County, New Brunswick, revealed to G. E. Foster, to say nothing of the other forty or so Maritime MP's, failure to meet constituency exigencies frequently led to what sociologists sometimes call intraorganizational conflict.[40] As E. R. Black, a political scientist, put it, "Particular configurations of centripetal and centrifugal forces within the federation may still be expected to be closely related to the vitality of individual concepts."[41] One may prefer André Siegfried:

> Dans la vide voulu des programmes, les questions d'intérêts matériels, de travaux publics à exécuter prennent vraiement une place trop importante. Il y a certes d'autres problèmes plus brûlants; on y pense toujours, mais les grands chefs voudraient qu'on n'en parlât jamais . . . ce n'est pas le parti qui est au service de l'idée, mais bien l'idée qui est au service du parti.[42]

NOTES

1. Campbell to Macdonald, 27 July 1873, cited in L. H. Thomas, *The Struggle for Responsible Government in the North-West Territories, 1870–1897* (Toronto, 1956), p. 61.
2. Canada, Senate, *Debates, 1867–1868,* 26 March 1868 (Ottawa, 1968), p. 145.
3. Cited in Gordon Blake, *Customs Administration in Canada* (Toronto, 1957), p. 70.
4. Canada, House of Commons, *Debates, 1867–1868,* 10 December 1867 (Ottawa, 1967), p. 231.
5. Ibid., 16 December 1867, pp. 292–93.
6. Ibid., 30 April 1868, p. 598.
7. Ibid., 16 December 1867, p. 287.
8. Ibid., 20 December 1867, p. 335.
9. Ibid., p. 337.
10. Ibid., p. 338.
11. Senate, *Debates, 1867–1868,* 6 December 1867, pp. 79–80.
12. House of Commons, *Debates, 1867–1868,* 19 March 1868, p. 372. The tariff on flour was eventually taken off late in the session, ibid., 18 May 1868, pp. 731–33. Macdonald wrote the archbishop of Halifax to tell him about the removal of the duty on flour, corn, and corn meal. Joseph Pope, *Correspondence of Sir John Macdonald* (Toronto, 1921), p. 68, Macdonald to Connolly, 1 June 1868. The tariff on flour was reimposed in 1870.

13. Senate, *Debates, 1867–1868,* 23 March 1868, p. 130.
14. Ibid., 15 May 1868, p. 321; 16 May 1868, p. 328.
15. Ibid., *Debates, 1869* (Ottawa, 1975), 16 April 1869, p. 14; 26 April 1869, pp. 36–37; 1 June 1869; p. 247–48; 4 June 1869, p. 277.
16. Noted by Senator Wilmot. Ibid., 4 June 1869, p. 273.
17. House of Commons, *Debates, 1869,* (Ottawa, 1975), 17 May 1869, p. 348.
18. Ibid., 17 May 1869, p. 365.
19. Ibid., 12 June 1869, p. 756; 16 June 1869, p. 806.
20. Ibid., 14 May 1869, p. 335, for the original locus of the phrase.
21. O. J. McDiarmid, *Commercial Policy in the Canadian Economy* (Cambridge, 1946), p. 139; K. G. Pryke, *Nova Scotia and Confederation, 1864–74* (Toronto, 1979), pp. 114–15, 136.
22. Library of Parliament, *Scrapbook Debates 1871,* 10 March 1871.
23. Nova Scotia, Assembly, *Debates 1871,* p. 273; Halifax *Morning Chronicle,* 18 April 1871. This editorial was used by the Conservative Montreal *Gazette* to show the folly of the conciliatory courses followed by the Ontario Liberals (22 April 1871).
24. The Report of the Mills Committee is in Canada, House of Commons, *Journals,* 1876, Appendix 3; T. W. Acheson, "The National Policy and the Industrialization of the Maritimers, 1880–1910," *Acadiensis* 1, no. 2 (Spring 1972): 3.
25. J. S. Willison, "Reminiscences, Political and Otherwise," *Canadian Magazine* 52, no. 6 (April 1919): 1028.
26. W. C. Bill to Thompson, Macdonald and Tupper, 6 April 1891, confidential, J. S. D. Thompson Papers (hereafter JSDT), vol. 126.
27. Macdonald to Thompson, 18 May 1891, ibid., vol. 128. The issue concerned the underestimate by contractors—good Conservatives—of the cost of excavation along a section of the Cape Breton Railway. Hard-pan is firm heavy clay and gravel compressed into a rocklike consistency.
28. Thompson to T. E. Kenny, 22 February 1888, private and confidential, ibid., vol. 233.
29. Thompson to Annie, 22 September 1887, ibid., vol. 290.
30. McGillivray to Thompson, 18 October 1886, ibid., vol. 45; 13 November 1886, ibid., vol. 46.
31. Power to Thompson, 9 December 1886, telegram, ibid., vol. 47; Pottinger to Thompson, 11 December 1886, telegram.
32. D. H. McDonald to Thompson, 17 January 1887, ibid., vol. 48. A condensed version of the Antigonish story is in P. B. Waite, *The Man from Halifax: Sir John Thompson, Prime Minister* (Toronto, 1985), pp. 176–77.
33. Pottinger to Thompson, n.d., endorsed on Thompson to Pottinger, 29 May 1887, private, ibid., vol. 52.
34. Thompson to Michaud, 15 April 1887, ibid., vol. 229; vol. 52 contains the incoming correspondence on this question.
35. Thompson to Macdonald, 21 September 1887, Macdonald Papers, vol. 273.
36. Thompson to Langevin, 23 August 1888, private; JSDT, vol. 235; vol. 76, Whidden to Thompson, 24 October 1888, telegram; same, 25 October 1888, telegram.
37. L. deV. Chipman to Thompson n.d., private and confidential, ibid., vol. 124; 19 March 1891, private, ibid., vol. 125.
38. Pope to Thompson, 1 March 1891, telegram, ibid., vol. 124.
39. Toronto *Globe,* 9 March 1891.
40. These concepts are outlined in Peter Clark and J. Q. Wilson, "Incentive systems," *Administrative Studies Quarterly* 6 (1961): 129–66.
41. E. R. Black, *Divided loyalties: Canadian Concepts of Federalism* (Montreal, 1975), p. 222.
42. André Siegfried, *Le Canada, les deux races: problèmes politiques contemporains* (Paris, 1906), pp. 180, 182. The references in the F. H. Underhill edition (Toronto, 1966) are on pp. 113, 114.

9

Managing the Periphery: British Columbia and the National Political Community

DONALD E. BLAKE

British Columbia is widely perceived as a province cut off emotionally as well as physically from the rest of Canada. As R. M. Burns put it, "Under most of its leaders in recent times British Columbia has been chiefly concerned with its own affairs and the pursuit of its own destiny, rather than with establishing itself as a vital and integral part of the Canadian nation."[1] Former Prime Minister Pierre Trudeau once likened residents of the province to those who dwell at the foot of the mountain but never climb to the top to meet those on the other side. His description even included provincial members of his own party, the audience before whom the remark was delivered. As several observers have pointed out, British Columbia has never produced a prime minister or even a leader of one of the major national parties, although it did provide seats for two of them (Sir John A. Macdonald and T. C. Douglas) when they suffered electoral setbacks in their home provinces. John Turner, whose political career began outside the province, may be an exception, if only for the brief interval between his swearing in as the member for Vancouver Quadra and his resignation as prime minister and for his decision to pursue Liberal revival from a B.C. base.

For their part, British Columbians apparently[2] share with other western Canadians a feeling that their views have a limited impact on national affairs because of their small share of Canada's population. They also seem to subscribe to the constitutional absurdity that the B.C. voice in the House of Commons was eliminated together with Liberal representation from the province in 1980 and was only restored with the national Progressive Conservative victory in 1984. The province was enticed into Confederation by the prospect of economic benefits, and while this put the province in good company, many feel that materialist motives are the major tie that binds British Columbia to the nation today.

This paper re-examines some of the problems in the relationship between British Columbia and the national political community from the perspective of the centre. In particular, it explores ways in which the central government might better manage relations with the province without completely undermining the legitimacy of the centre. In it I hope to dispel the notion that the people of British Columbia have no interest in and perceive that they have no stake in the national community. Alienation certainly exists, but it is bound up with attitudes towards the stewardship of Pierre Trudeau and his attempts to make French Canadians feel more at home in Canada, rather than to the federal level of government per se. It is possible that alienation will fade with Trudeau's departure from federal politics, but the argument advanced here does not depend on that.

The analysis of possible avenues for rapprochement will assume that current institutional arrangements will persist. Key aspects of the institutional dimension—federalism, parliamentary institutions, and the electoral system—have attracted considerable attention from scholars and have been the focus of several reform proposals. However, while it is undoubtedly important, this dimension is arguably the least malleable and the one for which the effects of changes are the most difficult to predict. Changes in the party system run up against the problem that British Columbia has evolved two separate party systems, a provincial one based on competing visions of the role of the state and a federal one where issues of left and right must compete with the politics of culture, national unity, and government responsiveness. The fates of parties and politicians at the two levels have virtually nothing to do with each other.

Yet, despite the peculiarities of its provincial system, British Columbia has never completely abandoned its interest in the divisions represented by the dominant federal parties. The Conservative party has been the major beneficiary of that link recently, but there may even be incentives for Liberals to include British Columbia in their calculations, although they are weakened by the province's relatively trivial contribution to parliamentary majorities. In other words, before engaging in institutional experimentation, we should explore possibilities provided by existing ties between British Columbia and the national political community. The results of the exercise may also illuminate the possible effects of different institutional changes.

LESSONS OF THE PAST

> ... by 1871 the sense of sharing a common nationality was sufficiently strong to offset the economic attraction of the United States and to break the direct political tie with England. In spite of strained relations between the provincial and the federal government following the entrance of the province into Confederation, Canadian sentiment among British Columbians was materially strengthened by the joint endeavour of Canadians from all parts of the Dominion to build the section of the national railway which lay within the province's limits.[3]

If Margaret Ormsby's assessment is correct, present conflicts between British Columbia and the centre must be considered relatively inconsequential. During its first fifteen years in Confederation, the province was a constant thorn in the side of the government in Ottawa. The provincial legislature passed secession resolutions in 1876 and 1878.[4] In 1881, B.C. was described as the "spoilt child of Confederation" by the British colonial secretary, who had been called upon once again to support the province's demands for speedy fulfilment of the terms of union.[5] Nevertheless, citizens of the province recognized that their fate was bound up with the fate of the nation. They remained staunch supporters of the federal Conservative party and of Sir John A. Macdonald, the architect of the National Policy, even to the extent of eschewing partisan, or at least Liberal-Conservative, divisions in the provincial legislature. The strong provincial rights and anti-imperial stance of the federal Liberal party had limited appeal in the province, given its dependence on the beneficence of the federal government and the use made of the former colonial power as an ally in the battle for better terms. It was ten years after completion of the railway before British Columbia sent its first Liberal MPs to Ottawa and seven years after that before Liberal and Conservative divisions appeared in the provincial legislature.

Some grievances were shared with other western provinces. British Columbia complained that it bore an unfair share of the burdens of Confederation because most manufactured goods had to be imported from abroad or from central Canada, thus incurring extra costs from tariffs and freight charges. Later, federal industrial strategies and the lending practices of the central Canadian lending institutions came under fire for their emphasis on the manufacturing industries of central Canada rather than on the potential of the province's resource industries. More specialized complaints centred on the added costs of building roads, railways, and other communications links given the province's difficult terrain; these were cited as justification for additional federal subsidies.

Serious jurisdictional conflict, on the other hand, has been relatively rare. The federal government disallowed some of the more extreme attempts by the province to exclude Asians from the rights of citizenship, from certain occupations, and even from the country, but both Liberal and Conservative federal governments turned a blind eye to franchise restrictions based on racial criteria at the insistence of their B.C. MPs. Provincial disqualification was also grounds for disenfranchisement in federal elections, an embarassment that was not remedied until after World War II.[6] John Oliver, Liberal premier during the 1920's, used to rail against the federal presence in the personal income tax field, but it was Premier Duff Pattullo who took the strongest action, conspiring with William Aberhart and Mitchell Hepburn to wreck the dominion-provincial conference called to discuss the Rowell-Sirois Report in 1940.

While the conflict was an important one, Pattullo's stand was widely criticized in the province. It was probably responsible for the poor showing of his party in the 1941 provincial election and his replacement as Liberal party leader. With hindsight, it appears that Pattullo's problem was mainly one of timing. It was considered unpatriotic to undermine federal authority during wartime. Today, it would be called province-building. His stance reflected a belief, developed in response to the Depression and pressure from the CCF, that the state must assume an increased responsibility for individual well-being, economic planning, and regulation of business in the public interest, a position that placed the provincial Liberal party well to the left of its federal counterpart.[7] Before the war was over, Mackenzie King had come to similar conclusions, stimulated by concern for the growth of the CCF, especially in Ontario.

W. A. C. Bennett was probably the province's most famous "fed-basher," and Burns's description of an aloof provincial leadership certainly applies to him. According to legend, Bennett required civil servants to seek clearance from him before journeying out of the province, and his major contribution to federal-provincial conferences was a proposal to redraw the boundaries of the province to include the Yukon. While federal action was necessary for the success of development schemes which hinged on the export of power to the United States or expansion of port facilities, Bennett insisted that federal participation be on his terms. When federal funding for the TransCanada Highway ran out, he ordered that signs be changed to identify it as "BC-1."[8]

Yet, Bennett's commitment to Canada never wavered, and other potentially serious conflicts were avoided. Unlike the other western provinces, British Columbia was given control over its own natural resources and public lands with entry into Confederation. In fact, exercise of this power became the raison d'être of provincial governments following the completion of the C.P.R., and it led to an orgy of railway building subsidized by provincial land grants. Provincial prosperity and the success or failure of provincial governments soon became tied to economic development issues and to the health of the resource industries, principally forestry and mining. Federal jurisdiction over tariffs and interprovincial and international trade had significant implications for these industries, but the federal government has rarely expressed an interest in them.[9] The province acquiesced to predominant federal jurisdiction in the fishery, perhaps because of its declining significance for provincial wealth or because its needs often conflicted with the more lucrative and powerful forest industry. Key political issues on the agenda of provincial governments, especially development and regulation of forestry and mining and conflict between labour and management, had only limited significance for federal politics.

British Columbia's resource base and the significance of hydroelectricity as an export earner and as part of the industrial infrastructure provided by the state give it interests similar to those of Quebec and Ontario. This similarity probably allowed British Columbia to benefit from Ontario's victories over the federal government on trade-related issues such as provincial legislation restricting the export of raw logs or requiring rudimentary domestic processing of forest and mineral products.[10]

The historical record provides little support for basing grievances on a quasi-colonial past or on federal obstacles to provincial prosperity. There have been no successful federal third party or protest movements in the province except the CCF, which could not base its appeal on the theme of central Canadian exploitation developed by its agrarian-based counterparts on the Prairies. Moreover, if one accepts my argument that the success of *provincial* governments is tied to economic development issues and that the province has prospered independently of federal policies, then the argument that the connection between British Columbia and the nation is based on materialist motives loses much of its force. In fact, this is one avenue federal leaders might explore as a way of convincing British Columbians of the utility of the federal connection. They must, of course, remain wary of the propensity of provincial authorities to downplay or ignore federal contributions to joint endeavours.[11]

INTEGRATION VIA THE PARTY SYSTEM

The pressures of federalism and federal-provincial conflict have weakened the links between provincial and federal wings of the major parties. The role of parties in aggregating interests and in the formation of public policy has been eclipsed by the expansion of public bureaucracies, executive federalism, and the proliferation of interest groups.[12] Roger Gibbins summed it up as follows: "The lack of harmonious integration is not surprising given the absence of shared electoral risks, a common ballot, an interwoven political career structure . . . or significant provincial participation in the selection of national party leaders."[13] Given the almost complete separation of federal and provincial party systems in British Columbia, the prospects for integration via the party system must be considered even more remote. Looked at more optimistically, the resurgence of the federal Liberal party in B.C., and thus the revival of a truly national party system, does not depend on the resurrection of the provincial party.

The divisions between Liberal and Conservative, the basis for divisions in federal politics, have always had a shaky foundation in British Columbia provincial politics. The overwhelmingly British and Protestant character of the white population in British Columbia in 1871 virtually eliminated religion and ethnic origin as a source of partisan division. Unlike central Canada, "there was no feud of ruling faces to allay, no Clergy Reserve to divide, no complicated fiscal policy to arrange."[14] In other words, when Liberal and Conservative labels were finally adopted in provincial politics, they came without the social and historical baggage which governed their adoption elsewhere.[15] The Canadian constitution encourages the separation of federal and provincial policy agendas, a division which has been accentuated by the decline of federal responsibility for setting goals in the areas of health, education, and social welfare.

The near irrelevance of federal partisan divisions to provincial politics is clearly illustrated (and was undoubtedly reinforced) by the coalition experience from 1941 to 1952. While the CCF was initially invited to participate in an all-party arrangement, the Liberal-Conservative coalition which emerged soon evolved into a device to counter the power of the left and ultimately redefined the basis of provincial politics. Co-operation within the coalition reduced Liberal and Conservative differences in their own eyes as well as in the eyes of the electorate; the very existence of the CCF as the official, and only, opposition raised the salience of the division between free enterprise and socialism, especially given the doctrinaire stance of the CCF leader, Harold Winch.

The federal parties, especially the Conservatives, mindful of the role played by provincial organizations in federal election campaigns ultimately opposed coalition, but the record since 1953 suggests their fears were groundless. Since then the fortunes of the Liberal and Conservative parties in federal politics have fluctuated independently of the level of support achieved by their provincial counterparts. The effects of the 1958 Diefenbaker landslide (49 per cent of the vote and eighteen of twenty-two seats in B.C.) were barely discernible in the results of the next provincial election. Provincial Liberal support in 1969 was similarly unaffected by Trudeaumania, which gave the Liberals 42 per cent of the vote and sixteen of the province's twenty-two federal seats.

The CCF/NDP enjoyed comparable levels of success in the two arenas, but the provincial party consistently finished ahead of its federal counterpart. Since its provincial victory in 1972, the gap has increased substantially. Social Credit obtained 25 per cent of the federal vote in 1953 and 1957, but since that time its federal showing has been only a pale reflection of the party's provincial dominance, despite W. A. C. Bennett's reputation. Since 1968, only a token number of Social Credit candidates have even appeared in federal contests.

The separation of party systems was dramatically illustrated by the results of the 1979 elections in the province. Twelve days after returning Social Credit to power in Victoria, the province's voters assisted in defeating the federal Liberals. The Conservative party contested 65 per cent of the seats in the provincial election and received only 5.2 per cent of the vote. The federal Conservatives enjoyed their best showing since the Diefenbaker landslide. The NDP, the only party with substantial support at both levels, received the highest provincial vote in their history, 46 per cent. Federally, they finished a distant second to the Conservatives with only 32 per cent of the vote, an improvement over 1974, but not much different from their long-term average.

In all, approximately 65 per cent of those who voted in both elections voted for different parties, following the patterns detailed in Table 1.[16] Despite the coincidence of federal and provincial campaigns, the NDP was able to deliver only 64 per cent of its provincial supporters to the federal party. Nearly 70 per cent of those who had voted Social Credit in the provincial election went on to support the federal Conservatives, but the fact that nearly 30 per cent voted Liberal (representing 60 per cent of the support given to the federal party) indicates that provincial Social Credit and the federal Conservatives are not simply clones. The Conservatives also attracted the support of over 20 per cent of those who had voted NDP provincially.

The movement from provincial to federal politics represents a move to different issues involving different strategic considerations, and voters react accordingly. Overlaying the left-right division so prominent in provincial politics are differences over government language policy, constitutional policy, and attitudes towards Ottawa generally. For some, alienation in 1979 became personified, bound up with attitudes towards Pierre

Trudeau, who was seen as aloof, arrogant, occasionally ruthless, and even foreign. For others, the main objection was to the perceived domination of the national agenda by issues of bilingualism and biculturalism and the demands of Quebec. An attempt has been made to capture these dimensions with three attitude scales measuring support or opposition to a

TABLE 1

Voter Migrations—1979
(Vertical Percentages)

FEDERAL VOTE	PROVINCIAL VOTE: LIBERAL	CONSERVATIVE	NDP	SOCIAL CREDIT	TOTAL
Liberal	87.5	13.9	12.6	27.5	21.8
Conservative	12.5	80.6	22.3	69.3	48.0
NDP	0.0	2.8	63.7	2.3	29.0
Social Credit	0.0	2.8	0.0	1.0	0.6
Other	0.0	0.0	1.5	0.0	0.7
	(16)	(16)	(278)	(309)	

TABLE 2

Attitudinal Divisions Among Federal Voters
By Provincial Party Support*
(Provincial NDP and Social Credit Voters Only)

	FEDERAL VOTE					
	LIBERAL		CONSERVATIVE		NDP	
PROVINCIAL VOTE: / ATTITUDE SCALE	Social Credit	NDP	Social Credit	NDP	Social Credit**	NDP
Alienation	2.01	1.79	2.75	2.79	—	2.45
Ethnocentrism	3.19	2.79	3.85	3.89	—	3.03
Individual/Collective Responsibility	3.42	4.07	3.24	3.94	—	4.23

* Entries are mean scores based on a range of 0–6 for individual/collective responsibility and ethnocentrism and 0–8 for alienation.

** Only 6 respondents reported a Social Credit provincial vote and an NDP federal vote, too few cases on which to calculate a reliable mean score.

strong role for the state in economic regulation and social policy (labelled "individual versus collective responsibility"), support or opposition to federal language and cultural policies and attitudes towards Quebec (labelled "ethnocentrism"), and attitudes towards centralization, the relative responsiveness of federal and provincial governments, and feelings of community with other Canadians (labelled "alienation").[17]

Table 2 illustrates the effects of these differences on the support patterns of federal and provincial parties. Differences *within* the federal Liberal and Conservative electorates on left-right issues are as large as those *between* the NDP and Social Credit provincially. Provincial voters apparently forget their differences on these issues as they choose parties which reflect their degree of ethnocentrism or alienation from the centre. The less ethnocentric or relatively unalienated gravitate to the federal Liberals; the ethnocentric or alienated select the Conservatives. Federal NDP supporters, virtually all of whom supported the NDP provincially, are as a group slightly left of provincial New Democrats who failed to support the party in the 1979 federal election. They also seem to be torn between feelings of alienation (which approach those exhibited by Conservative voters) and a low level of ethnocentrism shared with federal Liberals.

Although it is not possible to examine the details here, federal voting in British Columbia reflects divisions which appear elsewhere in Canada, even to the extent of involving a religious cleavage which is insignificant in provincial voting and which helps to determine the choice between Liberals and Conservatives among those who decided not to stick with the NDP when voting in the federal election. Class voting, while higher than elsewhere in Canada, is much lower than in provincial elections.[18] Despite the peculiarities of its provincial party system, support for the federal Liberals and Conservatives in British Columbia has been highly correlated (at .65) with the national level of support for the parties since 1921.

The separation of party systems and political agendas is in part responsible for the perception that British Columbia is a reluctant participant in national politics dominated by the national unity agenda. Provincial politics are about priorities in health, education, social welfare, economic development, and the state of industrial relations. In the 1970's and 1980's federal politics have revolved around the struggle over symbols of our national identity and access to power at the centre. The attempt at national reconciliation represented by Pierre Trudeau was apparently supported by nearly half the province's electorate in 1968, but concerns that a bicultural national community implicitly devalues British values and symbols so prominent in the province's history eventually played into the hands of the Conservatives.

Given the historical and constitutional basis for separation of the two party systems, it is unlikely that they can be linked in the forseeable future. Given the decline of party, it is questionable whether party system integration would matter in any event. However, the separation of party systems also presents an opportunity to federal leaders willing to risk the wrath of the provincial government by tapping divisions within the province on economic and social policy issues. Since I do not believe that "fed-bashing" has ever been a rewarding tactic in provincial elections,[19] and since neither the provincial Liberals nor the Conservatives have any support to lose from the use of such tactics, it is difficult to see why the opportunity is not seized.

The former Liberal government made a start with legislation penalizing provinces which levy user fees for hospital care, mindful of the large majorities in the provinces, including B.C., which oppose fee increases and cutbacks in hospital services. The present federal government might also reassert a national interest in the quality of postsecondary education by challenging provinces such as British Columbia which divert federal funds earmarked for education into general revenues.

The federal Conservative government cannot assume that it is invulnerable in British Columbia or that its strength in the province reflects majority support for a small "c" conservative position on social policy issues. Our data show quite clearly that the federal Conservative electorate contains many who do not share that value position but who voted Conservative to punish the Liberals.

The Mulroney government's massive financial commitment to reforestation in British Columbia is an example of how the federal government's contribution to the provincial economy might strengthen links with the centre. Here, however, it risks being outmanoeuvred by provincial politicians who wish to commit the federal government to the province's development agenda (which includes a gas pipeline to Vancouver Island judged uneconomic by federal officials) and who argue that federal contributions to B.C. are, on a per capita basis, less than those to Quebec.

THE TIES THAT BIND

While exploitation of the material basis for links between British Columbia and Canada is an avenue to explore, a significant reservoir of popular attachment to the Canadian political community already exists. Moreover, an analysis of attitudes at the mass level in British Columbia by David J. Elkins has convincingly demonstrated that alienation does not imply repudiation of a significant policy role for the federal government. Voters "called for *better federal policies* as often as they demanded that the federal government leave . . . matters to provincial or private control,'' increased centralization was often presented as a solution to problems in issue areas voters felt strongly about, and traditional western grievances about tariffs and freight rates were rarely mentioned.[20] In fact, a majority of voters felt that there was *more* at stake in the federal election of 1979 than in the provincial election which preceded it by less than two weeks.

In contrast to the situation in Alberta, alienation does not represent a consensus across social groups (it is somewhat more characteristic of the working class and the poorly educated),[21] and it is linked to populism, which is also more characteristic of blue collar voters. As noted above, and unlike Alberta, alienation is not strongly related to provincial voting habits. The historical record also provides a more limited basis for a collective memory of grievance in British Columbia. The province has been constantly renewed by immigration from abroad and from other provinces, and the development of community sentiment has been further retarded by obstacles to communication within the province.

A mammoth survey conducted in 1980 by Statistics Canada provides clear evidence of the links between British Columbia and the central and eastern provinces, particularly Ontario.[22] By their estimate, 9 per cent of the provincial labour force migrated to B.C. between June 1976 and December 1980, and fully one-third of Canadian-born migrants came from Ontario. Nearly one-quarter of the total number of migrants came from outside Canada, and they represent a group for whom the federal level of government should be especially salient. According to our 1979 survey, 50.8 per cent of the B.C. population has lived outside the province for a year or more, and 34.8 per cent have at least one close friend or relative living in another part of Canada. Some of these observations may apply with equal force to other western provinces, but so far as British Columbia is concerned, they suggest the absence of a firm historical and social basis for the development of a selfconscious provincial community.[23] However, if, as seems possible, native-born British Columbians become an ever larger proportion of the population, such a community may gradually develop, lending increased importance to the strategies pursued by federal leaders in making appeals to the province.

Institutional changes offer limited help. The adoption of some variant of proportional representation would not change the fact that British Columbia contains only 12 per cent of the nation's population. John Courtney has also challenged the assumptions made about the probable behaviour of politicians under such a scheme, and he argues that embarassment at being shut out in some provinces gives parties claiming to be national in scope sufficient incentive to persevere.[24] However, advocates of PR at least recognize the existence of divisions of opinion within the province on national issues. Various proposals to entrench provincial *government* power at the centre, strongly supported by the Social Credit government, play into the hands of provincial premiers who claim a monopoly on interpreting the interests of their populations. In British Columbia, such a claim can hardly be taken seriously given significant divisions within the province on economic, labour, social policy, and environmental issues.

The federal Conservative party continues to adhere to a vision of Canada as a community of communities; the Liberal party to a bicultural vision with conscience money available to "other ethnics." The way in which the Liberal vision has been presented has alienated a considerable number of British Columbians, perhaps a majority, and given over the province to the federal Conservatives despite limited support for the assumptions on which their vision is based. The NDP position on these matters, if known, is ignored by its federal supporters, who value its position on economic and social issues. It is possible that the federal Liberals, with Trudeau gone, might be able to reconcile British Columbians to their vision of the national political community, or at least to reduce the suspicion that the province is somehow being left out of it. There is certainly no reason to believe that the province's citizens have rejected Canada as part of their self-definitions.

However, another approach might be to revive federal initiatives in matters which now, partly by default, appear mainly on the provincial political agenda: issues such as health policy, education, social welfare, and environmental concerns. They are issues which divide the province, but they are also acknowledged to be issues for which the federal level of government has a legitimate role to play. By abdicating responsibility for setting policy in health, education, and welfare and by gradually yielding tax room to the provinces so direct federal contributions can be reduced, the federal government has even undermined the material basis for participation in the national political community. "Provincializing" the Charter of Rights and Freedoms may have been politically expedient, but it was not necessary in order to sell the Charter to provincial residents as opposed to the provincial government. Although we have been assured by some scholars that the existence of the Charter and the body of jurisprudence which will gradually develop around it will have a nationalizing influence, it will also take a long time.

The approach contemplated here would sometimes increase conflict between the federal government and the provincial government and sometimes reduce it, depending on the ideological matchup between governments at the two levels. But in cases of disagreement, the federal government would likely find an ally in the provincial opposition party. The absence of an integrated party system would make it that much easier. A realignment of federal voting habits might occur in the province, since the electorates of the two major federal parties currently contain within them individuals who are far apart on issues involving the role of the state in economic regulation and social policy matters. ''Province-building'' and decentralization in the policy areas I have mentioned may have already gone too far. However, the proposal has the merit of recognizing opportunities for including provincial voters in majorities which cut across provincial boundaries and which do not threaten the legitimacy of the central government.

CONCLUSION

It is fashionable and not wholly inaccurate to view British Columbia as unique. Politicians display and manipulate the powerful symbols of free enterprise and socialism, but a significant populist residue remains, affecting the style of politics as well as its substance. Labour leaders have described cabinet ministers as thugs, and ministers of the Crown have sneered at the alien influence implied by the British accents of labour leaders. In the most unionized province in Canada, the party of the right advertises right to work legislation as a gesture on behalf of workers. The party of the left supports the entrenchment of property rights in the Constitution. Allan Fotheringham has described it as the province where ''every pipefitter feels it is his inalienable right to have the same size ski condo at Whistler and the same price sailboat as his doctor.''[25]

Yet most of these images, however exaggerated, apply to provincial politics. British Columbians behave differently in the federal arena. The province's residents do have a keen interest in federal politics, and they divide on the same bases as other Canadians. The degree of mass attachment to Canada, both now and in the past, based on symbolic and emotional ties has been underestimated. Materialist motives may have been party responsible for B.C.'s entry into Confederation. Historians disagree on that point. But at the present time, given the preeminent importance of the provincial level of government in assuring economic well-being, this is an avenue still to be exploited by federal leadership.

However well-intended, reform proposals which treat the provincial government as the only legitimate voice for issues related to the federal connection assume that a consensus on the province's self-interest exists in British Columbia. They are unnecessarily deferential to the province's particularisms and fail to recognize obstacles to the development of a sense of community within British Columbia and the strength of ties to the national community. Nor does the historical record support attempts to portray Ottawa as a threat to provincial prosperity. Divisions exist within the province on social policy and economic development issues which provide opportunities for federal parties willing to insist that the federal government has a legitimate interest in such questions.

NOTES

*The generous support of the Social Sciences and Humanities Research Council for the research project on which this paper is based is gratefully acknowledged.

1. R. M. Burns, "British Columbia and the Canadian Federation," in R. M. Burns, ed., *One Country or Two?* (Montreal: McGill-Queen's University Press, 1971), p. 268.
2. I say "apparently" because British Columbians continue to exhibit high levels of political efficacy. See David J. Elkins, "British Columbia as a State of Mind," in Donald E. Blake, *Two Political Worlds: Parties and Voting in British Columbia* (Vancouver: University of British Columbia Press, 1985).
3. Margaret A. Ormsby, "Canada and the New British Columbia," in J. Friesen and H. K. Ralston, eds., *Historical Essays on British Columbia* (Toronto: Gage, 1980), p. 96.
4. Margaret Ormsby, *British Columbia: A History* (Toronto: Macmillan, 1971), pp. 269, 278.
5. The remark was occasioned by provincial demands for compensation for failure of the federal government to adhere to the promised timetable for completion of the CPR. See ibid., p. 283.
6. See Carol F. Lee, "The Road to Enfranchisement: Chinese and Japanese in British Columbia," *BC Studies,* 30 (Summer 1976): 44–76.
7. See Margaret Ormsby, "T. Dufferin Pattullo and the Little New Deal," in W. Peter Ward and Robert A. J. McDonald, eds., *British Columbia: Historical Readings* (Vancouver: Douglas and McIntyre, 1981), pp. 533–54.
8. Perhaps even Bennett's parochialism has been exaggerated. Kit Tam has pointed out that he endorsed the Victoria Charter, which did not give B.C. a veto on constitutional amendments and that he coupled his opposition to equalization with support for direct payments to poor individuals rather than to governments of depressed regions. See her *British Columbia: False Perceptions?* (M.A. thesis, Queen's University, 1981). Tam reviews the history of British Columbia's relationship with the rest of Canada and, as her subtitle implies, challenges the perception that B.C. is parochial, isolationist, materialist, and lacks emotional attachment to Canada.
9. A battle over offshore mineral exploration may yet emerge, depending on how the Supreme Court's support for B.C.'s claim to jurisdiction over waters between Vancouver Island and the mainland is interpreted.
10. See H. V. Nelles, *The Politics of Development: Forest, Mine and Hydro-Electric Power in Ontario, 1849–1941* (Toronto: Macmillan, 1975), pp. 172–75 and *passim.* To my knowledge, these parallels have not yet been explored.
11. For example, despite a contribution of $60 million towards the construction of the Vancouver region's Advanced Light Rapid Transit system from the federal government, the province apparently broke an agreement to display a federal logo on the exterior of the transit cars. The provincial logo was given prominent display instead. See the Vancouver *Sun,* 8 July 1983.

12. John Meisel covers these points and also cites the increasing role of the media in calling governments to account and in setting the agenda for public discussion, as well as "short-term" factors associated with Liberal domination of federal politics. See his "The Decline of Party in Canada," in Hugh Thorburn, ed., *Party Politics in Canada,* 4th ed. (Scarborough: Prentice-Hall, 1979), pp. 119–35.
13. Roger Gibbins, *Regionalism: Territorial Politics in Canada and the United States* (Toronto: Butterworth, 1982), p. 137.
14. Robert Hamilton Coats and R. E. Gosnell, *Sir James Douglas* (Toronto 1909), quoted in Allan Smith, "The Writing of British Columbia History," in Ward and McDonald, *British Columbia,* p. 21.
15. This analysis is pursued in more detail in my *Two Political Worlds,* especially ch. 8.
16. The survey data in this table and Table 2 are based on a survey conducted by David J. Elkins, Richard Johnston, and myself following the 1979 elections. For characteristics of the survey, see our "Sources of Change in the B.C. Party System," *BC Studies,* 50 (Summer 1981): Appendix. The data from this survey are available from the UBC Data Library or the Interuniversity Consortium for Political and Social Research.
17. These scales were created by aggregating responses to several sets of questions. They meet standard tests of scale construction. Details are available on request.
18. For additional details, see my *Two Political Worlds,* ch. 9.
19. Alberta seems to represent the opposite situation, one in which federal and provincial agendas are frequently aligned. For an analysis of the electoral consequences of separate and overlapping agendas in that province, see Terrence J. Levesque and Kenneth H. Norrie, "Overwhelming Majorities in the Legislature of Alberta," *Canadian Journal of Political Science* 17 (1979): 451–70.
20. See my *Two Political Worlds,* ch. 7. Emphasis in original.
21. Daniel Wong, *Western Alienation and Intra-Regional Variation: A Comparative Study of Regional Discontent in British Columbia and Alberta* (M.A. thesis, University of B.C., 1982), p. 59.
22. See "Characteristics of Migrants to Alberta and British Columbia: 1976–1980," in *The Labour Force,* cat. 71–001 (Ottawa: Statistics Canada, February 1982).
23. For a similar argument about the weak basis for the establishment of a sense of community in B.C. derived from an analysis of demographic differences among the western provinces, see W. Peter Ward, "Population Growth in Western Canada, 1901–71," in John E. Foster, ed., *The Developing West* (Edmonton: University of Alberta Press, 1983), pp. 155–77.
24. "Reflections on Reforming the Canadian Electoral System," *Canadian Public Administration* 23 (1980): 427–57.
25. Vancouver *Sunday Province,* 8 May 1983.

10

The "French Lieutenant" in Ottawa

JOHN ENGLISH

In November 1941, two political veterans met for what both believed would be the last time. As Ernest Lapointe lay dying, he told Mackenzie King that they had been great partners. King erupted with emotion, telling his Quebec leader that no man ever had a truer friend, adding that

> But for him, I would never have been Prime Minister, nor would I have been able to hold office, as I had held it through the years. That there was never a deeper love between brothers than existed between us. That we had never had a difference all the years that we had been associated together, in thought and work alike.

They kissed three times, and then Lapointe "drew his hands up toward his chest." It was, King later wrote, "a sort of *nunc dimittis*."[1]

King departed, knowing that Lapointe's death would remove the only successful Quebec lieutenant since the death of Cartier in 1873. He seemed irreplaceable, but in fact King soon found a replacement in the prominent Quebec lawyer, Louis St. Laurent, who served as King's Quebec lieutenant through the remainder of the war and through reconstruction and who succeeded King as Liberal leader and prime minister. No anglophone prime minister since King has been successful in finding a Quebec lieutenant.

In King's own view, his relationships with Lapointe and St. Laurent were fundamental to his considerable political success. His biographer Blair Neatby, in an important article on King and French Canada, agrees that "King's technique of always having a French Canadian as his closest and most trusted colleague is an essential part of the explanation of the dominance of the federal Liberal party in Quebec during his thirty years as party leader." Neatby argues that King's success in Quebec—with 86 per cent of all Quebec seats in federal elections while he led the Liberal Party—was not merely the product of the Laurier legacy. The success, in his view, required the careful nurturing of a special relationship with the province and the careful cultivation of a Quebec Liberal leader.[2] The formula worked; its preparation seemed simple. Nevertheless, no other anglophone prime minister has applied it effectively in the twentieth century.

That at least was the conclusion of the study of cabinet formation and bicultural relations prepared for the Royal Commission on Bilingualism and Biculturalism. In drawing together the conclusions of the separate studies of cabinet formation which comprised the volume, Frederick W. Gibson emphasized that only Lapointe and Cartier were given positions of "quite special influence in the making of the cabinet and, subsequently, in the councils of the Government." St. Laurent was also singled out as a special case because of his great prestige and success. Even these examples were not ones where the francophone "attained a position of full and recognized co-ordination with the prime ministers under whom they served."[3] They were lieutenants, but they were also something more than provincial spokesmen. And they most certainly did contribute to the success of the prime ministers whom they served. Yet, the exact formula for the successful lieutenancy has been most difficult to find.

Two anglophone prime ministers, Bennett and Diefenbaker, did not even try to find a Quebec lieutenant. In the case of Bennett, his cabinet was an army made up of one general and many privates. There was no room for any lieutenant, from Quebec or elsewhere.* Similarly, Diefenbaker believed as fervently in one leader as in one Canada. His cabinets aroused considerable criticism in Quebec because of their weak Quebec representation, both in number and status. Diefenbaker's low regard for the most prominent francophone Conservative, Léon Balcer, is well known. Balcer, Diefenbaker later recalled, was his "most bitter opponent in 1956."

> When the convention decided that I should be leader, he and his wife immediately rose and, with their group from Quebec, left the conven-

* An enduring monument to Bennett's familiarity with Quebec is the 1930 film in which he introduces his cabinet. Alfred Duranleau, the new minister of marine, steps forward. Bennett begins to introduce him but forgets his name.

> tion. His wife is reported to have said at the time that the blinds of Quebec would be forever drawn on my leadership. She would have made this so had she been able. . . . Although I found [Balcer] honest, no uxorious control have I ever known to equal that in which he was enmeshed.[4]

Neither henpeckery nor a French lieutenant had a place in the highest councils of the Diefenbaker realm.

Joe Clark and Arthur Meighen reigned too briefly to be judged, although in both cases their defeats resulted from their inability to make any inroads in Quebec. Brian Mulroney, though of anglophone background, has taken pains to establish his own legitimacy as a Québécois, thus making a "French Lieutenant" superfluous. Borden and Pearson, however, had longer tenures as prime minister, and both had considerable support in Quebec when they gained office, even though they spoke French poorly and had few personal ties with Quebec. Nevertheless, the Conservatives under Borden came to power in 1911 with twenty-seven Quebec seats (up from eleven in 1908) and with 48.1 per cent of the vote. In 1963, Pearson's Liberals took forty-seven Quebec seats (up from thirty-five), with 45.8 per cent of the popular vote. Both had achievements to build upon as well as Quebec lieutenants who were eminent and talented. Those lieutenants, F. D. Monk for Borden and Guy Favreau for Pearson, were men of considerable standing in Quebec when they donned the lieutenant's mantle. And both Monk and Favreau left politics as broken men. Their individual political histories left a legacy of shattered dreams and bitter memories which still endure. Their failures, this essay will argue, offer as much insight as King's successes do in the evaluation of the institution of the Quebec lieutenant.

Frederick Debartzch Monk seemed an ideal Quebec lieutenant when the new Conservative leader, Robert Borden, gave him that position in 1900. His father, Samuel Cornwallis Monk, was a distinguished Quebec jurist of the 1860's and 1870's whose family was among the most prominent Nova Scotia Loyalists.[5] On his mother's side, Monk was the grandson of P. D. Debartzch, seigneur of St. Charles and a rebel in 1837. The strength of the two traditions left its mark on young Frederick, who chose the law, as so many of his ancestors had done, but who also chose his mother's language as his first. Like his father, he quickly achieved prominence at the bar as a counsel and as a scholar. Elected to the House of Commons at the age of forty in 1896, Monk spoke strongly against the Laurier compromise on the Manitoba schools. He was a member of the best clubs, and even the *Toronto Globe,* the voice of Grit Ontario, noted that "his English speeches are remarkable for their excellent language and absence of French accent; whether in English or French, they are regarded as the utterances of a conscientious public man."[6] Such a conscientious public man from Quebec was precisely what the inexperienced Robert Borden needed to rebuild his Quebec party.

The specific reason for Monk's appointment is unclear. Borden's biographer speculates that the appointment was perhaps "a tacit acknowledgement by Borden of his own unfamiliarity with the political problems and aspirations of French-speaking Canadians."[7] There was, of course, the old memory of the Macdonald-Cartier partnership and the present reality of Sir Wilfrid Laurier's appeal to French Canadians. Monk, in fact, seemed ideal for Borden's purposes. They were both young politicians open to ideas of change in the party. They knew each other, having shared a front bench in the previous Parliament, and both had outstanding reputations as lawyers. Moreover, in an age when lineage was cherished, not least by Robert Borden, the preloyalist son of the Grand Pré stationmaster, Monk's direct ties to some of the most eminent figures in Nova Scotia's past should have offered reassurance. Further reassurance to Borden must have come from the fact that Monk, a descendent of Edward Cornwallis, had marched mostly in step during the difficult years of the Boer War. And yet the Monk-Borden partnership was a marriage made in Hell.

Within Quebec, in the early days of his lieutenancy, Monk was treated as the Conservative's co-leader. Outside Quebec, his eminence was also noted. *The Canadian Annual Review for 1902,* for example, reported that "the Dominion Leaders" R. L. Borden and F. D. Monk, addressed a large provincial Conservative dinner in Ontario on 21 February.[8] But Monk's position quickly deteriorated as J. Israel Tarte left the Laurier Liberals and began an earnest and protracted flirtation with the Conservatives. For Borden, Tarte's charms—his outspoken protectionism, his public support for Joseph Chamberlain's tariff schemes, and his reputation as the organizer who had carried Quebec for Laurier in 1896—made him irresistible. Very soon Tarte was appearing on Conservative platforms with Borden, and each declared their growing affection for the other. Monk was generally absent, and rumours of a rift soon developed. Public disavowals of such a rift followed private struggles among Quebec Conservatives and between Borden and Monk over Tarte's relationship with the party.

In the summer of 1903, Borden cut away the foundations of Monk's political position, all the while assuring the electorate of Monk's continuing leadership of the Quebec Conservatives. In early summer, Borden and Tarte plotted electoral strategy.[9] His bitterness towards Monk grew, as was clear in a letter to his wife on 24 July 1903. Monk, Borden charged, "spends the most of his time in brooding over imaginary conspiracies which he thinks are being hatched against him on every side."[10] The conspiracies, however, were not all imaginary. On 31 July, it was announced that L. P. Pelletier (who had appeared on platforms with Tarte) and M. F. Hackett had been appointed the party organizers in Quebec. Monk's understandable complaints about the separation of organization from leadership were not heeded.[11] In August, the veteran conspirator Hugh Graham reported to Borden that the deal had been sealed with Tarte and that Monk had agreed to "stand by and allow the procession to march along." He would not, however, speak from the same platform with Tarte.[12] The procession, like Leacock's horse, thus rode off in several directions at once.

On 21 January 1904, Borden told the press that

> Mr. Monk is the recognized leader of the Conservative Party in the Province of Quebec, and he is to-day putting up a splendid fight on behalf of the party throughout the whole province. He stands high in the estimation of the Conservatives of that Province and has gained materially in strength since he assumed his present duties. He has full control of the Conservative forces in Quebec, and possesses their confidence in an eminent degree.

Four days before Borden publicly expressed his confidence in Monk, Monk had written a letter of resignation. Eventually, the news seeped into the press, and on 20 February, Monk's resignation was finally announced.[13]

Monk's letter charged that there were "in our party here certain elements which clearly are not in sympathy with me, but which are hostile to me." He was, of course, correct. In late February, Monk attacked Tarte directly and Borden indirectly. In four important by-elections which had taken place on 16 February, Borden had permitted Tarte and Hugh Graham to run a strongly protectionist campaign. "Need I say," Monk told a Lachine audience, "that I was not consulted on the change which suppressed the old flag of our party, our mottoes, the glorious traditions of the party, and even the names of Macdonald, Cartier and Chapleau."[14] The tradition of a Quebec lieutenant lay in tatters, and Borden's attempt to stitch together an effective Quebec campaign for the 1904 election failed. The Laurier triumph did not lead Borden to a reconciliation with Monk. Indeed, in 1905 the Quebec Conservatives flirted with the notion of separating from Borden's party. Their anger derived from Borden's stand on the Autonomy Bills which created the provinces of Alberta and Saskatchewan. Monk led francophone opposition to Borden's amendment to the bills, which called for complete provincial freedom to make laws in the field of education. Borden refused to consider that the rights of western francophones merited any special protection. To Joseph Flavelle, who shared Borden's limited regard for minority rights, Borden expressed his exasperation: "One cannot say a single word in defence either of the constitution or the principle of national schools without at once being charged with fomenting religious discord and racial strife. The attitude of the French Canadian has always been a little peculiar in this respect."[15] Borden managed to escape much contact with such peculiarity for a couple of years, as leading Quebec francophone Conservatives refused to share speaking platforms with their national leader.[16]

Monk, in fact, had re-established his political influence in Quebec with his strong performance in defence of francophone rights in 1905. In 1907, some younger Quebec Conservatives called on Borden to reappoint Monk as Quebec lieutenant once more, but he ignored the pleas. After another election loss in 1908, however, Borden and Monk were ready to let personal antagonism take second place to political opportunity. In January 1909, Borden agreed to Monk's restoration as Quebec leader.[17] The political opportunity lay in the political excitement which Henri Bourassa and the young *nationalistes* were creating in Quebec. Borden saw that Monk could work with Bourassa, and he gave him the freedom to do so. For Borden, after 1907, Quebec would be a province unlike the others. His presence there became even rarer, and Monk's activities were, as far as possible, cloaked from Tory scrutiny elsewhere.

What happened is too well known to repeat in detail here.[18] In Monk's first term as Quebec leader, Borden had frustrated him by seeking an alliance with others and by interfering in organizational matters. In his second term, Monk was left alone, as Borden fastened his gaze upon English Canada, casting only furtive glances upon French Canada, where Monk joined the *nationalistes* in a bitter campaign to scuttle Laurier's Naval Bill and to defeat "Laurierism" forever. In January 1910, Monk wrote Borden that the views of the French-Canadian Conservatives "upon the naval question differ so greatly from those of our fellow members . . . I think it is perhaps better for each to follow our own course."[19] By dividing, they might conquer.

And they did. Monk's independent stand on the Naval Bill quickly won him *nationaliste* plaudits. Armand Lavergne, the former Liberal MP and the son of Laurier's close friend, Senator Louis Lavergne, wrote Monk at the beginning of the *nationaliste*-Conservative campaign: "Je n'ai pas besoin de vous comme je suis de coeur et d'esprit avec vous." In Lavergne's opinion, "le vieux parti conservateur français" had once again found its voice in Monk.[20] The bargain was struck with Bourassa and Lavergne to bring down the government. United by their distrust of Laurier and by a surprising sense of common purpose, Monk and Bourassa tore away at the pillars of Quebec Liberalism. Borden, for his part, ignored the tactics but welcomed the results. Craig Brown has succinctly described what happened.[21]

> The English-speaking Conservatives (in Quebec) and a few French Canadians with traditional sympathies fought one campaign. Monk and Bourassa fought another. Both groups desperately wanted to defeat Laurier in his home province. Beyond that, they had little in common. Borden stayed out of the province, neither blessing nor condemning either group publicly.

In September 1911, Borden's tactics and Monk and Bourassa's organization captured twenty-seven Quebec seats, the most the Conservatives had won in Quebec since Macdonald's death.

The victor, however, had too many promises to keep. Borden had promised Sir Clifford Sifton and other new supporters in English Canada that he would "not be subservient" to "Roman Catholic" and "Quebec" influence in either policy or patronage. In his public addresses, he had emphasized what Canada owed to Britain and promised that he would respond to Britain's needs in time of danger. The clouds which had shrouded the differences lifted away quickly once the Conservatives occupied the government benches.

The first spat came over cabinet representation. Borden did give Monk a veto, but some problems arose from the resentment felt towards Monk on the part of some Quebec Conservatives. In the end, however, the major problem was the overall weakness of the French-Canadian delegation in which, Craig Brown notes, "only Monk had sufficient stature to command attention either at the Council table or among his people."[22] Still, Monk had carefully consulted with Bourassa and Lavergne, and there were hopes that power would soothe the wounds of the past.[23] Unfortunately, it did not.

The delicate structure of the Conservative-*nationaliste* alliance, which had survived the campaign of 1911, tumbled down quickly in 1912. The first shock which weakened the foundation was a crisis over schools in the Keewatin district. The tremor which shattered the structure was Borden's decision in the early fall of 1912 to give an "emergency" contribution to Britain for its navy. To Monk, this was a betrayal of Borden's earlier promise that he would consult the people on the question of Canada's naval policy. To Borden, there was no time. This was a moment of emergency; Canada could not afford to dally with referenda or Quebec lieutenants while the Empire stood threatened. Bourassa and his *nationaliste* colleagues were outraged: *Le Devoir* published Monk's and other nationalist speeches from the 1911 campaign. Bourassa pointed out that Monk was a man of principle and such a man must resign when his party betrays his principles. And so, on 18 October 1912, Monk resigned.[24]

Two years later, Monk died. In his parliamentary eulogy, Borden praised Monk as "a man of very distinguished qualities," but then he added: "His character and his temperament in some respects were not suited to public life, for the reason that he was a man of singularly sensitive disposition, much more sensitive than, perhaps, those who did not know him intimately may have realized."[25] Monk finally found in death the intimacy with Borden that had evaded him in life.

In assessing Monk's career as Borden's Quebec lieutenant, the importance of the personal relationship between the leader and the lieutenant is obvious. Monk and Borden differed greatly in personality. Monk was warm and effusive; his correspondence with his family and with others bubbles with emotion and affection. Despite Borden's claim that Monk was overly sensitive, there is much evidence that he did not harbour grudges. He and Bourassa had opposed each other in the early 1900's and even in 1910 and 1911 on issues unrelated to the Naval Bill, but their correspondence in 1910 and 1911 reflects deep friendship and respect. The Borden-Monk correspondence, by contrast, is marked by formality and emotional distance. That distance probably conceals distrust, which is hardly surprising. Borden had ignored Monk in the first leadership period. Having appointed Monk as the senior Quebec counsel, he regularly sought out others. On the other hand, Monk also seems to have been suspicious of Borden's plans. Not surprisingly, when party dissidents challenged Borden in 1910 and 1911, Monk joined them, even though in terms of policy Borden was much more congenial than the alternatives such as the robustly imperialist Richard McBride. In contrast to King and Lapointe, Monk and Borden were neither true nor friends.

The personal difficulties do not explain everything. There were also two major problems in the structure which Borden used for his position of Quebec lieutenant. First, Borden did not link together the organizational responsibilities with the broader political responsibilities of the Quebec lieutenant. Other Quebec Conservatives, notably English Canadians such as William Price, Hugh Graham, and Herbert Ames, operated largely independently of Monk. The result was endless squabbles over patronage and position which demoralized the party. The second structural problem derives in part from this feudal approach to party organization. Monk's independent position and the weakness of traditional Conservative organization in Quebec did permit him to fashion the alliance with the *nationalistes* in 1910 and 1911. In doing so, however, he moved beyond the limits of freedom a national party can permit. He left himself and his party hostage to a group over which both had relatively little influence. A lieutenant must have the freedom to chart the course of battle but not to choose the battlefield. In this respect, Monk and Borden failed each other.

Personal, political, and organizational difficulties plagued the Borden-Monk relationship. In retrospect, divorce seemed almost inevitable between these partners who failed to consult, who flirted too eagerly, and who ignored the wounds they inflicted on each other. Because he could never understand what Monk represented, Borden could not respect him. Ultimately, Borden and his party lost much in Monk's demise. So did Canada, because it left Borden's government bereft of French-Canadian influence as Canada entered a war in which such influence was badly needed.

In the 1960's, Canada fought no wars, but, in the words of the Royal Commission on Bilingualism and Biculturalism, it was a time when Canada was "passing through the greatest crisis in its history." What the commissioners saw was a fundamental change: "it would appear from what is happening that the state of affairs established in 1867, and never since seriously challenged, is now for the first time being rejected by the French Canadians in Quebec."[26] When this preliminary report appeared in February 1965, Prime Minister Lester Pearson, whose concern about Quebec had led him to appoint the commission, was facing a potentially catastrophic collapse of the francophone representation in his cabinet.

Guy Rouleau, Pearson's parliamentary secretary, resigned in February after allegations that he tried to influence the bail hearing of the heroin dealer Lucien Rivard. A month earlier, Yvon Dupuis, the Liberal's roughly hewn answer to Réal Caouette, was fired from the Cabinet after being charged with corruption in arranging a racetrack charter. Maurice Lamontagne, the secretary of state and an intellectual leader in the party and the cabinet, and René Tremblay, the minister of citizenship and immigration, had lost their political utility and effectiveness as they withered under press allegations that they had received furniture from a dubious Montreal merchant who wanted political favours. Tremblay, who in fact had paid for furniture which had not been delivered and who scarcely merited the opprobrium cast upon him, was also a target because his special assistant, Raymond Denis, had tried to help Rivard. The Liberal Party in Quebec fell into disarray as the scandals accumulated. What made the crisis graver was the fact that at the moment when leadership was craved, leadership could not be given. Guy Favreau, the Quebec leader and minister of justice, was in a state of political limbo as Judge Frederic Dorion investigated whether Favreau had been grossly derelict in his duty to pursue the Rivard affair and, more seriously, to inform the prime minister. Favreau could not lead; the followers scattered.[27] In Peter Newman's view, "the whole sordid business," which took place between 23 November 1964, with the first charges of Erik Nielson, and 29 June 1965, when Dorion released his report, "seemed absurdly like an old-fashioned, low-budget gangster movie scripted by some third-rate dramatist with no regard for the authenticity of his plots."[28] But the players were not actors, and the farce contained much that was truly tragic.

What ended in a farce had begun, in the mind of Lester Pearson, as an epochal attempt to forge a new compact between French and English Canada. Pearson had indicated before his election in April 1963 that he considered "national unity" the most important problem his government and the country faced.[29] Pearson's commitment to dealing with the problem was unquestioned. The sincerity of his efforts and his openmindedness were in themselves a significant factor in maintaining "that continued—if frequently fragile—conviction that the Canadian experiment should not be allowed to fail."[30] But the sincerity and openmindedness of the prime minister were hardly enough. Quebec needed others who could lead from within the province.

Like all new prime ministers, Pearson owed many debts when he took office. One of the largest was owed to Lionel Chevrier, who had become the Quebec leader during the late St. Laurent years and who had given superb parliamentary service during the black years of opposition. Pearson, however, had profound reservations about Chevrier as his Quebec lieutenant. Although he sat for a Montreal constituency, Chevrier was a franco-Ontarien by background. In Pearson's view, this background made him an inappropriate Quebec leader.[31] Moreover, Pearson was aware that Chevrier, who was first elected in 1935, was perceived as "old" at a time when the new was very much in vogue. The first Quebec reactions to the Cabinet Pearson announced in late April could only have intensified Pearson's worries. The "old guard" took the pre-eminent positions; the "new guard" remained a row behind.[32]

Given the press reaction, it is not surprising that Pearson was especially impressed by a memorandum written by a prominent young Quebec Liberal which arrived on his desk in early May and which he circulated to his closest colleagues and commended to them. The perspective was interesting, for this young Quebec anglophone, later a Trudeau government aide, argued that "in granting increased recognition to Quebec problems . . . far from alleviating the present restlessness, it will probably increase." What was needed were strong francophone leaders who could "demonstrate the progress obtained, and, thus . . . keep within bounds the inevitable pressures from Quebec." Above all others there must be a *chef,* and this position had special qualifications. The individual chosen must

1) be accepted as a French Canadian in Quebec.
2) be "of the spirit and generation of New Quebec."
3) have "political knowledge, aptitude, and desire."
4) be "a professional in his field who knows what he is talking about."
5) be "a forceful orator and a dominant personality, which does not mean he has to be a Caouette."

Lionel Chevrier did not fit; by the end of 1963, he had gone to London as high commissioner.

Maurice Sauvé thought himself eminently qualified for the position, as did numerous journalists who promoted him. The Quebec caucus, the Cabinet, and the prime minister disagreed. Maurice Lamontagne had many qualifications, including personal friendship with Pearson, but he recognized his unsuitability for the political rough and tumble that the position required. Moreover, Lamontagne's friendship with the displaced Chevrier may also have prevented him from considering the position. The choice, therefore, fell upon Guy Favreau, who had entered the House of Commons in 1963 and who was minister of justice and Liberal house leader.[33]

Guy Favreau had much to recommend him. He possessed great personal warmth and had an outstanding reputation as a counsel. He had served as associate deputy minister of justice under the Conservative Davie Fulton, yet he managed to maintain strong links with the reform wing of the Quebec Liberal Party. As in the case of Louis St. Laurent, who had brought Favreau to Ottawa in 1951, the respect for Favreau transcended politics. And like St. Laurent, Favreau had virtually no political experience, but in all else he had proven a quick learner. Moreover, affection and respect were valued currencies in the political trade. Pearson seemed to have good reason to hope that Favreau would be to him "what Ernest Lapointe had been to King."[34]

Favreau quickly moved to the forefront of Canadian politics. His work on constitutional reform in the summer and early fall of 1964 (the "Fulton-Favreau formula") won him considerable public and private acclaim. Pearson wrote privately to his close friend Senator John Connolly about the "wonderful job" Favreau had done in dealing with the provinces in the thorny constitutional negotiations. Connolly urged that Favreau's work should be publicized, especially in Quebec. "This will put him a cut above the turmoil there."[35] But the turmoil had already engulfed him, and his work was getting bad as well as good reviews.

Hal Banks was his first hurdle, and he stumbled in explaining how the notorious labour leader managed to escape Canadian justice. On the CBC programme "This Hour Has Seven Days," in early October, Patrick Watson interrogated Favreau. In reviewing Favreau's performance for Pearson, Press Secretary Richard O'Hagan reported that Favreau "did not do himself or the government any notable good." O'Hagan was especially concerned about the extent to which Favreau's "command" of English affected the clarity and precision of his replies.[36] Favreau's appointment as Quebec leader at a time when Quebec's position in Confederation was the foremost national issue placed a harsh national spotlight on Favreau. He began to wince.

Seeing the weakness of their prey, Erik Nielson and John Diefenbaker moved in for the kill on 23 November 1964. Favreau scurried to the defence, but he only exposed himself more fully. Decoys failed completely. "When a big hunter is after big game," Diefenbaker taunted the Liberals, "he does not allow himself to be diverted by rabbit tracks."[37] The charges were indeed serious: that Favreau had not consulted his departmental officers before deciding not to prosecute Raymond Denis; that he had not informed the prime minister of his decision or about the involvement of Guy Rouleau in the bribery scandal; and that he had protected his friends. Favreau reacted bitterly as day after day the Opposition pursued their wounded quarry. The mood of Parliament turned foul.

In desperation, Favreau asked for an inquiry in order that the merciless parliamentary onslaught upon him could be halted. Pearson quickly agreed, but then he left on a western tour, leaving the impression that he did not stand behind his minister. More devastatingly, he did not inform the House of Commons that Favreau had in fact told him about Rivard on 2 September, not in late November as Pearson had suggested before. Pearson's failure to speak up at once disappointed even his closest aides. Jack Pickersgill and Tom Kent, in Kent's recollection, "almost wore out our welcome with Mr. Pearson, urging him day after day that the only thing to do was to make a statement."[38] But no statement was made to the House. Pearson instead wrote Mr. Justice Dorion, informing him of the earlier decision of Favreau. The information came too late.

The Quebec caucus was furious; English-Canadian Liberals, however, hesitated to rally to Favreau's side because of an editorial thunder against corruption in government. One who did rise to Favreau's defence, Walter

Gordon, received a note from Favreau indicating how isolated the Quebec lieutenant felt. Favreau thanked Gordon warmly for his encouragement and added: ''I shall never forget . . . how you dared rise in the House in my defence, at the very moment when so many were speechless and I myself was performing badly.''[39]

Pearson's mail, however, bulged with demands that he ''clean up'' his party. Old friends, such as the prominent United Church minister, Rev. George Goth, harangued him on the need to expunge evil from his midst. A distinguished historian's observation that there was much rot in modern Canada provoked a most interesting response from Pearson:

> As I have recently been accused of being personally responsible for the debasement of public morality in this country, your observations are very pertinent. Seriously, however, I do not agree that there are ''large areas of rot'' in our country. I do not agree that the conduct of Mr. Favreau, Mr. Lamontagne, and Mr. Tremblay, however inept and ill-advised, represents any form of corruption or lack of integrity on their part.

The historian had not mentioned the three Quebec ministers.[40] Pearson, nevertheless, thought of them at once and even granted their ineptitude. It was a telling reaction and a reflection of the fury in English Canada.

When the Dorion report of July 1965 found that Favreau had shown bad judgment, Pearson readily accepted Favreau's resignation, but he kept him as Quebec lieutenant and, more controversially, made him the president of the Privy Council.[41] The compromise satisfied no one. Only the husk of Favreau's former prestige and power remained. Like Monk, he lived only two years after his fall from political grace.

In the minds of the Quebec MPs, Pearson's failure to defend Favreau energetically marked him as insensitive to the true nature of the situation. In this vein, Auguste Choquette, the member for Lotbinière, told Queen's University students that since no one doubted Favreau's integrity, the commotion was simply another Diefenbaker attack on French Canada. He did not need to add that a Liberal prime minister should have fought off the attack with all the power at his command.[42] Tommy Douglas is, perhaps, most persuasive in his explanation of why Pearson acted in the fashion he did. In the British and Canadian tradition, Douglas claims, a prime minister does not rush in to defend the government: ''You let the Minister defend it, and if he can't defend it then you throw him to the wolves.''[43] This time, however, the minister dragged along others with him. He was, after all, the Quebec lieutenant, a minister unlike the others.

In the 1963 memorandum which had urged Pearson to find a solid Quebec lieutenant, the author had warned that a poor leader "would probably do more harm than good to the Federal Liberal cause," because he would become "the butt of attack." It was an accurate prophecy; Favreau was the last Quebec lieutenant. The office was refused by Jean Marchard, who thought the whole concept was outdated. Pierre Trudeau's long prime ministerial tenure eliminated the need for a "French lieutenant," although it did raise some new questions about the need for an "English lieutenant." Perhaps, however, a future anglophone prime minister will again face the question of a Quebec lieutenant. How should he or she answer it?

The Quebec lieutenancy has worked rarely, but when it has, it has worked very well. Conversely, when it has failed, its failure has created much worse problems than would a normal ministerial resignation. The nettles surrounding the opportunity are thick; but are we to conclude that only the deft political fingers of Mackenzie King could successfully pluck it? I think not.

The failures of Monk and Favreau have many common features. In both cases, their leaders did not give them the impression that they had their full support. This was true of Borden from the earliest days, and of Pearson from the moment of first crisis. Moreover, both Borden and Pearson, especially the former, gave their lieutenants a sense of independence but not a sense that they had influence. The contrast with King is striking, for in his case, his lieutenants were consulted not only on Quebec, but also on a broad range of subjects affecting the government. As Blair Neatby has written, the prestige of Lapointe and St. Laurent "began with their status, but it grew with the cumulative evidence of their political power."[44] Conversely, the prestige of Monk and Favreau fell as evidence of their political impotence grew. Simultaneously, the power of those who had denied them influence diminished.[45] The reciprocal nature of influence is thus most apparent.

The most effective and enduring leaders, James MacGregor Burns writes, are those who possess "the ability to lead by being led."[46] Both the lieutenant and the prime minister must possess this ability. If either lacks it, there will be an inevitable drift towards more independence on the part of leader and lieutenant. Independence, however, corrodes influence. With the Quebec or "French" lieutenant, the appearance of influence has always been more politically useful than the appearance of independence. When influence is denied, or appears to be denied, as in 1912 with Monk and in 1965 with Favreau, resentment surfaces quickly among Quebec members. The demise of Favreau and Monk did not arise from the unwillingness of Quebec ministers to follow them; rather, it developed from the prime ministers' unwillingness to support them. Perhaps they had no choice, but the consequences were serious.

Ramsay Cook has argued the "goal of French Canadians has always been security; the strategy for its achievement is the recognition of equality."[47] An effective French lieutenant can offer security; his existence is a form of recognition of equality. In navigating the passages which lead towards a national political community, the French lieutenant has sometimes been the most useful oarsman. At other times, the leader and the lieutenant have taken different strokes which threw them onto dangerous shoals. History does provide some clues for finding the proper rhythm.

NOTES

1. J. W. Pickersgill, *The Mackenzie King Record 1939–1944,* vol. 1 (Toronto, 1960), p. 287. The volume is dedicated to Lapointe, devoted comrade in arms in the longest and closest partnership in the political life of Canada, and to Louis St. Laurent.
2. H. B. Neatby, "Mackenzie King and French Canada," *Journal of Canadian Studies* (Fall 1976): 13.
3. F. W. Gibson, "Conclusions," in F. W. Gibson, ed., *Cabinet Formation and Bicultural Relations* (Ottawa: Information Canada, 1970), p. 155.
4. John Diefenbaker, *One Canada: The Years of Achievement 1956 to 1962* (Toronto, 1976), pp. 43–44. Since Diefenbaker, the percentage of French Canadians in Canadian cabinets has increased considerably over earlier levels. As Diefenbaker pointed out, King at one point had only one French-Canadian minister.
5. See Pierre-Georges Roy, *Les Juges de la Province de Quebec* (Quebec, 1933), p. 385. S. C. Monk, who sat on the Court of Queen's Bench in Quebec, was praised lavishly for his knowledge of French: "Sa connaissance des langues française et anglaise était si parfaite et sa prononciation si correcte, qu'un étranger pouvait difficilement dire à laquelle des deux nationalités il appartenait."
6. H. J. Morgan, *Canadian Men and Women of the Time* (Toronto, 1912), p. 815. On Debartzch, see Morgan's earlier *Sketches of Celebrated Canadians* (Quebec, 1862), p. 357, where Debartzch is accused of contributing "in a great measure, to excite the people to the lamentable outbreak of 1837."
7. R. C. Brown, *Robert Laird Borden: A Biography. Volume 1: 1854–1914*. (Toronto, 1975), p. 56.
8. J. C. Hopkins, *The Canadian Annual Review for 1902* (Toronto, 1903), p. 45.
9. Tarte to Borden, 6 June 1903, vol. 350, memoir notes, 5696–7; and Tarte to Borden, 18 June 1903, ibid., 5699, Borden Papers, Public Archives of Canada [PAC].
10. Quoted in Brown, *Borden,* p. 57.
11. J. C. Hopkins, *The Canadian Annual Review for 1903* (Toronto, 1903), p. 98. Monk to Borden, 18 November 1903, vol. 350, memoir notes, 5782–84, Borden Papers.
12. Brenton Macnab, editor, *Montreal Star,* to Borden, n.d., 5737 and 5739, ibid.

13. Quoted in J. C. Hopkins, *The Canadian Annual Review for 1904* (Toronto, 1905), p. 29.
14. Monk's speech and letter are quoted in Hopkins, ibid., pp. 30–31 which is an excellent account of Monk's problems. See also Brown, *Borden,* 1: 55–59; Réal Bélanger, *L'impossible défi* (Quebec, 1983), pp. 23–25; Laurier Lapierre, "Politics, Race, and Religion in French Canada: Joseph Israel Tarte" (Ph.D. diss., University of Toronto, 1962), p. 490 ff; and Réal Bélanger, *Paul-Emile Lamarche: Le Pays avant le parti (1904–1918)* (Québec, 1984).
15. Borden to Flavelle, 8 April 1905, vol. 350, memoir notes, 6052–55, Borden Papers.
16. Albert Sévigny to Borden, 1 December 1919, vol. 137, 72540, Borden Papers; Hugh Graham to Borden, 15 October 1905, vol. 327, 192963–8, ibid; and Bélanger, *L'impossible défi,* p. 37.
17. Memo of Conversation between Messrs. Borden, Monk, and Casgrain 29 January 1909, vol. 351, 6508–13, Borden Papers.
18. On the 1911 election, and its Quebec background, see Bélanger, *L'impossible défi,* pp. 88–113. Also, Brown, *Borden* 1, chs. 8 and 9.
19. Monk to Borden, 28 January 1910, vol. 352, memoir notes, 6787, Borden Papers.
20. Lavergne to Monk, 16 November 1909, vol. 1, pp. 99–100, Monk Papers, PAC.
21. Brown, *Borden,* 1, p.188. For a good analysis of what Borden knew, Bélanger, *Le défi impossible,* p. 98 ff. Also, see Bourassa's own account in "Le Nationalisme et les partis," *Le Devoir,* 28–30 May 1913. See also, Roger Graham, "The Cabinet of 1911," in Gibson, *Cabinet Formation and Bicultural Relations,* pp. 47–62.
22. Brown, *Borden,* 1:211. See also, Henri Bourassa, "Le nationalisme et les partis," *Le Devoir,* 4 June 1913.
23. See Bélanger, *L'impossible défi,* p. 118 for a discussion of the extent of consultation with Monk and Lavergne.
24. Bourassa editorialized in *Le Devoir* on 4 September 1912, demanding that Monk resign if he could not halt the Naval Bill.
25. Quoted in Henry Borden, ed., *Robert Laird Borden: His Memoirs* (Toronto, 1938), 1:401. Monk sat quietly on the backbenches until his death. Monk to Borden, 24 March 1913, vol. 1, pp. 236–37, Monk Papers.
26. *Preliminary Report of the Royal Commission on Bilingualism and Biculturalism* (Ottawa, 1965), p. 13.
27. J. T. Saywell's account of these events in *The Canadian Annual Review for 1965* (Toronto, 1966) stands up very well. See also, Peter Stursberg, *Lester Pearson and the Dream of Unity* (Toronto, 1978), ch. 8; Lester Pearson, *Mike: The Memoirs of the Rt. Hon. Lester B. Pearson,* vol. 3 (Toronto, 1975), ch. 6; and Peter Newman, *The Distemper of Our Time* (Toronto, 1968), ch. 20.
28. Newman, *Distemper,* p. 264. Pearson, in his memoirs, describes the period as "one of the most sordid and vindictive episodes in the history of the House of Commons," Pearson, *Mike,* p. 151.
29. See Pearson, *Mike,* pp. 67–69 for his 17 December 1962 speech in which he proposes the future Royal Commission on Bilingualism and Biculturalism; and Stursberg, *Dream of Unity,* ch. 1, for his colleagues' reactions, which varied greatly.
30. Ramsey Cook, *The Maple Leaf Forever* (Toronto, 1971), p. 19.
31. Pearson, *Mike,* 3: 38–39. See also Newman for a strong criticism of Chevrier from Maurice Sauvé's viewpoint. *Distemper,* pp. 244 ff.
32. André Laurendeau wrote of Pearson's Cabinet: "nous gagnons en nombre, mais guère en qualité et en influence." *Le Devoir,* 23 April 1963.
33. Newman's account indicates that a triumvirate was proposed by Pearson. Other information suggests that Sauvé proposed the triumvirate when his own hopes for the lieutenancy faltered. See Newman, *Distemper,* pp. 246–50. Contrast with the interview with Lamontagne in Stursberg, *Dream of Unity,* pp. 211–12. Confidential sources indicate that Lamontagne's account is accurate.
34. Pearson, *Mike,* 3: 214.
35. Connolly to Pearson, 15 October, 1964 and Pearson to Connolly, 19 October, 1964,

vol. 74, file 301, personal and confidential. Pearson Papers, PAC.
36. O'Hagan to Pearson, 5 October 1964, MG 26 N3, vol. 74, file 31212 Justice, ibid.
37. *House of Commons Debates,* 26 November 1964, 10562.
38. Stursberg, *Dream of Unity,* p. 221.
39. Walter Gordon, *A Political Memoir* (Toronto, 1977), p. 198.
40. Pearson Papers, vol. 3, file 313.29L (22 December 1964).
41. The *Globe and Mail,* 8 July 1965, denounced Pearson for retaining Favreau, "a man who has demonstrated lack of judgement."
42. Cited in Blair Fraser, "Favreau, Pearson and a Sick Feeling Inside," *Maclean's* 78, no. 1 (2 January 1965): 2.
43. Stursberg, *Dream of Unity,* p. 223.
44. Neatby, "King and French Canada," p. 13.
45. Gerald Wright, commenting on prime ministerial power, argues that "power, in this context is the ability to achieve one's desired objectives through the agency of others whose cooperation is indispensable but whose acquiesence is by no means automatic. It is measured by the frequency with which these objectives are attained" (G. Wright, "Mackenzie King: Power over the Political Executive," in Tom Hockin, *Apex of Power,* 2d ed. [Scarborough, 1977], p. 285).
46. James MacGregor Burns, *Leadership* (New York, 1978), p. 117.
47. Ramsay Cook, "The Paradox of Quebec," in R. Kenneth Carty and W. Peter Ward, eds., *Entering the Eighties: Canada in Crisis* (Toronto, 1980), pp. 46–59.

Contributors

CHRISTOPHER ARMSTRONG is author of *The Politics of Federalism: Ontario's Relations with the Federal Government, 1867–1942* and essays on the history of Canadian politics. He is a member of the history department at York University.

DONALD E. BLAKE is a professor of political science at the University of British Columbia. He recently published *Two Political Worlds: Parties and Voting in British Columbia.*

R. KENNETH CARTY is a member of the political science department at UBC. He is the author of *Party and Parish Pump: Electoral Politics in Ireland.*

JOHN C. COURTNEY is a professor of political science at the University of Saskatchewan. Author of *The Selection of National Party Leaders in Canada,* he recently edited *The Canadian House of Commons: Essays in Honour of Norman Ward.*

JOHN ENGLISH is a member of the history department at the University of Waterloo. He has written *The Decline of Politics: The Conservatives and the Party System, 1901-1920* and numerous other studies of twentieth-century Canadian politics.

MARGARET PRANG is a professor of history at UBC. She is the author of *N. W. Rowell: Ontario Nationalist* and many articles on modern Canadian political and social history.

DAVID E. SMITH is a professor of political science at the University of Saskatchewan. He has written *The Regional Decline of a National Party: Liberals on the Prairies* and "Party Government, Representation and National Integration in Canada," for the Royal Commission on the Economic Union and Development Prospects for Canada.

GORDON STEWART is Professor of History at Michigan State University in East Lansing. He is the author of *A People Highly Favoured of God: The Nova Scotia Yankees and the American Revolution* and a forthcoming study of nineteenth-century Canadian political culture.

P. B. WAITE is a Professor of history at Dalhousie University. The most recent of his many books on nineteenth-century Canadian politics and society is *The Man from Halifax: Sir John Thompson, Prime Minister.*

W. PETER WARD teaches history at UBC. He has written *White Canada Forever: Popular Attitudes, Public Policy and Orientals in British Columbia.*